NOTES

FROM AN

UNDERWATER ZOO

Notes
from an
Underwater
Zoo

DON C. REED

The Dial Press
New York

Published by
The Dial Press
1 Dag Hammarskjold Plaza
New York, New York 10017

Manufactured in the United States of America
First printing
Design by Francesca Belanger

Library of Congress Cataloging in Publication Data

Reed, Don C
Notes from an underwater zoo.
1. Marine World/Africa USA.   2. Reed, Don C.
3. Marine aquariums, Public—California—Employees—
Biography.   I. Title.
QL76.5.U62S287   639.3'42   80-28420
ISBN 0-8037-2181-1

To
the Sea

Acknowledgments

There are so many people I would like to thank: Mike Demetrios, president of Marine World/Africa USA, for his un-
stinting cooperation and total absence of censorship; Brad
Baruh, who first dreamed and built Marine World; my
friends at the Fremont Library, who have been so kind and
supportive for years; Ken Shiels, my brother in all but blood,
for the thousand reasons of the best of friendships; J. P. Held,
the voice teacher who first made me aware of the beautiful
sounds of the English language; all my English teachers, who
attempted to impose order on chaos; and Jeannie, Roman,
and Desireé Don Reed, the most important people in the
world to me.

I would also like to say a grateful thank you to all the
photographers and artists, many of whose works we were unable to squeeze in owing to space limitations, including but
not limited to: Dave DiFiore, principal photographer of the
book, who contributed so much talent and hard work; Lou
Silva, reknowned wildlife artist; Lindy Mitchell-Cook and Pat
Foster-Turley, who each contributed several irreplaceable photos; Steve Castillo, park photographer, who somehow found
the time to take special photographs for the book; Bonnie
Sanderson, and Ken Silverman, who shared our white shark
experience and captured it on film. All these people and
more helped so much to bring this book to life.

Lastly, I would like to pay tribute to the memory of my

sister, Patricia Christine Reed, who I wish so much could have lived to see this book done. Leukemia tore her from us so bitterly soon, but the spirit of loving kindness she lived, lives on.

Contents

NOTES

FROM AN

UNDERWATER ZOO

1

My First Shark Dive

~~~~~~~~~~~~~~~~~~~~~~~~~~~~~~~~~~~~~~

The shark spat out a mouthful of sand and raised itself up off the floor. Poising on flexible fin tips, a wide-headed, mocha-brown selachian surveyed me, the invader of its tank. I could read no expression in the tiny golden eye fixed on me.

"Good morning," I mumbled to myself. "I'm the new underwater janitor, come to clean your house." Neither of the two sharks moved, and as I could not see both at the same time anyway, I reluctantly turned my wet-suited back on them and attached a round iron suction cup (the kind glass movers use) to the variegated fiber glass wall. My wire brush bit into the thick purple-brown algae.

The labor was hard and simple, and I liked it. I wore no swim fins, the better to walk on the wall, and I felt like Tarzan hanging there by one hand, almost weightless in the water. My right arm grew warm; I switched hands, gripping with my resting arm, scrubbing with my left, and my work exposed clean, textured fiber glass.

A swirl of displaced water touched me, and I turned my head. The nurse shark was swimming: confidently, calmly, but with an appearance of definite effort, as if it was a labor to get up off the floor. It was really only looking for another, more congenial place to settle down. It found one and did.

I tried to remember what the books said about nurse sharks. *Bottom feeders . . . rooting around the ocean floor, using their heads like shovels, these harmless* (unless provoked) *creatures locate their hard-shelled prey* (crabs, oysters, and the

1

like) *by means of fleshy whiskers on their snouts. Bathers should be careful to shuffle their feet in sand, so as not to step on a sleeping nurse shark.*

Harmless . . . unless provoked. Only what constituted provocation to a nurse shark? Did they protect territories? Did they have emotional attachments to each other? In the tank with me there were two of the rough-skinned fishes (technically not fishes: sharks are actually a separate line, lacking bones and the more advanced gill structure of true fishes): Were they husband and wife? Would they defend each other? I had no idea what went on in the mind of a shark.

I did know they were good movie sharks, featured bit players in virtually every underwater epic from *20,000 Leagues Under the Sea* and *Beneath the Twelve Mile Reef* to *The Deep*. They were large (5–14 feet) and bigheaded and had wide, flaring fins. Sweet-natured, they wouldn't go far away, usually waiting on the bottom until a stunt man stirred them up. Then they would cruise, adding menace and atmosphere, while they searched for a peaceful spot to lie down.

But even nurse sharks have their limits, as one stunt diver found out. Not trusting a particularly photogenic nurse to stay in the desired area for the next day's filming, he'd lassoed the slow-moving bottom feeder and left it to writhe and struggle and try to free itself, through the long dark hours. Now, I would be pretty irritable myself if somebody tied me up and walked away, and when that stunt man came back and untied his unpaid actor, it glommed onto his shoulder and tried to do what it did with its natural prey, i.e., crush. I'm not sure if the diver regained the use of his deltoid, but I am fairly certain he didn't rope up many more nurse sharks.

When my suction cup broke loose from the wall, the extra-heavy lead weight belt around my waist dragged me backward and down. My finless feet kicked and cut vainly through the water as I fell, and it seemed pretty funny until my rear end sat down on the nurse shark's head.

As the muscles of my flinching buttocks contacted the rough cartilaginous skull, I distinctly remember thinking, "If

I get bit back there, I won't even be able to show off the scars!"

Then the nurse shark shrugged and pitched me off like a troublesome kid and, grumblingly, lumbered away, to a more sedate section of the tank.

And even though this incident was the beginning of a false confidence around sharks that lasted until precisely January 1, 1979 (on which date my opinion was forever altered), still I was very grateful that one nurse shark had not chosen to live up to its notorious reputation and considerable abilities—as a bottom feeder.

2

Dolphin Catch in Shallow Water

~~~~~~~~~~~~~~~~~~~~~~~~~~~~~~~~~~~~~

"Make 'em think God's got 'em!" the rough-voiced head diver had said. "Don't make your move until you're ready, and then boom! Go all the way, don't hold back."

And that's just what I had done, I thought smugly to myself, mentally replaying the instant before. One moment I had been standing in the waist-deep water of the lowered dolphin pool; the next a beautiful *Tursiops truncatus*, an Atlantic bottle-nosed dolphin, glided before me, and I lunged.

She had not even struggled. My lunge transfixed her in her path. A soft smack as my chest and her gray side collided, and I pulled her pectoral fins in to her, "so's she can't steer," as Ted Pintarelli had told me. Now I held the ocean's most beautiful animal, gentle in my arms.

The silk-clean delicate texture of her hide amazed me. Soft, tough, with tiny lines, barely visible indentations in the skin to give it added flexibility, so that it could actually change shape slightly as the animal swam, conforming even more perfectly to the varying forces of the water she hurtled through, leaped from, or lazied in. Even the painting of her coloration reflected the hydrodynamic nature of her element. For when scientists painted a wooden model of a dolphin and put the wet-painted model in the watery equivalent of a wind tunnel, the pattern the rushing water made on the paint was just like the swirls and whorls of shaded gray on the dolphin beside me.

This is easy! I thought as I waited for the vet to finish his

4

work, taking his blood sample from the edge of her tail flukes. Catching dolphins is no problem, not for us former weight lifters anyway, I told myself puffheadedly. The very next dolphin changed my opinion. Her name was Ernestine. She wasn't large—perhaps 220 pounds, 7½ feet long—and her sleek shape was unmarred by shark scars, rake marks, or fight wounds of any kind. Shouldn't be too tough, I thought.

But when Ted lunged and I followed, aiming to the right of his disappearing wet suit because I could not see the dolphin in the kicked-up foam, something like a heavy construction beam smashed me off my feet and continued on. When I regained my balance after a gasping eternity of bubbles and shock, Ted's back was emerging, and another diver was beside him, and they were being tossed by waves where there should have been no waves.

Quick as I could get to them I waded into the dolphin-made maelstrom and grabbed what slammed me in the ribs. I held the narrow up-and-down blade (called peduncle) just before the tail flukes, and I locked my arm and armpit around it, and I would never have dreamed anything so soft could have hurt like that. The bladelike edge dented my bicep.

Five of us, all husky divers with an average weight of at least 185, and we could not hold that little girl dolphin still. I would have been embarrassed if I hadn't been so busy. Not only were we tossed irregularly up in the air and yanked down, but she also played crack-the-whip side to side with us, by way of variety. I tried to find the floor with my feet, but it was pretty much all I could do to hang on, let alone brace myself and slow her down.

It took 45 minutes to hold that dolphin still enough for the doctor to get his needle in her tail and take a blood sample. When at last the reluctantly welling purple filled the syringe, and brown coagulant on a gauze pad pressed against the needle prick had stopped the bleeding, Ted said, "Okay, on three." His voice echoed in the cavernous, near-empty show tank. It was 22 feet from the floor we stood on in the shallow water to the normal surface level, and the silence as we waited to release was somehow eerie, like being on a darkened stage before an unoccupied auditorium.

"Three!" We opened our cramped arms.

Ernestine rolled an eye back at us. If she'd had an eyebrow, she might have raised it, twice, like an allusion to mischief. She waited a few seconds, in case there was any more party. Then she gave the dolphin equivalent of a shrug, arching away casually to the side, dismissing us from consideration. Her body motions were fresh and light, revealing not the slightest hint of fatigue, though she had tossed nearly a thousand pounds of humanity around for three-quarters of an hour.

"She doesn't look too awful terrified to me," I grumped, rubbing my arm.

"Ernestine?" responded Pintarelli. "Naah. She just likes to get it on, make it tough for us. It's a game to her." His eyes followed the female dolphin as she rejoined her friends.

Then his face tightened, as if against the wind. "Now there's the stud can give us trouble," said the wet-suited man. I followed the direction of his gaze.

One large dolphin, separate from the pack of others playing, was watching us. He had a short beak, and his eyes were not friendly. There was a small, round, purple mark on the left side of his face: incongruous, like a beauty mark. His melon, the massive foreheadlike area, was unusually heavy, and he was exceptionally thick between the hunched-forward pectoral fins. His powerful gray body was lined straight up with the small knot of divers. He hung very still in the now-quiet shallows.

"Him? The easy one?" I spoke up too quickly, remembering the dolphin who had stayed so quiet, allowing us to approach and take him, offering no more resistance than luggage at the station.

"He *let* us take him," said Ted. "That's Lucky, the king bull dolphin, the baddest dude around. Except for me of course," he added lightly. "Lucky still thinks he's in the wild."

"I'm gonna take away this ladder!" shouted somebody from above and playfully laid hands on our only means of exit from the tank. A rush of water foamed in from the inlet pipe, and it began to be time to turn away to other things.

But I was still watching Lucky and Ted. I felt a shiver along my spine. There was almost a visible energy between the diver and the bull dolphin. A sense of differences unresolved, as if two great warriors had glimpsed each other across an ancient battlefield. Each seemed to recognize the other as dominant among his kind. Was it inevitable that they would one day clash, and resolve their dominance dispute once and for all?

I could not know, of course, that their disagreement would end in death for one and breakage for the other.

3

A Walk Around the World

~~~~~~

The Pacific Ocean, or more specifically that arm of San Francisco Bay called the Belmont Slough, laps unspectacularly at the northeast corner of Marine World/Africa USA. Just a quiet marsh it looks like back there, mud and tough salt grasses and sea gulls flying over, and at low tide the sea retreats, so that a determined struggler could actually walk across that tidal basin, if he or she didn't mind getting muddied to the waist.

But life, the multitudinous microscopic beginnings of the great food chain, sleeps here, and, more immediate to Marine World's need, this is where the tide comes in, and men and machines snatch up a portion of it, to be cleaned and filtered for the animals of an artificially created sea.

Laboring pumps suck the bay water across a ridge and into a black vinyl-lined bed, like a colossal swimming pool. Here the water rests, and the heaviest particulate matter settles to the floor. Chemicals, soda ash, potash, chlorine, lime, are added in substantial but carefully monitored amounts. This process, called shocking, kills the bacteria and makes the water crystal clear. If you fell in before the excess chlorine had a chance to cook out (it gasifies and leaves), your skin would bleach, and your eyes might be permanently damaged.

But in a day or two the saltwater will be safe and clean and ready. Then a man like John Pipkin, lean and hard-muscled despite his more than sixty years, will walk out on the path between the marsh and the bed of treated water, almost as long as a football field. He'll stop at two huge rust-red barrels, surrounded by a maze of gray pipe and gauges and levers.

Studying the gauges, he'll place his hands on one certain lever and—delicately—heave. Carefully, for if the valve opens too swiftly, the onrushing water will break the pipe. The water roars into the rust-red barrels, which are filled with sand, to sieve out further impurities.

The water goes from the barrels to the pipes underneath the park, through an intricate network of lines that no one person totally knows, for those who laid them are no longer here, and there have been changes since then, and there are no maps. It is certain only that the water arrives at the various clusterings of tanks, there to circulate and be filtered again.

The filtration department tends the pumps; water quality people add the chemicals; and we, the divers, scrub the tanks that the channeled waters feed.

Every morning we take a walk around the world: or at least that portion of Marine World whose cleanliness we are responsible for. The walk, which takes 14 minutes if alone and more if in company, begins just past the elephant barn and the filtration shack.

Training tanks A, B, and C are essentially long capsules of concrete, open-topped, sunk deeply in gravel-topped earth, and filled with saltwater, dolphins, and an occasional whale. Here "naive," or untrained, dolphins learn to exchange their natural behaviors, leaps, bows, tail walks, for a fish and a signal.

Next door is Seal Compound, where a variety of pinnipeds, or flipper-footed animals, either train, or won't. Some, like the massive Steller's sea lion, don't have the patience to put up with much trainer nonsense. Others, like the elephant seal, bulging the fence as it scratches, lack the energy and inclination and would dismiss a trainer like a fly at the beach. These animals will be here, with a private swimming pool and the company of their own kind, until

they are either traded or get their own exhibit, or a transfer
to the naturalistic habitat of Seal Cove.

From here we walk past a pleasantly dilapidated wood
building with a grass roof in perpetual need of thatching.
That's our place, the dive shack. It fronts the lagoon, just
across from which is Sarge, the water buffalo. "Sarge," says
the tour boat which passes by several times an hour, "has
been on the Johnny Carson show and has starred in several
movies. But he's typecast now because he always plays . . .
a water buffalo." It's humorous enough, the first few hundred
times you hear it.

Across the bridge is the dolphin show and the reef aquarium complex. A windowed tunnel winds around the two
tanks. Follow the carpeted hallway down, and you'll first
have fish on both sides of you. Individual, or "jewel," wall
tanks on one side, and the beginning of a half-million-gallon
reef aquarium tank, one of the largest in the world, on the
other. Progress further, past the eels and seals and giant
booming groupers, and you'll come to my favorite spot in the
park.

At the lowest reef-tank window you can stand in the shadows and watch the life rippling slowly past you, while at your
back dolphins check you out from the other giant tank. Here
is where I like to linger, between the buoyant vivacity of the
dolphins and the slow-moving fish. Here also I take my son,
Roman, and my daughter, Desireé, and we stand and watch
and dream.

But up the hall and around is the sunlight, and that too
has its call. Just ahead is the koi pond, filled with the fat,
multicolored cousins to the goldfish, and beyond, the Seal
Cove, and to the left, that mound of earth and flowers with
a path leading up, that's Jungle Theater, where lions, tigers,
elephants, and chimps work and play and delight the folks.
Divers don't help much there, or at the ski show.

But beyond, there in the distance where the white pillars
intermingle with the trees against the sky—that's Oceana,
where the killer whales live.

4

Kianu

~~~~~~

There are two pictures in my scrapbook that I would not trade, though they are blurred and dim almost beyond recognition. The first depicts a small object with arms and a scrub brush, beside and below a black and white mass the size of a boat. The blur with the scrub brush is me, and the other is Kianu.

Kianu means "big woman" in Aleut, and the name fit her because the female orca, or killer whale, weighed somewhere in the neighborhood of four tons and was the largest performing female killer in the world.

In those days, before the killer whale troubles began, we would clean the orca pens with the animals still in them, and that was what I was pretending to do today. Arm bent at an appropriate underwater janitoring angle, I posed for the camera of a friend. He had just built an underwater housing for an ancient camera and wanted to test them. I had no photos of me and the great lady so I had volunteered to clean the already-clean pen.

Though her size was always just a little unnerving, Kianu's presence was warm and friendly, like a grandmother in the room. She spread her great pectoral fins, either of which would have overlapped a desk, and settled gently, almost but not quite to the floor, next to me. I felt the physical heat of her nearness in the cool water.

One poor fellow had had his diving career cut short by Kianu. Not that she'd been cruel: she hadn't bitten, hit, or broken him: she had just lain down on top of him. By way of a joke or an itch or some other killer whale reason, Kianu had gently lowered her vast bulk onto the new diver, until all but his little arm disappeared. His wrist and scrub brush stuck out, still twitching, as if he was going to scrub that tank no matter what. It must have felt like a living water bed on top of him. He wasn't hurt when she lifted off, but he gathered his gear and left the park in dignified silence, and we never saw him again.

Once I had been scrubbing the tank for real, and I'd felt a tugging on my air line. Just a little pull, and I figured a surface person was trying to get my attention. If it had been another diver, he'd have given a good healthy yank, but the topside people were more cautious with our air supply.

But as I rose, I'd been horrified to see, dim in the algae-clouded water, the unmistakable form of Kianu, *all tangled in my air hose.* There must have been ten coils around her, fore and aft of her high dorsal fin.

I couldn't leave her to go get a trainer; she might drown before I got back. But if she panicked and thrashed while I cleared her, I might get mashed against the wall. It would be like a bus falling over on me. I stared irresolute for several seconds, then kicked toward her forward half.

Her head moved. She'd seen me. I paused, then came ahead slowly, hoping she would understand.

She did. For as I approached, she seemed to sigh, and then her head arched up, and her pectoral fins came to-gether. The yellow coils I'd thought were snarled lifted up from her chest. She arched forward, graceful as a platform diver, and the back loops of air line freed up and floated. ("Oh. 'Scuse me, Kianu, I thought you were in trouble.")

What amazed me the most was not the escape, but the entanglement. While I am not as sensitive to the where-abouts of my air line as a hard-hat diver—who works at far greater depths (our deepest tank is only 22 feet) and to whom that line is definitely life—still I have some awareness of the location of the rubber hose attached to my back. But so per-fect was Kianu's mastery of the swimming motion that I had no knowledge that my lifeline was being played with until she had almost its entire length wrapped around her. POOF! The camera flash blinked me back to the present. One picture down; let's get another. And a good one, I thought to myself.

The second picture in my scrapbook shows the diver with his arm out, apparently petting the killer whale. But I was not expressing a natural affection when I started over to touch the whale. That clownish urge that drapes strangers' arms around celebrity shoulders in pretended intimacy motivated me. This was going to be my Killer-Whale-and-Diver Photo.

Kianu did not want it. She did not nod her head sharply down and up (yes means no in orca), and she did not clap her jaws. Her body bent inward, cringing genteelly away from the indignity—but she was too polite to really object. And I didn't take the hint. I wanted that picture!

As my hand approached her gently pointed snout, I felt a fuzzy, prickling force around her, like an aura. I shoved my hand through the energy and touched her.

Her eye took me over as if it was on a movie screen 20 feet across. Her red-brown eye with flecks of gold, overlaid with a blue sheen.

Just for a moment ego left me. I felt like a small, insignificant monkey, crouching before the ocean, staring out at unknowable all. I felt the foolishness of the vanity that makes us think we were the first and only rulers of the earth.

I took my hand away, but the great eye still held me. I felt, or wanted to feel, an enormous warmth enveloping me.

Now it is the nature of humans to put labels on unlabelable things and to attribute their own emotions to other life forms. Anthropomorphization, the scientists call it. I cannot say I am right about what I thought Kianu felt. Maybe, when I looked into her eye and thought I shared her soul, she was only thinking about food: about rich red mackerel or white slimy squid: or about sex, or the sun on her back. Maybe I was no more to her than a piece of interesting driftwood.

But what I felt, for her and from her, was love.

5

When Dolphins Fight

When dolphins fight among themselves, they deal in blows that look fit to shake the sides of buildings. Against humans, dolphins will (usually) hold back, moderating their violence for the relative fragility of our frames so that a beating-up is like a punch-out from an older brother who might knock you out but wouldn't kill or cripple you. Most often, dolphins or whales will refrain from violence against humans altogether, and indeed it used to be thought that dolphins would *never* strike humans under any circumstances—but this is an exaggeration of a general truth. The clan of whales, large and small, is an extraordinarily generous-spirited tribe, understanding (as we have not yet learned to do) the responsibilities of enormous power. I would go swimming with a 60-foot sperm whale if ever I got the chance, sure in the belief that he or she would be careful and not carelessly crush me with a finger-snap exertion of that monstrous mountainous power; even so, there are exceptions to all rules, and there are individuals who go against the norm. Such a one was Lucky.

The first time I saw Lucky fight, I thought I was in trouble myself.

I had been scrubbing the dolphin tank floor when I heard the KLONK! of a dolphin-aggression signal. I knew what that meant. Stop what you're doing and look around. Maybe Lucky wanted to clear the tank of humans, in which case I would climb out and sit for ten minutes and then try to sneak back in and do my work, or maybe it would be enough to just back up and look humble for a bit.

14

But it wasn't me that Lucky was warning. The KLONK! KLONK! (scientists aren't sure if the noise is a snap of jawbones coming together or the tongue being sucked rapidly across the roof of the mouth like kids making hoofbeat noises) was directed toward a large bull dolphin named Arnie.

The two dolphins nodded their heads sharply—making their noises—and charged. The speed was so great my mind registered only glimpses of gray blurs hurtling toward each other. At the last instant their forces veered, and as they passed (WHUNK!WHUNK!) the impact of tremendous tail slaps echoed, blows that would have broken a man.

As momentum separated them, one dolphin turned and shot back around in an incredibly quick turn, but the other combatant kept right on going, and all Lucky could do was pursue and rake the fleeing tail flukes of Arnie. Lucky's almost one hundred needle teeth scored cat's claw gouges in Arnie's gray skin and the tough blubber beneath, but the point had apparently been made, because the action was short-lived. Presently the two males were swimming together calmly as though they'd never fought. (Sometimes, however, the fights would continue for five to ten minutes of turning, charging, and sledgehammer blows.)

Once, almost by accident, I *hit* Lucky.

Dolphins like to rub on people. And not just for backscratch reasons, though that is certainly part of it. They will rub the lower portions of their bodies very roughly on a diver's leg or back, and what happens to an excited male mammal, happens. They are not inhibited sexually.

At first this was very embarrassing to me. They were not the least bit discreet about it, uncaring of the sensitivities of our guests peering in through the windows. And while it was surprising when a female enveloped my heel (FLOOP!) with her vagina, it was another thing altogether to have a male come at me with the intentions of a teenager in spring.

An adult male dolphin's penis (whatever testicular arrangement they have is internal) is about 12 inches long, gray pink, blue-veined, bent, and with a hook on the end. The structure is designed for making love on the run. Dolphins will often copulate in stillness, but they can also couple at 20 miles an hour, which is convenient when you consider they have enemies who could eat them both like a dolphin sandwich if they had to be motionless in mating.

When Lucky was in the mood (which was most of the time, but especially so in summer) he might ignore his gorgeous girl friend and charge my leg, shoving me across the tank with his lunging genitalia. "Go get Ernestine, you idiot!" I would shout in my mind while I tried to fend him off with my feet.

I was humiliated and enraged about this for years, because even when it ceased to be offensive to me, I figured the folks looking in the windows would be shocked and disgusted and think there was something wicked about me the diver—as though I had any control over it.

But gradually it filtered through to me that people either did not know what was going on ("Aww, look at the cute dolphin playing with the diver!") or understood and laughed. Like the grandmother I saw watching me through the windows once, when it was happening. She had her hands up to her face. Her wrinkles and age spots said seventy years and maybe widowhood because she was alone at the window. But the expression on her giggling face said twenty-one, and if I'd been working in a bar, I'd have asked her for her ID card.

So now I mostly just endured the semiassault of the dolphins. It did give me a different perspective, though, on waitresses and other women who have to work around guys who can't keep their hands to themselves. I hated being a source of sexual friction to someone much bigger and stronger than I was.

Lucky, in the innocent fury of his pleasure seeking, would sometimes shove me across the floor so that I kept missing algae as the concrete went by and would have to go back and do that part over.

On the day I speak of, Lucky whammed his maleness suddenly down on the back of my left knee. This knee had been injured slightly by the sport of Olympic weight lifting, which used to be my life. It gives me twinges now and then and is sensitive.

When Lucky ground my knee into the concrete, the pain was like an internal explosion. I could have drawn a very good diagram of the interior of my knee joint right then because it seemed to be coming apart, and I knew where each ligament and nerve ending was.

I punched Lucky in the beak. My fist stopped with a shock on that rock-hard rostrum dolphins use to wreck sharks, and there was one cold instant for me to think: What have I done?

There is a phrase the French use, lese majesty, and it means an unforgivable assault on a king: treason, the kind of thing people were killed horribly for, lest they dare get the idea a king was only a mortal. I had hit a king who happened to be able to defend himself.

Waves of dolphin anger flooded around me, and I knew I was not going to just get bonked on the head for this. Lucky was going to treat me as he would another dolphin.

His mouth opened and shut. His massive head nodded, and the sound of his jaw-snap challenge reverberated in my brain. My limbs were numb; I could not even think to cover my head and vital organs. I knew how a seal must feel when it has dodged and twisted to no avail and a killer has crunched it to helplessness for its children to practice on.

I will always believe that Ernestine rescued me. For, as Lucky's body seemed to swell, almost to vibrate with overflowing power, Ernestine, that small, lovely female dolphin, shot down between me and Lucky. And she was vocalizing, *ee-ee-eeeEEEE*!

Lucky jaw-snapped again, violently, and I saw the ridges on his torso. Ernestine continued to squeak in a sound range I could hear.

It was as though I was a teenager who had wisemouthed a professional boxer into rage, and the boxer's wife had stepped between us. ("Don't beat him up: you know you can take him—he's not worth it. Come on, let's go get some air. Okay sweetie—?")

Tension leaked away. The two dolphins turned and headed up for the surface, Lucky allowing himself to be tamely led away.

But just before they broke into the sunlight, Ernestine turned back toward me and abruptly snapped her jaws. And if she had really been the boxer's wife, she would have said: "All right you smartass kid, I saved your bacon just this once, but don't you ever mess with my man again!"

Lucky was, of course, back on my leg in about fifteen seconds.

How hard could he hit if he wanted to let loose? Arnie, a dolphin whom Lucky routinely fought and defeated, was once put into a tank with a huge Pacific guylli (gill-eye) dolphin named Gordo. Gordo means "fat one" in Spanish, and it fit because Gordo weighed at least 600 pounds, roughly two of Arnie.

We didn't figure Arnie and Gordo would fight, because Gordo was happy-natured and Arnie was too small—we were wrong. No sooner did Arnie's body slide out of the dolphin transport stretcher than the surface of the tank turned to foam, and we could hear the thunking sound of blows being struck underwater.

Gordo's black marble bulk lifted sideways into the air. It took a moment for us to understand what we had just seen, and then we could only shake our heads, or whistle, or softly swear. For Gordo had not leaped. His 600 or more (his weight has been estimated as high as 1,000) pounds had been knocked out of the water by the force of Arnie's tail kick.

What impact would that power have upon a human?

6

The Cowboy Diver

~~~~~~

When Ted Pintarelli grinned, he did so with front teeth that were not his own, except by right of purchase. The originals had been removed by a kicking horse, and the replacements shattered by a killer whale. I don't know who the horse was, but the killer whale's name was Ramu.

Ramu (not Namu or Shamu, those are other orcas) had been resting at Marine World on his way to Sea Life Park in Australia. Being moved is dangerous for orcas; some die. For though they breathe air like all mammals, killer whales need the supporting buoyancy of the water around them: without it, they must lift a portion of their own great weight every time they take a breath. It must be like having a couple of men stand on your chest. You could go on breathing for a while, but not long. So Ramu, who had been caught in Alaska and boat-towed in a floatable pen from there to here, was recuperating and building up strength before the long overseas air flight.

"We was trying to force-feed him, and he got excited," said Ted when I asked him how he lost his teeth the second time. "Got me with his flukes." He shrugged, about to dismiss the incident, then paused, tapped a blunt finger on the desk. "I like to think it was an accident," he added slowly, "because if he'd done it on purpose, he'd 'a' killed me easy." Then he nodded, having settled it in his mind.

Ted Pintarelli, head diver at Marine World when I first joined, was a part-time cowboy. He broke broncs and wres-

19

tled steers in weekend rodeos at Halmoon Bay, and a bull had horned him, under the chin.

"A brangus bull half brahma, half angus. Funny thing, too. My little buddy, Brien—he's five, and ever' time he'd fall, I'd tell him, 'fore he'd start to cry, 'Aw, shoot, that just makes you tough!' So when this brangus throws me and comes back around snortin' and hooks me under the jaw and I get away and there's a lot of blood and I'm trying to hold my jaw together with my hands, ol' Brien hollers down from the stands, 'Aww shoot, that just makes you tough!' "

Tough. That was the word for Ted. His face looked like somebody had taken a cheese grater to it and then healed the wounds with fire. A fist crashing into those red, scarred cheeks, you felt, would be inclined to glance off.

Maybe it was his eyes—large and brown and looking for an excuse to laugh—that made ladies get breathy in the voice when they talked to the head diver. Or maybe it was the unconscious aggressiveness in the easy way he moved his 200 pounds. When he leaned back, relaxed, bare feet crossed on the wooden desk of the divers' shack, his muscles lay in fine flat lines. When he stretched, he ridged and knotted all over, and when he moved, it was in sudden swiftness—that invisible speed that marks the animal and the athlete.

I saw Ted wrestle once, on the concrete behind our grass-thatched shack, a big burly fellow from the Midwest, named Sidney Bittle. Blond hair, blue eyes, healthy, square-cut biceps that crowded the elbow, and the comfortable moves of a cat in control of his neighborhood—Sid was hard. And when he went at Ted, at first the match went so fast I couldn't follow it, like one of those lion-tiger fights Clyde Beatty used to stage. But gradually a pattern began to emerge. They'd move swiftly—and stop. Move swiftly—and stop. Ted was playing. He'd wait, seeming to listen, uh-huh, uh-huh, as Sid threw a quick series of moves—and then Ted would defuse them and wait for the next batch. When it became apparent that the blond man was running out of new moves to try, Ted got bored, gathered Sid's head and knees together, and held him on his back.

And there'd been the time when Ted rubbed a giant's back in dog droppings and the time Ted took a dive into a vat of paint to find a treasured watch for a friend—can you imagine that? Paint? Ted had even been a whaler, for a time.

"Me and ol' Whitey the whaler, we used to work out of Oakland when they still had the rendering stations there. Killers, pilot whales, couple small sperms . . . One day Whitey says to me, 'Did you know a whale'll spout fire?' And I say, 'Whitey you're full of it—whale won't spout fire.' So he bets me: I have to clean the boat if the next whale we hit does do that. I forget what he put up, but I was waitin' and waitin' because I know whales don't spout no fire!

"Next whale we pull alongside of, Whitey harpoons him—in the lungs." Ted stopped short, the joke ended, even his hard face turned cold after what he'd seen.

"Whale spouted *blood*. All over the sky, all over the boat, or all over us. Red, everywhere." His voice trailed off, picked up. "Damn if it didn't look like fire!"

And then, very faintly, as though he was alone in the room: "Something like that . . . you don't forget."

7

Bradycardia

∿∿∿∿∿∿∿∿∿∿∿∿∿∿∿∿∿∿∿∿

Bradycardia, my dictionary tells me, means a slowing of the heart rate, sometimes occasioned by cold. Among deep-diving marine mammals like the sperm whale, bradycardia becomes a trick of survival, enabling the animal to slow down the flow of blood to its nonvital body parts temporarily so that the one vast lungful of air will last long enough (30 minutes? Longer?) for the hunter to find, fight, and feed upon his prey: the giant squid.

For us, the Marine World divers in the winter of 1973, bradycardia meant a place. The grotto.

The grotto was where the dolphins lived, but they are not important to this story. Indeed, the sex and violence they sometimes brought would have been welcomed, almost, as a diversion. Against the cold.

There was ice on the dolphin stage, a thick film to be stepped on and broken into spiderweb cracks and kicked aside in piles of slush so that our bare feet could grip. The muscles under the soles grew so numb that we seemed to stand on stumps. We made our preparations deliberately, plugging in the hookah lines, *click-hisssss*, and watching the pressurized air stiffen the yellow coils: we tugged swim fins onto white, deadening feet, spitting in our masks with commendable thoroughness, tracing the saliva that served as an antifog solution all across the faceplate lens—anything to put off the jumping in.

As we sat on the edge of the platform, dangling our feet, we'd look off into the gray sky and hope someone had something to say.

"Say, did I ever tell you the story of my life?"

"Why no, not this morning at least, and I'd love to hear it! Do please begin at the beginning, and leave nothing out."

"Well, I remember the womb. . . ."

But finally the words would die. We'd look at each other, in case there might be just one more story or comment or any excuse whatever to put off the going in. We'd scoot an inch closer to the edge but still holding on, like penguins reluctant to step off the ice floe.

"NOOOOOOO!" somebody would scream and commit to the plunge, and everybody else would follow into the freezing bubbles of his entry.

"The painnnn," as Bill Cosby once put it, "was amazing." The brain seemed squeezed in an ice vise—you know the headache you get from eating ice cream too fast? Uh-huh, only longer.

Our heads, like our feet, were bare. We wore neither the diver's rubber bootees, nor hoods. I don't know why. We weren't trying to prove our courage or lack of intelligence. We just didn't wear the warmth-retaining gear, and I couldn't have told you why.

There were two ways, neither satisfactory, of dealing with the freeze. One was to hug the heat we had carried from the surface, turtling our head and neck to our shoulders, clamping elbows into our sides, scrubbing with the smallest possible strokes, trying to ignore the unsubtle shoots of ice water down the neck and spine. In 20 or 30 minutes, the first discomfort would diminish. The second method was the charge. Rush down through the heavy-feeling water as fast as we could move our limbs, hit the floor and scrub in a frenzy, roaring the wire brush back and forth in a desperate attempt at increasing body temperature.

This all-at-once maneuver did keep the mind occupied while the body flailed and the adrenaline rushed, but I always wondered if my heart might not one day rebel and just stop. I'm told there are people called ice bathers who do this sort of thing unpaid and without coercion. These brave souls go in among the snow and icebergs (if available)) wearing nothing more than a swimsuit, for the sheer exhilaration of it. Personally, I prefer a warm bed and a book. I never went into that freezing tank without the conviction that I was doing something dreadfully wrong.

It was better not to wear a watch because if those slowly moving hands were available, our eyes would be drawn to them. The time passed more slowly (What?! Only that long?) for our awareness of it.

Better to think of the hard, dark green algae on the floor. Winter algae, tough algae, sneering at the supposition that one-celled plants needed warmth to grow. Smooth algae, with no rough surface for the wire brush to catch and dig into, clung like paint. The wire brush had to be turned on edge and driven forward with all the force of the arm and shoulder behind it. Sometimes our best efforts only scratched bristle marks in the green so that we had to repeat the scour, shoving the brush in the same inch-wide, foot-and-a-half-long stroke, and sometimes it took four or five strokes to get it clean.

The cold came in waves, and we'd fight the creeping-in numbness by increasing effort on the brush, shifting hand to hand, eight strokes right, eight strokes left, heave ourselves against the floor, and the cold would back away a little. But it was just waiting.

We might delay the victory of the winter for two hours, three, or even four. But then would come exhaustion, and the frost would settle in our bones. The body retreated to its last defense, shivering in a desperate friction, rubbing itself together for warmth that would not come.

Pale fingers weakened until the loose circle they formed around the brush handle guided more than held, and sometimes the brush flipped over as the grip lost power and control.

When the floor at last was more white than green, the algae was judged to have conceded the match. In a few days it would have regrown completely, but for now we had only to kick blindly for the surface and get out by leaning on the stage with our bellies and sides because we did not want to use our hands just now.

The hands became instantly red, swollen, and heavy with the blood that fell into them as we stood. If we'd had to fight anybody now, we'd have to use our knees and elbows, because the fingers felt weak and brittle enough to snap off like carrots.

But if we could just gather our gear and make that one awful leaning step up from the dolphin stage onto the reef-tank platform (some small movements require an agony of internal effort) and a few easy steps and down, a paradise awaited us.

A dream of warmth and light and beauty so completely out of synchronization with what we had just suffered that it seemed at first a fantasy, conjured up by our freezing, dreaming minds.

8

The Paradise of Life and Death

~~~~~~

Our immediate need, as we stumbled down the steps into the reef tank in the winter of 1973, was warmth. And the first gift the reef gave us was heat. Tropic temperature, bathlike and radiant into our numbed cores so that we could have shed our wet suits and swum naked. We did not, of course, for not only were there visitors peering in through the windows, but there were little fish who would peck and bite at anything unusual. But we didn't need to skinny-dip to get the pleasure anyway.

We'd sit in the flume (a small shallow tank that used to connect the grotto and reef) and let our internal temperature rise.

Sitting in blissful silence, luxuriating in the warmth, closing our eyes to enjoy it more. The cold had wound our life clocks way ahead so that we seemed to be a stiff and shaking seventy—the warmth turned the clock back, and undid the years. Our tight limbs loosened, and we were young again.

And when our arms could stretch out freely and we'd begun to get just a little bored sitting still, it was time to duck out the reef-tank entrance.

Into technicolor.

Even now, years later, sitting at my desk with my notes all around me, I can hardly accept the memory of that beauty in my mind.

Colors on fish that looked up startled: yellow, *bright* yellow, sunspots of yellow (you could warm your hands by that yellow); orange, flashes of it, vivid like fire; and iridescent purple like a black-light poster. Fish I had no names for then, and even now I do not know them all. Surgeonfish, angelfish, sturgeon, jack—some were shy and hid, darting behind a sheltering arm of the fiber glass reef and peeking out.

Others were bold and perky, and the boldest and the perkiest was the damselfish. The brown, dancing damselfish, 3 inches long in the body and with filamentous tail, brave as six lions. POCK! My mask jarred, the first time I met the savage, finger-long damselfish. POCK! POCK! It took me a minute to realize what was happening. I didn't associate the snapping peck on my mask with the darting little brown fish. "Huh? What? Was that you?" "Yes, it was me, you idiot four-leg, get out of here, or I'll bite your face off!" In the wild, I'm told, this tough little character will attack the fearsome barracuda, charging and snapping at the big, savage-toothed predator. The barracuda reportedly tries to ignore it, maintaining dignity by paying no notice, but it gets out of the damselfish's yard.

A sausage-shaped fish, cream-colored, with chocolate brown spikes along the sides. Approach too closely and pop! it becomes a blowfish, a round, spiky ball full of sea. Couldn't swim much, inflated—you could poke it with a finger, and it'd just bob around. It must have been frightened though. What would it be like to be a blowfish and have a slender gliding blue shark approach you? You'd puff up immediately. How much effort did that take? Like holding a deep breath? Could you maintain it while the blue shark cruised around you, maybe nosing you with its pointed snout? Might even take the spiky ball of your cream-white body inside its mouth. Would your defenses hold? Could you maintain the integrity of tightness? Or would the teeth slice through and end everything—POOT! The blowfish became a sausage again and flitted away.

Once in a book I saw a picture of the Amazon jungle, and the artist had crowded the canvas with animals. On that one double-page spread picture was an example of almost every South American creature. Boa constrictors coiled in trees. Anacondas swam in the river. Eagles perched high, and monkeys swung and jaguars stalked. You couldn't have put your foot down without stepping on some beast in that painted jungle. For a long time I thought of the jungle as being that jam-packed. It's not, of course, but the reef *was*.

Sturgeon—strange-looking, lumpy relative of the goldfish. Ridges and bony plates all over, with a catfish mustache, body 6 feet long and giving a colossal impression of dumbness, underslung mouth pooched out and so slow-moving it gave not the slightest hint of threat despite the bulk. I could have used it for a couch, I think and it probably wouldn't have noticed.

Surgeonfish, with natural switchblades behind their ears. Their bodies seemed colored by a mad-genius painter who thought gaudy but painted with taste.

Tarpon. Silver, sharp-angled, gorgeous. Hanging in mounted stillness. Scales as big as silver dollars armoring their man-lengthed, shining forms of latent energy. Frightening—not for their teeth (which I never saw) but for the sudden *snap!* speed of their departure. One instant immobile; the next, a silver frame in your memory.

Gar. Alligator gar. Prehistoric alligator gar, going back till time unmeasured. They reminded me of Texas fish I'd seen, in brown lake stillness and heat. Nothing moved. Except them, the quiet, dinosaur fish. They were long-snouted, the alligator gars, and with teeth that seemed unnecessarily huge. I never saw them fight, or hunt, but I swam up to one once and touched its hard tail. The recoil almost broke my wrist. The dead eyes looked me over, and I did not mess with it again.

Moods in the reef tank—what Jacques Cousteau, that colossal pioneer and champion of the sea, calls "ambience," the feeling all around you. Like when you walk into a room full of people and you pick up on their emotion. Maybe friends had been arguing, and they stopped on your arrival, and you feel the anger, though nothing is said. If you were blindfolded you could still probably sense the tension—especially if it was you they were angry at.

So it was in the reef (brain waves, I suppose), and when the shock of information overload had passed and I didn't have to keep thinking "What's that?" all the time, then I liked to try and pick up on the brain waves, to figure out what was going to happen from the interlocking moods.

Some days it seemed a truce had been called. The fish moved calmly in the lazy, summerlike warmth, and the human mind relaxed. Beams of sunlight waved on the bottom, and there in the farthest corner of the reef was a sight almost not to be believed.

Two dozen giant sea turtles all stacked up. Loggerheads and greens, piled up in a snoozing heap. Turtles don't burn much energy holding still, and they could apparently hold their breaths for many hours.

And woven among the smooth dark ovals of the greens and the rough irregularities of the loggerheads were moray eels, poking their heads up like snakes by tombstones. Normally the turtles would eat the eels if they could catch them, but during the truce all that seemed to be forgotten.

Those were the days it was safe to practice flying, and envy no man, on Earth or off. The astronauts got several bounds on a lowered-gravity moon, and some weightless moments in the sterile vault of outer space. But my sky is alive, and flying is the way we do business here.

I liked to take my fins off and, my weight belt loaded heavy with gray slabs of lead, climb up on the reef like a mountain climber, poise at the top, balance, and dive off. The shove would carry me out and up, to the interface of water and air, and it seemed sometimes I could keep right on going and glide into the sky. But the sea is enough, even a small bubble of it, and I preferred not to even stick my hand out, into the dry air, but would arch at the top, my belly almost breaking the surface, and arch backward, toes pointed, peeling off in a soaring arc toward the floor, 20 feet below. The lead weights pulled me down in a dive—faster and faster—to land on one finger. And push off, jump up, and play some more.

Oh, for an oceanic vocabulary! My landlocked words can only barely convey what divers share. The Eskimo, I hear, have thirty-three names for snow: snow falling softly, snow that sticks, snow to make fresh water from—many words for the element that is so important in their lives. Some day, when millions of people live and work routinely in the sea, we will have the words.

But now, for that endlessly varied motion that is almost an emotion, that interaction with the liquid element, the flying, gliding, arching, soaring, wheeling, rushing, charging, racing, poising—the delicate but strong calculations that seem to happen automatically, the outward pushing of the fingers and hands for direction, the massive shovings of the thighs when the body really has to move, emergency kick, the forearm pulls for polar bear surface paddling, the twitching flexions of the knees and ankles for casual transportation, for all this and more I have only—*swimming.*

One of my favorite swimmers in the reef was the brown stingray, which glided across the bottom, wings rippling like an endlessly unfurling cape. The stingray is a menace to heavy-footed surfbathers, who really should shuffle their feet in the sand to give this mellow cousin of the shark a chance to get away . . . and not have to use its stinger. (I would be inclined to object too, if somebody stepped on my head.)

The stinger, mounted at the base of the whiplike tail and resembling a narrow ridged sword, carries either poison or infection (scientists disagree) so that a foot lanced by that weapon would be a foot plunged in agony. But, if not stepped on, stingrays are the sweetest of fishes.

Never did a stingray try to strike me, or any other diver whom I know about. (The electric ray, with malice toward all, was another matter altogether, but that's a different chapter.) We would feed them at the windows, holding up our hands like stop signs for the stingray to jump into. Rays have large brown eyes that apparently don't work well at all; these animals live in a kind of happy fog.

They'd perch on our hands like hesitant butterflies, and we'd give them squid to eat. Their smile-shaped mouths would inhale—floop—and the ray would flap off with part of the squid protruding underneath, like Churchill's cigar. One fellow trusted the good-naturedness of the stingrays so far as to thrust his thumb up inside one's mouth, to see what would happen. He had forgotten, I suppose, that stingrays very often deal with hard-shelled animals, and even their tolerance was not without limits. I was not present at the experiment, but I'm told it was quite interesting. I asked the subject to repeat his venture, but his scientific curiosity seemed to have dried up. He wouldn't even let me look under the bandages.

The eels too were a surprise in the reef. With plenty of room for both moray and diver to retreat in, a wary kind of mutual tolerance could be developed. The eel would leave the small, dark, safe places, and the diver would feed squid or mackerel to it. We could touch them, and their soft, muscled bodies felt like wet velvet. Over time, enough confidence could be built up by both parties that the eel could be handled, poured over the hands like a living rope.

Only once did an eel bite me in the reef, and then it was a small eel and a small bite. I had just been handling it too long, showing off for someone in the window, and the 18-inch baby turned and SNAP! bit me on the index finger of my left hand. A quick nip and let go, none of this "hang on till death-do-you-part" stuff you read about in adventure books.

The reef morays did not make me feel threatened, though—not at all like the small wall tank that displayed forty morays living close together. Going in that tank was an exercise in self-control for me, and even now my breath comes short, and my stomach freezes when I think about it: all those slimy armless bodies, and the teeth. Some eels were coiled and some swimming, and when you scrubbed, the algae would cloud the water and the swimming eels would brush you in the dark. (I did not think about the moray eel tank often.)

It was possible, of course, to misread the moods of the various life-forms. One such misunderstanding I had involved a sergeant major who I thought liked me. He did, but not in the way I intended.

Black and silver stripes, hard gray lips he could crush coral with, wide and flat and upright in the water, he was as big as the lid of a garbage can. I would scrub the floor, and the sergeant major would spend time beside me. Occasionally he would putter away long enough to break off a chunk of fiber glass reef (apparently for the algae flavoring it), but mainly he hung out with me.

I liked his companionship. I even had a stray thought or two (blush, blush) about how maybe I could train the sergeant major and have the one and only world's first performing sergeant major fish act.

But he only wanted me for my body. CHOMP! He took a chunk out of the back of my elbow. I spun and punched the water where he'd been. Sergeant major shot in a 6-foot circle that brought him back within my reach. "Dagnab fish doesn't realize how dangerous I am. Dumb thing anyway, we could 'a' had Broadway, we could 'a' been a team," I babbled to myself as I turned back to my scrubbing and the sergeant major bit me again—same elbow, same spot, like I'd fallen on asphalt, liked it, and done it again.

"All right, fish, you're gonna get it. I am going to punch your lights out. But cleverly. With strategy."

I had been scrubbing. I continued scrubbing. But, slowly and unostentatiously, I gathered my right leg under me, trying to appear natural about it, as though it was my unvarying custom to lie down with my belly on top of my heel. "I'll teach you, you miserable fish, to respect me"—I sprang!

The sergeant major retreated, but his heart wasn't in it. Mine was though, and I chased him furiously till he zipped around behind the reef and disappeared. But, haha, I knew my opponent, I knew his habits, and I knew precisely by what route he would return.

Giggling softly, I crept along the side of the fiber glass reef and set myself in deadly ambush. When that fat garbage-can lid came around the corner like he always did I was going to give him such a sock, he'd never bite me again! I'd—I would—he—where *was* that stupid fish? I raced around the corner, nothing—back again, nothing—? I looked *up*. The sergeant major was resting comfortably on top of the reef, as if leaning on its fins looking down. Observing me. I chased that fish till I sweated in my wet suit. At which point I reflected, pant, wheeze, that the poor dumb animal was probably in terror for its life, nnnnn-hah, and I took pity on it, and did not terrify it anymore.

There were other times in the reef, times when I knew something was hunting. I could feel the violence about to break, tension building like lightning about to strike from thick gray skies. Then my eyes tried to take in everything, from the motions of the animals to the shadows under the reef.

Once I *heard* an eel kill. A soft pop as of something breaking. My head yanked around, and only then did I see the moray in the middle of its kill. Eels cannot swim fast; what it must have done was brace against something solid—a coil or two like a spring compressing—and jumped and bit and broke the crevalle jack, for such it looked to have been, though it was difficult to tell with the bits of white fish flesh exploding upward and the moray weaving backward quickly, desperate to reach cover before something bigger came along and took its meal away.

There were fish in the reef that could do it too, and inhale the eel in the bargain.

9

Groupers: Mr. and Mr.

~~~~~~

There were no sharks in the reef tank then. They would come later. But there were two strange fish who liked to snack on small sharks and who would have given even the largest of predators cause to reflect.

These were the groupers or giant sea bass. Jewfish, Junefish, Him-with-the-Big-Mouth. Definitely "him," too, for all giant sea bass begin life as females, bear their young, and then switch sexes, spending the rest of their lives as males.

We had two. One weighed 450 pounds, and that was the small one. The larger weighed 550 pounds and had lips like Volkswagen bumpers. Skin green-tinged, speckles and dots, and the textured complexity of its hide had a purpose, for it could change color.

If a grouper got nervous (which did not happen often) it could disappear. Once two smallish groupers, 200 pounds apiece, were unloaded into a wall tank. We watched and helped dump the stretchered fish in, then ran down from the top of the tank and around to the hallway to see how the groupers looked in their new residence. But when we stood in the carpeted hallway, and peered in through the glass, the big fish were gone. Vanished, as if they'd been stolen. It took us ten minutes to figure out where they had gone, which was nowhere. They were right in front of us, but we could not see them until one big, independently roving eye moved— look! There—see it? If you kept the eye in sight, the rest of the grouper's body could gradually be picked out. But what

34

perfect camouflage! For not only had they made themselves the exact shade of brown the wall was, but they had made *shadows* appear on their sides, so that the bumps and hollows of the fiber glass seemed to continue on their bodies.

Groupers. Almost too big to be afraid, like the elephants in Africa. Skin divers used to kill the huge cave fish with relative ease. The groupers expected no threat from the scrawny hunter struggling down so clumsily from the surface. They watched, curious, until the spear crashed into their bodies. So did the elephants die, allowing the safari hunters to walk right up near the wrinkled gray sides, so close that only a light rifle was needed to kill, until the mastodon's descendants learned caution.

But there was no sport killing done here; there were no spear guns in the park. Well, one: a huge, double-rubber-belted cannon that fired a shaft about an inch thick. We used it once to destroy a bass with possibly communicable fungus, lest an epidemic start and wipe out the tank. I did the executing, sliding up beside the corroded bass and squeezing the huge trigger. The spear as big as a pole went through the sick fish, killing it instantly, but I felt as though I'd used an elephant gun on a gopher. We've still got the enormous weapon, which was apparently intended to fight white sharks with, but it's up on a wall now, in decorative retirement.

A diver without a spear gun is apt to be realistic. I had no illusions whatever about who ruled that tank. And I remember well the first time the grouper showed me who was the monarch of this patch of sea.

BO-OOOOOMMM I *felt* the sound, vibrating)))))((((through my ears and innards, and I looked up from my scrubbing. Nobody had to tell me whose chest had produced that long, drawn-out explosion.

There he was, King Rubbalip, chesting his way across the algae-covered floor. That mouth looked big enough to swallow me and a couple of cousins, and I could read no expression in the bulging, obelisk eyes. I'd seen him eat before; I knew his method. He did not merely swallow the fish, no: he vacuumed up the immediate neighborhood as well. CHUFF! The gill covers would flare out and flex shut. And the intended dinner guest would be inside.

My cheek on the just-scrubbed concrete before me, like naptime at kindergarten except no "blankie," I lay perfectly still. I saw the folds of gray, loose skin that let the gill covers expand so widely: I saw the gills themselves, red fibrous combed strands. I saw the belly of the great fish as it swam over, and the wide tail brushed me. The grouper had neither accelerated nor moderated its pace as it passed the human beneath it. It simply continued, as though nothing of consequence had occurred.

But something puzzled me. The enormous mouth . . . I could see no *teeth* in it. I knew the grouper swallowed smaller fish directly down the throat, and I had heard its stomach walls were muscular and could squeeze and pulp like a garbage disposal—but still, no teeth?

It was only a casual curiosity. I wish I had never learned the answer.

10

The Dolphin Strike

~~~~~~~~~~~~~~~~~~~~~~~~~~~~~~~~~~

Lucky put the dolphins on strike: canceled the shows.

Now you might wonder how even a dominant dolphin like Lucky could exercise authority over humans, but it was actually very simple.

When a veteran trainer like Jim Mullen would whistle all the dolphins to stage-side, Lucky let them go. He also allowed the other dolphins to accept food from the sandy-haired trainer, but nothing more. No further human commands would be obeyed. Jim might blow his whistle till his lips chapped or swing his hand in signal till his arm unscrewed, but when Lucky turned his head slightly to the side and gave the gentlest of jaw snaps, not a dolphin would budge for the trainer.

All the guests in the grandstand got to see was a group of lazy-swimming dolphins, sometimes taking a casual dive down to the inlet pipe to watch the current, but mostly lolling on the surface, enjoying the warmth of the sun. The people shifted on the hard wooden bleachers, and the announcer explained and explained and tried to think of something else interesting to say about dolphins.

Mullen, playing that mental game that training is, would try to build an interaction, to touch a personality and get the behaviors (trainers never say "tricks"; everything dolphins do in a show is an extension of their natural oceanic behavior) moving. "Hi, Ernestine!" Jim would call and toss a silver smelt to the lady tursiops. Ernestine's jaws would snap out accurately, and the fish would be lying lengthwise on the dolphin's pink tongue. She might flip the food around a bit or store it beneath her tongue or swallow it immediately, but when the old pro trainer would try to build on that contact and issue a command, Ernestine's eye would go to Lucky. Permission denied. Ernestine would go back to playing, breaking the link Jim had built. The people would leave the stadium muttering and looking back.

You can imagine how the trainers felt, not being able to deliver a decent show: Trainers are also show people, and any performers worthy of the trade suffer agony when they cannot deliver.

One young trainer got so crazy with the frustration of a no-dolphin dolphin show that he jumped into the water with his clothes on and swam through the show himself. He Australian-crawled through the hoops, beached himself on his human belly on the stage, and even accepted a fish reward in his mouth. The people cheered, even the dolphins seemed impressed, and Jeff Pulaski's name will long be remembered in Marine World lore—but even that sacrifice play could hardly be considered a substitute. Come to Marine World and see the performing trainer?

Still and all, the dolphin strike was only an embarrassment; what was serious was the fact that Lucky had gone off his feed. He wouldn't eat: not the fat herring, not the small "tinker" mackerel, not the white small squid, not the shining silver smelt. He might mouth a crisp fresh smelt, even puncture the light scale armor with a needle tooth or two. But the juices did not tantalize. He would disinterestedly take his jaws out from under, or even pitch the fish away and watch it sideslip softly to the bottom, where a diver would have to retrieve it. None of the other dolphins would touch a piece of Lucky's food.

Lucky would have to be pulled and taken to one of the back training tanks. There the vets could watch him more closely, and the trainers would try to stimulate his interest in performing by giving him more attention one to one. If the problem was medical, then what could be done, would be done. Dolphin medicine is still in its infancy, but there were at least antibiotics to fight infection and steroids to increase appetite and protein utilization.

The vets, management, and trainers decided and passed the word along to the divers, who would do the catching.

To avoid throwing away several hundred dollars' worth of filtered, treated water, the catch would be tried first in deep water. If it proved impossible, the water level could always be dropped later, but Ted Pintarelli would never have been the man to call for that. The head diver's attitude was that of the late great football coach, Vince Lombardi, who once said that he had never lost a football game; he'd just had the clock run out on him a few times.

"I saw Ted in a bar fight once," said Dave Worcester, blond-haired and blue-eyed like his brother Keith, who would later become one of my best friends and a fellow diver.

"This big guy tried to cold-cock Ted with a sucker punch, brought his fist right off the bar and all his weight behind it. Ted wasn't braced, and the blow knocked him flying. But he hit in a roll and got up smiling and went right to work. Cleaned the other fellow's clock, too."

In high school, I'd heard, Ted's football coach had promised a painted lightning bolt for anybody who knocked out an opposing player on the field. Ted earned so many lightning bolts he ran out of space on his helmet and had to paint them on his locker door.

With Ted the question wasn't *if* he could capture a dolphin, but when. He'd bide his time and wait, and BAM! make his move. And if one trick didn't work, Ted knew another and another, and he'd never give up until his arms locked around the gray smooth sides. Ted was inexorable: inescapable, like time.

But Lucky's time was almost gone. We could not believe anything would harm Lucky seriously; he was too strong! In actuality, however, the ocean mammal was dying.

But Lucky was still Lucky. He was the dolphin king. And there were yet deeds to do.

11

Nepo and a Glimpse of Yaka

~~~~~~~~~~~~~~~~~~~~~~~~~~~~~~~~~~~~~~~

"Hiya, Neep!" I said, just a little too loudly, to the killer whale beside my legs. My heart seemed to flutter as I sat on the stage, with my shins and feet in Nepo's pen. I'd cleaned Nepo's pen with the juvenile killer inside, oh at least a dozen times, I reminded myself. And he'd never given me trouble.

Nepo. *Orcinus orca*, killer whale. Or, more properly, whale killer, for this is what the predator of the great cetaceans used to be called before the name and the image got twisted around. "KILLER WHALE EATS 14 DOLPHINS AND 28 SEA LIONS!" the tabloid headlines would shout, every so often, always quoting the same source, Captain James Scammon. But what the 1890s whaler and naturalist had actually *said* was that he'd found the *remains*, fragments of ear bones and the like, of those forty-two animals in one killer-whale stomach.

If the ingested animals had been whole (even assuming a low average weight of 300 pounds per individual), their combined weight would have been 12,600 pounds, which is quite a lot of stomach contents, particularly since killer whales don't usually weigh that much themselves. Our orcas ate between 80 and 120 pounds of food per day. In the wild they would have eaten less regularly and therefore more at one time, but 12,000 pounds at one sitting? They would have had to have a stomach bigger than they were, like a blimp with a bigger blimp in its belly.

"You're just a big pussycat, aren't you, Nepo?" I said to the orca at my feet. My voice came out boisterous because I was scared inside. I didn't like to admit that to myself, so I reached over and patted Nepo's huge head, slap slap.

The "big pussycat" jerked his head sideways, and his teeth halfway snapped where my hand had been. Not a complete closing of the teeth, not a "KLOCK!" jaw snap, but a sudden narrowing of open jaws. Definitely not a gesture of friendship either; the emotion transmitted, or at least perceived, was "keep your damn hands off." Okay! That's fine! No problem! I was perfectly willing to be less demonstrative.

What I should have done would have been to let the male orca alone altogether. At least give him time to change moods. Sometimes whale irritation can vanish as quickly as chalk off a washed blackboard.

But I was still at the stage where I watched John Wayne movies for personality guidance, and I thought a *man* would never back away, as if a person was like a car with only one forward gear, and no reverse.

"O-kay, here I come!" I said to Nepo, and left the security of the stage. As I slipped off the edge, I made more noise than I usually like to.

It was autumn, and the Oceana algae were in full bloom. Brown lumpy layers of it, fertilized by the extra waste orcas produce in cold weather, by-product of the increased food they need to keep up warmth. Hard to believe this tank had been cleaned just seven days before.

This is when I like to scrub a tank, when I'm needed to make a difference. I feel like I'm fighting monsters ("Attack of the Slime"!) as I pick up my weapon and look grimly at the floor. "Can you do it, great hero, sir?" "I don't know, Smedley, a man can only try." And then we lock in mortal combat, my enemy the algae and I.

ZWISSH, SCRUB, ZWISSH, SCRRUB—the outward stroke away from the body takes off the topmost layer of algae, and the inward pull scours down to the clean. The first slash of white breaks the brown, declaring my intentions, laying down the glove of challenge. Then only work will answer, widening the combat. For while I have the brush, the slime has the numbers, uncountable trillions of entities, united in an advancing horde.

I lose if I leave skip marks, both figuratively and literally. For if the scrubbed-off algae settle back to a smooth, perfectly scrubbed surface, they will not be able to latch on as quickly, and the filtration system has a chance to suck more of the enemy away. But if I allow the thin brown hairline smudges of algae at the outer reaches of the brush stroke to remain, then the million billion algae brothers hanging in the air will have something to adhere to.

If we do our work right, no one will notice. They will see only the grandeur of the animals, which is as it should be. People don't visit parks to think about scrubbing floors. Only another working diver, or a filtration attendant or a water quality person, might look at a tank and know the work it took to make it clean.

My wife Jeannie cringes when I refer to myself as an underwater janitor, but she shouldn't. As anyone who has lived in both clean and sloppy neighborhoods can tell you, cleanliness means pride. Above water or under, janitors make the place look proud.

A shadow spread coolness on my back. I turned and saw the inside of Nepo's mouth. The teeth like ivory thumbs. The enormous tongue. The pink and black-spotted gullet. He wants a fish, he wants a fish, I told myself. Sorry Nepo, got no food in my pockets. No pockets either, for that matter.

I tried to return to my scrubbing and dreaming, but the peace was broken. The nervousness rose in me, even before something clamped on the back of my thigh. High up, just before the buttock and the groin.

Nobody had to whisper what had grabbed me. I knew enough to hold very still, so as not awaken the feeding response. For what would a killer whale automatically do to a struggling lunch?

Rotating my head very slowly so as not to twitch my fragile leg, I turned back to see Nepo's truckhood-sized snout. Limitless power, poised.

My lower limb numbed. I thought about the great femoral artery, the pipeline of blood that winds around and through the thigh. Sever the femoral artery, and the life will pump away in short order.

I thought about what a turkey leg looks like when the knife only does part of the work and the carver wrenches off the rest: ligaments and bone exposed and muscle fragments where the meat tore.

Oddly, though, I could not feel the individual points of his teeth. I had no information to judge with (never having been eaten by a whale before), but the generalized squeeze felt almost as if he held me in his gums.

Nepo let go and backed away. I remembered to breathe.

But do you know what that big sucker did next? He looked over to his left, to a square-cut hole in the cinder-block wall.

And there, peering in that window, was the red eye of Yaka, the young female orca.

My mind was filled as with coarsest laughter, and the emotion in that tank read clear as words on a printed page: "HAWWW! DIDJA SEE ME FREAK THAT DIVER?!"

Showing off for his killer-whale girl friend.

12

The Last Confrontation
of Lucky and Ted

Lucky knew why we were in his tank. Divers with nets and no scrub brushes in their hands. The thick-torsoed dolphin watched closely as we settled to our prearranged positions on the floor. Ted dominated the right third of the net-enclosed area, I waited in the middle, and Keith Worcester poised himself alertly on the left.

What was it Keith had said about Lucky? "First time I went in with Lucky, everybody'd told me what a killer he was. I figured I would be dead before I hit the bottom. But Lucky came over to check me out, and he looked at me like 'I'm here, and obviously you're afraid of me, so I'll just go over there and leave you alone.' He did, too, except that he liked to chew on my swim fins. And once when Delbert [another large male tursiops] was hassling me, Lucky chased him away."

Like a statue of an ancient dolphin god, Lucky loomed over me now. I saw the short stub of beak, and the round spot of purple on the right side of his snout. The brown, black-flecked eyes peered into me.

I had been balancing lightly on my fin tips. I pulled my arms in close and crouched, scarcely crediting my good luck as the bull dolphin, body upright like a man, eased his white belly forward, toward me. His pectoral fins stretched out like hands. Another few inches closer and I was going to get a

grab on the dolphin king. My first deep-water catch, and if
I could put the tackle on Lucky—

I leaped from the floor. I weighed 210, and I had once
lifted 345 pounds overhead in an official weight-lifting com-
petition. I was strong, and I could move, and I did not hold
back.

I couldn't tell you how many times Lucky's head and tail
bashed me. I felt like a boxer's speed bag, and I forgot what
I was in the water for. When I remembered, there was a blue
blur all around be, and saltwater gagged my throat.

Air being my first requirement, I fumblingly followed my
regulator hose down to the end, found the mouthpiece,
shoved it in my mouth, purged, breathed. I located my mask
which had been knocked up into the hair on the top of my
head. I pulled the mask down over my nose, and punch-
drunkenly snorted too much air out of my nostrils, to clear
water from the mask and restore vision.

Lucky—old, sick, hunger-weakened Lucky—still "stood"
before me. And while scientists will tell you dolphins can't
change their facial expression, anybody conscious could have
read the expression in Lucky's red-brown eyes.

"Would you like to try that again?" the emotional message
snapped across the gap between our eyes. I would because I
had to, but I definitely did not want to.

Maybe I could kind of sneak up on him? I turned my gaze
away from his sleek power but sidled in his direction. After
I had imperceptibly (I thought) edged 5 or 6 feet closer, I
snapped my head around. Lucky was precisely the same
lunge-length away. He had that distance figured to the inch.
He was tantalizing me, knowing precisely the distance a diver
could jump off the floor before that momentum died and
had to be replaced with the relatively snail-paced swimming
of a four-limbed human.

Lucky turned and flicked away. I wondered why the sudden respect, until the reason for it tapped me on the arm.
Oh. Hi, Ted.

Ted had a trick in mind. He pointed to his own arm, then

to Lucky (20 feet away in the narrow envelope of water between net and wall) and then back to himself, putting his finger to his mouth and tapping his twice-broken teeth. He bit his own arm, pointed to me, and made a tackling motion. Discounting the possibility that Ted had gone mad, I believed he wanted me to tackle Lucky when the dolphin bit Ted. I kicked after the rising bubbles of the former whaler. Lucky did not look much inclined to run. Ted put his forearm up and bored in like a slow-speed ram. Lucky stayed, but he seemed puzzled as to what he was expected to do with the proffered forearm. Dolphins are not biters. They rake with their eighty-some teeth; they'll use the needle-sharp grabbers to catch fish and hold, but they don't crush. Nevertheless, Lucky obligingly mouthed Ted's arm.

I lunged in from the side, and it almost worked. My arms encircled the rubbery back and chest, 4 inches more and I'd have had him wrapped. But "close don't count" as the saying goes, and Lucky spit out the arm he was working and rolled, twisting my arms and breaking my grip. Then WHACK to Ted's head went that great dolphin's tail, and WHOOF to my belly went that beak like a rock, and if he'd been human, I'd have said Lucky laughed.

When the bubbles cleared away, Ted kicked up topside for something, and I watched his fins kick back and forth as he treaded water to talk. Then he dived back down, and we tried some more.

We braced in the indentations of windows and shot out as Lucky passed. Lucky swivel-hipped neatly and slapped our faces for us.

We lined up three at once, top, bottom, and Ted in between. Lucky evaded, blinking into invisible speed with a pop of his flukes, leaving a swirl of water distortion to mark the spot where the big gray ghost had been.

Ted took his kinked-up air hose, separated a tangle in a tight-knotted section, handed it to me, and pantomimed me suddenly twisting it shut. Like a trap. He followed this energetic closing of the hose with a thumb jerk to his chest and a clamping motion of his arms.

Oh, no, Ted, you don't want me to try to lasso Lucky with a length of rubber hose? But Ted's eyes were bulging, and Ted was Ted. I'd have given it a try, had not Lucky changed the situation.

With easy strokes of his powerful tail flukes, Lucky made for the surface, hardly bothering to put on speed. A brief burst of power just before his nose broke the join of water and air, and his body became a leaping line. He was jumping out of the netted area. We would have to reposition the net and start again.

I waited for the clean cut of his diving reentry, but instead there was a great splash and then the undersides of wet-suited trainers heading out from the stage to the center of the tank. Lucky was tangled!

When we broke the surface, there were people and nets all over the now-quiet animal. I swam my nose into his netted side and grabbed tight and closed my eyes and listened.

"That's why I called for the second net," said Ted, his deep rough voice triumphant, "because I *knew* he was gonna jump, sooner or later."

We bumped the stage. I opened my eyes and helped to peel the nets back gingerly, terrified lest Lucky break away before we got the stretcher on him.

But the dolphin king only stared straight ahead and made no move.

Lucky was placed in A training tank, with a smaller dolphin for company. Dolphins are supremely social animals, needing friends almost as much as food. It makes me miserable to see a dolphin alone in a tank, even if it's for the most logical reason, like an infectious disease such as erysipelas. Erysipelas rots dolphin's skin and spreads like fire, wiping out whole herds in the wild. But a dolphin alone can die of sadness, and I was glad that Lucky had someone to be with.

The water was lowered to a compromise level between the dolphin's need for swimming room and the divers' need to be able to catch him. There was about 4 feet of water in the tank. Ted remembers this differently. Ted, whom I spoke with eight years later, has it fixed in his mind that the water was deep first and was later lowered.

I remember the last time Lucky hit me. We had been catching him twice a day, and this day he was looking poorly, listing to one side like an old grandfather who can only hear well from one ear. I thought about how he had been, the mightiest leaper in the show, water droplets gleaming, flung from him at the top of his leap.

Lucky kicked me in the shins. I made myself not move and said, in a voice pitched a trifle lower than I normally can muster, "Lucky, that was not nice." And sure enough, somebody behind me said, "Now that man is cool!" I was just loving it until Lucky came up and kicked me again, which caused me to consider the advantages of the other side of the net. Ah, well, so much for coolness.

We had been force-feeding Lucky, holding his jaws apart with towels while a vet's Vaselined arm jammed mackerel down the dolphin's throat and into the first of his four stomachs. Lucky, surprisingly, had cooperated.

But Lucky had been vomiting up the broken fish. Sometimes immediately, sometimes hours later, but in any event, he was not keeping food down. Not enough. He was losing weight. The delicate ribs, no thicker than a pencil, had begun to show.

The vets found he could retain a predigested slurry of ground fish, poured through a high-held tube while divers restrained his discomforted struggles, but it was very awkward for the vet to keep holding the can of predigested food high, standing waist-deep in water. We needed him out on dry land where we could control him better.

So on this day we caught Lucky easily and walked him over to the waiting stretcher, which was hooked up to a crane. We adjusted Lucky's sleek weight in the stretcher, checked to make sure his pectoral fins were tucked in to his sides (this stretcher didn't have "pec" holes for the fins to stick through), and tied the two heavy iron poles together over Lucky, totally encasing the dolphin in canvas. Houdini would have had trouble escaping.

We signaled, and the crane began to raise the stretchered dolphin. We kept our arms over the tied-together poles because you never knew with Lucky, but it was over, and we were thinking about how we better get topside and help swing the animal over the tank side when the crane stopped.

Rrrrrrr—nothing. "What's the matter—what's going on? Hurry up, he won't take very much of this!" "Arright, arright, I got it." The crane started again. Whew.

Lucky rose in the stretcher, as a cobra rises. Were there poles in the way? They bent aside. "Stop the crane!" "No, take it up!" "Hurry!" "Slow down!" Ted was off duty then, and everybody there had a different opinion.

Lucky propped his pectoral fins on the stretcher one instant, during which he surveyed the situation. Then he dived for the water below.

But if his upper body was free, his tail flukes were inextricably fastened, caught between canvas and rope and tied-together stretcher poles.

He exploded. His body hurled itself in unbearable circles, propeller spins your eye could not follow except when he changed direction, which happened with the speed of a boxer changing hands. It would have been death to touch him then. He'd have popped a man's skull like a blown eggshell.

It would have been his own death if he touched the wall at that speed. He was within inches of the painted concrete during that entire incredible gyration. But he did not touch. Even in frenzy, Lucky was a self-guided missile.

It was clearly impossible for dolphin muscle to rip through the combination of heavy canvas, rope, and tied-together stretcher poles. But when stability returned to the world, there was Lucky, sailing calmly about in the water, as if it had never occurred to him to unleash his strength.

But hanging on the wall behind him were two bent and twisted, ruined iron things, wrapped in rags. Hard to believe they had been a stretcher 60 seconds before. Looked like wreckage from a fire now.

The vet said: "He's too stressed today. I don't want to bother him anymore just now."

To which there was no disagreement.

I am not positive, but I think the reason I missed the last confrontation of Lucky and Ted was that I was having a nose job. Not for looks, but for the proper operation of my eustachian tubes. The nose-ear connection, the eustachian tube, is a vital tool to the diver. Eustachian tubes let the diver adapt to the crushing pressures of water, which would otherwise pop the eardrum, like a giant pushing pencils in. The deeper a diver goes, the greater the weight of the piled-up water around him and the greater the pressure on the eardrum.

Dive 20 feet down without "clearing," i.e. neutralizing this pressure, and your eardrums will rupture. But a functioning eustachian tube lets people dive without danger to their ears. By "clearing" or blowing gently through the nose while the nostrils are pinched shut, air travels through the eustachian tubes to the eardrum and balances the outward pressure with inward pressure. Otherwise, all divers would be deaf.

A piece of gristle called a septum was slightly out of place in my nose, (i.e., "deviated"), narrowing the passage to my ear. As a result, any slight cold closed off the eustachian tube, and I couldn't clear. And a diver who can't clear, can't dive.

I have what follows from a number of people: eyewitnesses, Ted himself, those who happened upon the scene immediately thereafter, and those who heard it first.

Ted was working with a new guy, whom we called Band-Aid. Band-Aid talked like a duck, with a nasal, quacking monotone, and he was frail to the point of scrawniness. He had nothing going for him, physically, but he was always willing, and he was one of us. Willing or not, he was too light to be of much help in a dolphin catch where things go wrong.

Even in shallow water, we used a net when we caught Lucky, and the tank was divided into a section that had Lucky and a section that didn't. Lucky on his side KLONKED his jaw at the divers. Maybe at one diver more than the other.

Ted looked at Band-Aid's pale, thin arms, then back over at the unwilling dolphin with the short snout and the heavy-muscled torso. "I'll catch this dolphin by myself!" he said, in a cartoon macho way. People laughed, and Band-Aid obediently stepped back. "Ride 'em cowboy!" somebody shouted, but the jokes all stopped when Ted slipped over the rope.

Four feet of water isn't much, breast height, but it's enough. Lucky was on Ted immediately, flashing at the man, ramming with his rock-hard rostrum. Ted covered himself, with forearms and raised knees, and the dolphin glanced off like a deflected arrow and turned again.

Probably Ted could have crawled back across the net and been safe. No one would have thought less of him. But there was that feeling between them which stands between the wild horse and the wild horse breaker. Ted had once attempted to break a stallion at midnight, and the horse flung him off against a barn. Ted had gotten up, grinning in the moonlight, and in the morning he was riding.

No, the great disagreement was out in the open now and would be settled, with neither nets nor teammates to interfere: just the man who wrestled steers, and the dolphin who wasn't afraid.

It was not a long fight. Lucky's endurance was too limited; he had a liver dysfunction, and the poisons the liver normally filters had spread throughout his system. The fatigue toxins could barely dissipate; the dolphin's strength was nearly gone.

"He dived, and I went down after him," said Pintarelli years later.

"He weren't too hard to find, rammin' and pokin' the way he did, and me trying to ward him off with my elbows and waitin' for an opening. It came, and I got my arms around him, but he wrestled me off.

"I ran out of air, and I guess he did too, because he came up beside me. He breathed, and his breath smelled real bad, like his insides was all wrong.

"Then he threw himself forward, and his tail came up."

All the bystanders saw was a white wall of water rising, and falling down, on the diver's blocking forearm.

When the white wave receded, and the water went still again, Ted pulled himself across the net, with his left hand. "What's the matter, Ted?" "You okay, Ted?" came the voices from the walls.

"I think my arm's broke," said Ted very low. His face was white like a paper mask with holes punched in it for eyes. The one brief statement his only complaint, and the first doctor at the hospital wouldn't believe the arm was broken, because, first, Ted wouldn't let the interns cut the wet-suit jacket off his arm ("Wet suits cost money," Ted said.) and, second, there was a pretty nurse at the reception desk. Ted wasn't *actually* flirting with her, but anyway the doctor didn't think the diver was too badly hurt, until the X rays came back. And then the medical man's lips separated.

"A dolphin did this?" the doctor said. "It looks more like the work of a sledgehammer!" Both the major bones in the forearm were shattered, and it took several operations, two metal plates, twelve screws, and a year in a cast to make Ted's arm be right again.

Back at the park, killer whale trainer Dave Worcester was called out of a show, and Dave got hold of his brother Keith, and the two put on wet suits and went in for Lucky. "You can imagine what we were feeling!" said Keith later, "but he just gave up to us."

The great dolphin never fought again, unless you count his dying flurry when he flung off the diver who held him upright in the water and leaped his last and fell back still.

Everyone had something to say about Lucky. Each had a story, and where the strict recounting of fact ended and imagination began was not easy to tell. Lucky was an amazing animal, and nothing seemed impossible for him. Had the dolphin king once attacked a killer whale for interrupting his lovemaking? Had he truly punched out seven divers in as many minutes? Had he once leaped twenty feet to try and knock a hated trainer from a ladder? I don't know. I've tried to stick to stories I can verify, or those I've lived myself.

But it's fitting, I think, to let the last word on Lucky be said by the man who would forever wear the dolphin's mark, the man whose forearm had to be opened up like a hamburger bun, for the pieces of bone to be realigned and pinned and plated back into place.

I asked Ted, did he *like* Lucky? Ted's red face pulled back, his large eyes squinted as if the question was in some way improper.

"*Like* him?" he said. "Of course, I liked him. I respected him. He was a good ol' boy. He whupped me, sick." He nodded. "He was Number One."

Lucky's antagonist leaned back in his chair and crossed his cowboy boots on my desk. His scarred face grew soft.

"Say, that old bugger could whistle Happy Birthday!" said Ted Pintarelli, of the dolphin king.

13

Before the White Shark

~~~~~~~~~~~~~~~~~~~~~~~~

I heard the meshing click of teeth. I felt a different stirring in the muscles beneath the rough hide of the animal I held. Then, with a violent twist that numbed my hand, the shark wrenched out of my grip. A great white shark: *Carcharodon carcharias*, "man-eater," "white death," "Jaws," the symbol of all that is insensate and savage, was loose in the darkened waters of Marine World/Africa USA, at three o'clock in the morning, with one very vulnerable human being.

How does a (relatively) normal citizen get into a situation like the above?

Well, it took thirty-one years, but don't worry: I'm not going to ask you to sit through all of them.

Briefly, though, I was born knowing how to swim and then forgot. If I'd been a South Sea Islander, I'd have been paddling in the lagoon before I could walk. It is much easier for a baby to swim than to struggle against gravity, to teeter outward from the center of the earth and make the staggering, controlled forward falls that add up to walking.

But I joined the world in Berkeley, California, and had to wait till the age of seven before being introduced to a body of water bigger than a bathtub. The Richmond Plunge. I'll never forget that stinking chlorine pond. Clutching on the overflow drain, looking up at the amazon thighs of the bored lady lifeguard who said "kick, kick, kick," I remember being shocked that I had to *learn* to swim. I had assumed that it came with the package. Actually, I think the ability to swim is innate in all of us, but if we wait even a few years, the knowledge slips away, and we have to begin again—maybe like I did, red-eyed and clumsy in a sweat-warm pool.

Sometimes I thought the bottomlessness had me, and would drag me down and drown me. I tried to run from it, which is of course the worst thing to do, trying to adapt land skills to the water, and I choked and couldn't see: only the white domed light and my blurred fingers struggling for the wall. What relief to feel my flung arm lock onto the drainage gutter! Something solid to cling to.

Couldn't float; never could, still can't, and the lifeguard would yell "FLOAT! FLOAT! FLOAT!" as though the command would make my sinking scrawny limbs rise up. But I did discover that I would not sink forever, but only a few inches below the air, and that I could play at that level until I needed a breath, and then pull once with my arms and maybe twitch my toes a little, and I'd reach the gaseous oxygen.

Drown-proofing, that's the name for it nowadays. The knowledge that all free swimmers are tied to the surface by an elastic band of buoyancy, no matter if we can float or not. Armed with that understanding, a virtual nonswimmer can stay afloat in deep water for 20 or 30 hours. Just sink down, rest some seconds, let the arms drift up over your head. Pull down leisurely with the straightened arms and flattened palms and tilt your head back so that you barely have to break the surface to breathe. Exhale, inhale, let yourself sink down again, with your arms drifting over your head. Drown-proofing.

The ocean was a roar of surf to be tumbled about in like a washing machine—until I learned what goggles were for and met Lloyd Bridges on TV.

To me and millions like me, Lloyd Bridges will always be Mike Nelson, scuba-diving star of *Sea Hunt*. That program became almost the center of my life. Somebody actually living and doing underwater. I watched with my eyes wide, practically glaring at the set, desperate lest I miss a watery instant. You have to understand, "Sea Hunt" was practically my only underwater contact. Oh, I had read fish books under the desk in geography class. and put on my goggles to study the bathtub drain, and I knew what the muddy bottom of our local lake looked like, but Mike Nelson worked in the sea. He was, in a way, more fantastic than my other childhood idol, Tarzan of the apes.

I could understand Tarzan. Given his upbringing, the adventures that befell him and the heroics he performed to get out of tight spots seemed only logical. But Mike Nelson was a person! A real, live, actual human individual!

And if to me Lloyd Bridges was barely believable, then Jacques Cousteau was hardly human. The coinventor of the Aqua-lung? The man who has done more than any other to show people the majesty of our sea? Jacques Cousteau turned public awareness to the ocean. If our sea can be saved—and it must be if our world is to work—it will be to no one's credit more than that fragile, soft-voiced Frenchman.

When high school, the army, and my attempt to become the world's strongest man (seriously: Olympic-style weight lifting was my life for seven years) was over, I was looking for another direction for my life, and my friend Ken Shiels gave me the best advice I've ever listened to:

"Why don't you become a professional diver?"

14

Chopper One

~~~~~~

Twenty-six sea turtles, greens and loggerheads, hawksbills and ridleys, lived in the tropical reef tank. Only one had a name.

Each species had its own reasons for beauty and uniqueness. The ridleys, white, all irritable swiftness and speed were supposedly the product of a loggerhead/green mating and, like the mule, which is the offspring of a donkey and a horse, reportedly sterile. The greens weren't green but a mixture of light and dark: mottled shadow. The hawksbills had narrow-shaped mouths like birds, as their name implied. And the loggerheads in general were impressive creatures, with their strange combination of massive bulk and grace.

But Chopper, named for a cartoon bulldog who protected a pesty little duck named Yakky Doodle, Chopper was never an "in general." Chopper was always specific, an identifiable individual and more. Chopper had that undefinable something extra: star quality. She was always *the* turtle. It wasn't just her size. There were other loggerheads as long and broad as a dining-room table and with heads as wide as a typewriter. It wasn't her configuration, for her shape and uniform were regulation loggerhead issue. Belly the yellow of old cream and the top a proper rough bark brown. The armor had the required number of loopholes—six. The tail hole, of course, for waste disposal and for sex. The male's tail apparently contains sex organs (females like Chopper have either no tail or one so short it's not visible from the outside), and when loggerheads make love, it is like walnut halves joining together the wrong way, flat belly against round back.

The arm and leg holes sprouted arms very much like chicken joints, if chicken joints turned into massive brown paddles tipped in dull, fingernaillike claws. The yellow claws at the end of the wide, flat paddles had no purpose I could discern.

The sixth and final armor opening provided a space (and a partial protection) for Chopper's triangular head. Her skull was of brown armor guarding the top, yellow shell on the sides, and a white semileather underneath. The beak, composed of an overhanging top three-quarters section with the bottom quarter fitting neatly up inside, was of a substance that looked like ram's horn. The edges were thick but tapered to a nasty sharp narrowness, backed by enormously powerful jaw muscles. We'd seen Chopper chewing on the hard fiber glass reef, where a piece of the rocklike material projected and she could get a beak-hold. Soon there weren't many projecting places on the fiber glass reef, but only holes where they had been. The head was mounted on a muscular neck, usually retracted in the shell. The neck could act like a spring—SHOOT! Six inches forward her head could reach, very, very fast.

Once Chopper autographed my hand.

I'd been doing an underwater feeding show, swimming backward, flinging squid to the cloud of onrushing turtles as quickly and accurately as I could, trying to feed the aggressives enough to keep them off me while at the same time reaching the weaker ones as well. The fish were darting in and out too and I was moving quick and paying attention.

But as the feed bag emptied and the edge of hunger dulled among the inhabitants of the reef, I relaxed, slowed down, and watched them eat. The eels were the most cautious, easing warily out from under the sheltering reef, not comfortable in the open, snatching a fish and ess-ing back to cover fast as they could. They knew what turtles could do. I had seen Chopper once with a moray in her mouth, munching calmly as the eel fought. The crystal teeth splintered on Chopper's horn-hard skull, affecting not one whit the crush-

ing death in the moray's middle. When it was over and the
eel was two, Chopper inhaled one half, and a grouper got
the other.

A searing vise seized my left hand.

Chopper's head covered my hand, as if my wrist ended in
turtle. I could feel the bones bending. I dropped the feed bag
and though it was almost empty, the other turtles were instantly on it, biting holes in the canvas to get at the squid
inside. Even in the pain, like red-hot metal slowly severing
my hand, I knew I'd better keep moving, or something else
might sense my weakness.

I slammed the heel of my closed fist on the "eyebrow"
ridge of her skull, brought my knee up violently to the underside of her throat, trying to make her gasp and release me.
Neither action accomplished a thing. There was no more
time. I had to fight dirty.

I went for her eyes. The span of my free hand from thumb
to forefinger whammed down on the narrowing section of
her triangular head. Too wide. I couldn't reach both her eyeballs. I slid my hand over, tried to sink my fingers into one
socket, while my mind screamed and screamed and tried not
to go blank with the pain.

Her eyelid closed, a leathery shield. I could not reach her
eye. I squeezed in on the thick pile of eyelid anyway, knowing nowhere else to go. Was any discomfort penetrating?

Something hard bonked my shoulder from behind. Another turtle! I arched my head sharply and felt the satisfying
clunk of my skull banging into another. My shoulder came
up, too, shrugging, pitching the startled turtle a few inches
to the left, and I ducked under and moved, trusting in the
turtle's monumental ability to forget what was not immediately before it.

The edged pressure eased fractionally, and I yanked my
hand, not caring if it tore, just so I got the majority of it
back.

Free. My hand was mine again, no longer a part of a turtle's luncheon. I absentmindedly brought my fin up and

shoved on Chopper's hulking shell, pushing some distance between us, just in case. But Chopper wasn't attacking. Her bulging black eyes, open now, stared at me with the saddest expression, as though she were a puppy and I'd kicked her. She was just a turtle, after all, and she'd seen something white and drifting, and that was a squid, right? Turtles are supposed to eat squid, aren't they? She had just been doing her job. Why, then, had I given her pain?

She lifted her long wings and stroked sadly away, as though brooding on the perfidy of humans. But . . . but . . . I looked at the back of my hand, the zipperlike opening and the meat and pieces of broken fat showing through. A vein had been cut, and a spiral of blood lifted slowly. The whole appendage throbbed.

Why, then, did I feel like apologizing?

15

Car-Wash Tunnel
and the Deepest Dive

~~~~~~~~~~~~~~~~~~~~~~~~~~~~~~~~~~~~~~~

"Why don't you become a deep-sea diver?" my friend Ken
Shiels had asked. Why not, indeed, I wondered, sitting in
front of the car-wash tunnel, at the gas station where I
worked. Sure wasn't doing any too well here. Barely making
eating money as it was, and a baby on the way?

A big Lincoln Continental pulled in honking, and I
jumped off the chair, hustling out to meet the obnoxious
driver. Whether they were the kind of people who snapped
their fingers at attendants or not, I had to get them in a good
mood, make them receptive to my car-wax pitch. The trip
through the car-wash tunnel came free with a fill-up of the
moderately overpriced gas, but the hot-spray-wonderful-wax-
make-your-car-look-new-again cost 50 cents extra. I had to
sell a lot of waxes because I kept forgetting to tell people to
pull their electric antennae down, and the scrub rollers in the
car wash yanked them out like weeds (two yesterday). I'd
found the shiny metal rods, one wrapped around a roller, the
other flung useless in a corner. That meant (if the drivers
figured out where they'd lost their antennae) a minimum of
sixty bucks the station would lose on account of me, a fact
I'd had drummed into me at the last lecture.

I was near getting fired. And Jeannie had just found out
she was expecting. Ever since I'd been fired from a job as
reporter, nothing had gone right. I had deserved the firing
from the reporter job, I admitted to myself if no one else.

Because reporters have to be always on the move, have feet like iron, and it helps if they don't get tired. Reporters farm news, watching the stories grow, fertilizing the beds with friendship and small talk, constantly developing contacts, keeping track of dozens of developing plots. They know everybody on the beat and constantly produce copy, five or six stories a day.

That hadn't been me. I wanted to take one story and do it in depth, researching, revising, rewriting, polishing, pondering over phrases and thinking about it—but that's how a book writer works, not a reporter.

I was assigned three cities—Fremont, Newark, and Union City—and I had to cover all the crime and government stories in that beat. A likely combination, but I did not do it well.

I produced one good article, for instance, on the life of a policeman, but it took me two months. Sixty-four hours in and out of a squad car, interviewing all the policemen I could talk to—and even then I knew I wasn't getting the true picture because I was only getting their side of it. The article came out serge blue, and with a badge pinned on it.

Reporters have too much to do just for an outline of the what; they almost never have the time to try and figure out why.

Besides, a portion of my mind was always working on my first book, a novel, about The Sea and Man and Sharks and Politics and Weight Lifting and Women . . .

The newspaper fired me, and rightly so.

I guided the Lincoln into the car-wash tunnel, didn't punch the wax button, did scrub the back bumpers, and watched them disappear into the spray and multicolored brushrollers, wondering for the umpteenth time if I could run through the tunnel safely.

I picked up the brochure again. Mike Rugged's School of Deep-Sea Diving, we'll call it. Mike Rugged looked wonderful in his hard-hat gear, heavy polished helmet on his lap as he sat. The school sounded thorough. Small boat handling

. . . underwater welding . . . Looked like everything a commercial diver would need to know.

I didn't trust Mike Rugged, though. I'd been over to the school, and the first sight through the office door was an enormous mural painting of a hard-hat diver with a knife, defending a barebreasted mermaid, while a nearby octopus guarded a box of overflowing treasure. Mike R.'s sales pitch came across the same way. "One hundred ninety-one dollars a day or any portion thereof! One young man worked eighteen months, saved his money, bought three bars, and quit!" And had I heard big Mike (who had put on quite a bit of weight since the brochure picture had been taken) say something about "guaranteed job placement for graduates"? I felt sure I had. Though I didn't like the way he'd looked around when he'd said it. As though watching out for witnesses.

The money (twelve hundred dollars) would take everything we had and could borrow, but I had my GI-bill benefits to live off while I went to school for the three months.

Still, could I really do the work underwater? I had no skill with tools, and one thing Mike Rugged had said did make sense: "A commercial diver is not a diver who works, but a worker who dives. It's not if you know how to dive down, but what you can do while you're down there." Mechanically, I could just barely change the oil in my car. I didn't know what I was getting into.

As the sudsy Lincoln made its way slowly through the tunnel, I thought of the very first time I'd ever had air tanks on my back. I didn't know it, but it might have been the deepest dive I would ever take. It almost ended my career before it began.

Scuba Point, Texas, I remember it was, and I'd been delirious to get away from the boredom and endless inspections of the peacetime army. My three years' volunteered time was nearly up, and everything about the service had begun to pinch. The clouds of mosquitoes who not only drank your blood but couldn't even be quiet about it. I can still hear that ZEEEEEEEE they continuously made, above the swamp of

Fort Wolters, where helicopter pilots were trained for Viet-
nam. I was an electronic-warfare specialist, which meant I
had six months' electronics school behind me and spent my
days cleaning trucks in the motor pool. Once we built a
barbed-wire fence and tore it down, just for something to do.
And the little snotty new second lieutenants, who tried to
look hawklike and succeeded in looking ridiculous. On post,
they had what power a gold bar and swagger stick could give
them. Off post, we took their girl friends away.

But on one great weekend, just before my time was up, I
discovered Scuba Point, a submerged valley where gear could
be rented and there were no embarrassing questions about
certification cards or qualification or anything except did you
have the three dollars and that was it; "Here's your gear—
have a good dive, kid. Next!"

I could barely carry everything they'd pushed across the
counter at me. Scuba tank, backpack, double-hose regulator, weight belt, fins, mask, snorkel, and an enormous
spear gun. Huge thing, that last, weighed almost as much as
the bottle of air and looked as if it might have seen duty
against Moby Dick. Boy, did I feel macho as I walked out on
the baking dock!

Slipping on my fins at the end of the low pier, I lowered
my hot heels toward the water. Now before you can appreciate what happened next, you have to know how hot Fort
Wolters, Texas, can get. One hundred degrees is an ordinary
day, and the humidity is always just an inch off rain. You
could hardly write a letter home because the sweat rolled off
your hand, obliterating the writing and ruining the paper.
Even with salt tablets on the mess tables, you sweated all the
salt from your system so that the flat pools of perspiration on
your forearms had no taste, and men fainted easily. The people who lived here year around, lifetime in, lifetime out, had
air-conditioning and dehumidifying equipment everywhere
possible so that they moved quickly from one cool, dry place
to another. But the paint-peeling barracks had only two so-
called air conditioners apiece, and all they were good for was

to chew up mosquitoes and blow them, crushed bits and blood, upon the unhappy soldier whose bed was beneath the fan. No one else benefited.

But when my heels and ankles touched the coolness of that brown Texas lake, I knew I was home free. "There's a car 70 feet below; just follow the rope straight down!" shouted somebody wet and sneezing—wet and sneezing because he was *cold*!

Darkness, coldness, and relief flooded over me as I fell down through the fresh, murky water. A submerged valley. Artificial lake.

My eyes found the white rope, followed it down out of sight. Leaving all my petty cares and hassles topside, I gripped the rope and swam down.

Pale hands, my own, traded places before me on the rope. Surroundings faded.

The weight of the water oppressed me. The cold which had been such relief before seemed less of a friend. Oppression, suppression, repression, compression—all applied. The blackness below seemed a living entity, a something that would envelop me and chill my core and kill me, encyst my soon-to-be-shivering body, and I'd never see the sun again. Ha ha.

Just as I began to seriously consider turning back, a white blur loomed below, seeming to rise up the rope toward me, though of course it was just the reverse.

The car. White, and with an unexpected appearance of emanating evil. Like a mud-covered trap, the outlines of which the mind can only dimly sense.

The windows were like dead eyes. I wiped a film of freshwater algae off the glass and peered inside. Saw nothing.

I wanted to push that car around, show it I wasn't afraid. My palm reached out and touched the chalky, slimy side. It seemed to recoil from me. I tried the door, against my will. Perhaps if I went inside, sat in the seat where maybe dead folks had been, I could exorcise the fear.

There was a horrible gloom, a rottenness about that car,

and I was delighted when I could not get the door open and had a legitimate excuse to swim chilledly away.

Over a ridge and down.

A strangeness. A layer of light and warmth and clarity like brown glass. I glanced uneasily over my shoulder, wondering if I had somehow got my directions mixed and was swimming ashore? But no, the darkness framed me, mud below, muddy-colored water above. I was deeper than I'd been with the car, but I was more comfortable in every respect. It was my first experience with that delightful phenomenon called thermocline. Water lives in layers, and their temperature and life content are not always predictable.

My fin tips disturbed the soft mud floor, leaving trails of murkiness behind. It was as if no one had ever disturbed that silt before.

A fish! An actual trout! I was going to walk out of this lake with a kill on my spear!

I whipped up my spear gun with both hands and fired. Then remembered that these things have to be cocked. Let's see, um . . . yeah, this has to pull back over here, while the handle goes into my stomach—hang on, fish, this'll just take a second!

The trout, innocent of its mortal peril, continued about his business, doing whatever an idle trout may do.

There. The gun was cocked, uh, yes, the safety was off, ready.

Doom stalked the 10-inch trout. I steadied the weapon, sighted in (the fish was so close I could have counted the speckles), squeezed the trigger slowly as the army had tried to show me on the rifle range—the strands of heavy rubber *twanged* the spear forward, straight and true.

The spear stopped short. As if invisible fingers had pinched it, clip, and at the same instant a sharp jerk almost tugged the spear gun from my grip. The trout looked up, flexed its gills twice, and was gone.

It took me a moment to realize that the fish I'd thought so close was at least 40 feet away, because the spear had run out that length of retrieval line before yanking to a stop. A trick of magnification in that clear brown water. Oh well, at least no one had seen.

I played perhaps an hour before my air ran out. It wasn't difficult to tell when the supply ran low, as it became harder and harder to breathe. Imagine breathing through a straw, and imagine the straw partially collapsing, so that you must suck harder and harder for less and less air. Eventually the effort of breathing drains more oxygen from your system than the narrowed straw—or empty tank—gives back.

Aha, I thought, when my chest heaved for air and almost nothing happened, it is time to go. I was back in low visibility now: either the thermocline had left me, or I it. But I could see the bubbles rising, so I knew which way was up. If in doubt (as in night sea), I had read, I could have taken my mouthpiece out, exhaled, and *felt* for the bubbles, following them up by their tickle on my palms. I was in no difficulty, except that I was going back to the oven of Fort Wolters, Texas, and even that did not seem altogether bad, so much body heat having now left me.

I stopped short, as the spear had done. As if I, like it, was tied. Couldn't move. Kicked hard with my fins and pulled with my arms, but there was no corresponding motion rush of water against my face. I tried to arch up but couldn't. Something had me. I weaved to the side and attempted to retreat. Nothing helped. What was happening? My fingers found emptiness before me. I flailed the spear gun over . . . encountered resistance.

My hands shot up, found something both rough and slimy. It felt like an algae-covered tree limb. Ridiculous. Oh. That's right, this was a dry land valley once. If I didn't get off quickly, I would have an interesting epitaph: "drowned in a tree." Or suffocated, actually, because I've heard the lungs lock and prevent the entry of water until the body decomposes, which was somehow comforting.

Being careful not to drop the spear gun, because I didn't want to have to pay for it, I reached up over my head and locked my hands around the branch of the waterlogged tree. I pulled down with all the strength of fear.

With a wonderful sound of wood fiber tearing, the rotten tree limb broke. Remembering to breathe out, lest the little air remaining expand in my lungs and pop them as the pressure decreased, I ran for the surface, clawing with every available appendage to get to that air! If I had thought to wiggle my ears, I would have. Breaking the surface was like climbing a ladder, and I sucked in that hot, sticky good old air.

I must have looked unusual, coming out of the water with a piece of forest stuck in my backpack. The air bottle barely hissed when I took off the regulator and cracked open the valve. "Why didn't you just undo your chest straps and ditch your gear?" a diver friend asked me later. Oh well. Next time I swam onto a tree, I'd know what to do.

The roar of the blower at the end of the car-wash tunnel sounded, disturbing my reverie.

I knew what went on inside that tunnel. Knew the movement of every man-high roller, knew the timing of the conveyor belt and where not to put your feet. One poor guy had got his foot caught and crushed and cut off, in slow motion, while he screamed for help, which arrived too late.

I turned and ran in. It was cool inside the tunnel, and the wall of noise was like a waterfall, so loud and constant you could not hear.

I ducked under one roller, stepping quickly to avoid the white hooks on the conveyor belt, and stood while the spray-spinning vertical scrub roller approached; I waited until it almost touched and dodged around, timing the move so I could weave behind the next roller, laughing as the spray rinse hit me, lunging low beneath the hot air dryer, running soaked out into the sun.

Even the honking of the next impatient customer did not dampen my spirits.

Because I knew I was altogether too dumb to work on land forever.

16

Death of a Neighborhood

A flash of white that didn't move drew my attention downward. The angelfish lay on her side, the paleness of her belly showing. She had been one of the tank's most beautiful inhabitants: bright yellow, fringed with light-show blue. Now her colors were becoming drab, like the paint on an old building.

I slid my fingers next to her, hoping she would dash away. But she only trembled, once, and then went limp. I pinched the tiny joining of her gill slits underneath and dragged her tiny carcass out.

The fish in the tropical reef had begun to die.

No one could tell why. There were no marks, no spots, no lumpy, chancrous cancer; just the white bellies shining up at us from the bottom of the tank. We gathered them, sticking our fingers reluctantly into the gills from the underside (as this was virtually the only way to grip their slippery bodies), and took them to the fish curator, Paul Hoekenga, a big, blond, compassionate Dutchman. He took the fish apart, dissecting, checking out the insides, both by gross observation and slides.

He could find nothing wrong. And the fish continued to die. In larger numbers now. Ten, fifteen dead on the floor in the morning. "Deadie in the reef tank!" somebody would say, and we'd mumble, "Yeah yeah," because we didn't really want to know.

Hoekenga was a good and dedicated man. He consulted

Steinhart Aquarium, taking tissue samples up for their expert opinion. He spent hours in the library, yanking through the pages in search of an answer, or at least a cause, to have some idea what we were fighting! He ran up a long-distance telephone bill calling other oceanariums to ask for their experience. He kinked his neck, crouching over a microscope with slide after slide. He grew bitter, snarling at people who approached him with small talk, because he hurt inside.

Meanwhile the divers collected the dead. Twenty, thirty dead in the mornings now, and we had to use bags to carry them, there were so many. We had to hurry, too, to get their trembling bodies before the visitors came in: we didn't want our sadness to be passed on to them.

Fifty dead, and we could no longer get them all in the morning but had to keep collecting through the day.

Our eyes numbed with so much death that we, who were normally playful as otters, sat still staring at things when we were not working.

One hundred dead in a day.

The stingrays lost their beauty and became flat slimy things that were difficult to retrieve. Sometimes we'd find them with their white undersides turned up, and the little smiling circles of their mouths showing. The gaudy flash of the tropicals' coloration faded, as one by one they kicked and trembled, lying on their sides in the final stillness. The silver tarpon, gray in the uncaring sunlight. The stupid, ugly sturgeon, ridged back and mustache and pooched-out mouth, ridiculous even in death.

"Did they find out anything?" was the first question we asked in the morning, and the last at night. Other departments too would ask us if there was any progress being made, and always, "No." Like the tolling of the bell for the dead.

At first the turtles would dine upon the victims, and we pulled up bodies that had pieces missing, and this was comforting because at least someone had benefited. But even turtles, who eat almost nothing in the winter and almost everything in the summer—turtles who reportedly have eaten until they vomited and then calmly redevoured the spewed stomach contents—even turtles have limits. As the floor covered over with finned and twitching bodies, the turtles could eat no more.

Moray eels, on whose bodies there was no place to grip so that we had to carry them out of the tank, draped flaccidly across our fingers—we could recognize individuals; that was the eel who had killed the kelp bass, that was the little guy that bit my finger. Dead, dead.

The tiny fierce damselfish who had attacked my mask so savagely—POCK, POCK!—was helpless against this unseen enemy. He—or she—became a pile of filamentous jelly in my hand.

The sergeant major, whom I had once thought of taming and training, developed a bend in its back, a crookedness of the spine. I feared to look for it lest I find it like the others.

The groupers left their cave. Normally they led quiet lives, preferring privacy and shadow to the exposure of the sun. Usually when they came out in the open, it was only to exercise or hunt or inspect their domain, affirming their dominion over all.

But now the enormous, granite-skinned fish were dying, and they appeared to know it. In the cathedral beams of sunlight they lay, head to head for several hours, as though saying good-bye. The silent companionship, the being together of two strange creatures who were strange only to others, not to themselves, was ending. They separated, swimming with that gigantic dignity to different sections of the tank, looking their last. They settled down, and their coloration faded. When the greenish, granite patterns on their sides had turned a uniform mottled cream, the groupers were dead.

Men with ropes were brought to the top of the reef, and Keith Worcester swam the huge bodies up. Even in death they moved easily.

Keith passed a heavy manila rope through the distensible mouth and out the gills. He tied the rope and raised his hand out of the water in signal for the men to pull.

They heaved, and the thick manila rope separated. Easily. Keith examined the rope, and it was severed. Cut through as if a knife had done it.

The diver looked again at what we had thought was a relatively toothless jaw. And true, there were no fangs, but—oh, my goodness, look at that.

Unobtrusively, almost buried in the gums, were translucent slicers, like embedded half-dollars, and the exposed edges were sharp as razor blades. The groupers did indeed have teeth.

Finally there came a day when there were too many dead for the bags I had brought with me, and I had to fill the sacks and take them to the flume tank at the reef exit, dump the bodies there in the shallow water, and go back for more.

I worked for hours, and when I had finished, there were more than two hundred fish around me. Some still moving. They had struggled when I'd picked them up and put them in the cramped confines of the death sack.

A surgeonfish with dying colors flexed the knifelike spine behind its ear. I'd been careful when I'd picked it up, opening the metal-reinforced mouth of the bag wide around the hand-sized fish, and even then I'd been startled to see the spine suddenly protrude through the heavy weave of the canvas. Small incised slashes on the still bodies of the fish around it showed it had made the last moments of others unpleasant. I should have brought the surgeonfish up separately, I thought wearily.

The spine stabbed upward, as if in helpless fury. But it was no weapon against what was killing the surgeonfish, and the rainbows colors faded, and the little fish shook in that peculiar, ugly, convulsive shudder I now knew so well.

The alligator gar, link to a prehistoric past, lay on its side. The long snout of teeth separated and closed, softly. Even dying, it had the dignity of ages.

These fish I knew not just as species, but almost as individuals.

I was supposed to gather up everybody and put them in a

plastic bag, a trash-can liner, that was waiting by the air-hose outlets. But I didn't. Couldn't, wouldn't. I'd done it days and days on end, but now the twitching, palsied bodies of those I'd known folded me at the stomach, and I covered my mask with my hands and ploughed out of the shallow tank and dumped the chore on somebody else.

As though by running I could make it not be so.

In three weeks the fish-kill ended, for the simple reason that there were almost no fish left. Two thousand fish had died. Only a handful (the sergeant major!) survived: they and the twenty-six turtles. It was strange to see all those turtles and so few fish, and so the front office okayed the release of most of the heavy-shelled reptiles. Greens and loggerheads, hawksbills and ridleys, were piled in puzzled stacks on the back of a flatbed truck, and taken down to the ocean, by Monterey, where the trees are bent by the wind and blue waves break white against the rocks, and artists groan at the impossibility of getting all the beauty in. Lovers' Point, Monterey, where the skin-diving classes make their first ocean dives.

Turtles. Leathery limbs flopping as they resisted being carried from the truck. Grunting men staggered down stone steps to deposit them on the sand before the sea. They dragged themselves laboriously across the yards and yards of white, ground-up rock. Their chitinous beaks dipped hesitantly into the surf. Then one green plunged, and the others followed, and the bay was briefly alive with the backs of turtles, heading out of the cove and turning left. South, toward the warmer waters of Mexico.

I was glad to see the park choose the animals' freedom instead of a profit. Because the possibility had been raised that we might sell the turtles to a local *soup* manufacturer.

We kept Chopper, two greens, and a hawksbill, and collecting trips began again to revitalize the giant aquarium tank. The heaters had to be turned off (to accommodate the new fish, all locals), and the water in the reef grew cold.

Management tried to keep up our enthusiasm; "we'll get some *sharks*!" they said, for by then the novel *Jaws*, by Peter Benchley, had begun to infect the nation, stirring up an antishark hysteria that has never quite died down. As divers, we were both excited and worried about the possibilities of something spectacular swimming around behind our backs while we scrubbed the windows and vacuumed the floors.

We never knew for sure what killed our neighborhood of fishes. Possibilities were raised—pollution in the bay, the wrong kind of glue used in a filtration pipe through which the water circulated—but we didn't know. Fish curator Paul Hoekenga left the park shortly thereafter and went into real estate. He drives a royal purple Mercedes-Benz now and seems content. But I've always believed (though he's never said a word to confirm this) that the loss of all those finned lives burned too deeply into Paul, and that if the kill hadn't happened, or if he could have found some miraculous way to stop the dying, you couldn't have driven the Dutchman from the park with a two-by-four.

And for a long time the reef was like Dorothy's return to black and white Kansas after the rainbow-colored, magic land of Oz.

17

The Man Who Could Skip Rope Lying Down

~~~~~~~~~~~~~~~~~~~~~~~~~~~~~~~~

Mike Rugged wasn't alone when I came back to his dive school with a check for all the money I had and could borrow. Twelve hundred dollars, that was a sum. It wasn't only money, either. It was my family and my future. Another life was growing inside my Jeannie's belly, a life for whom we were both responsible, and if that wasn't enough, there was the inescapable knowledge that if I blew this chance, that was the end of Jeannie and me together. Once before, when I'd been out of work three months and showed no great enthusiasm for a factory job (I wanted to work on my book!), Jeannie had suggested that I get the hell out. If I quit the job I had now and went through deep-sea dive school but didn't end up with a job—an actual paying job—then I'd lost my wife. "I've got to think of my baby," she said. "I've got to have a good provider, or else do it by myself." Jeannie was tough, and capable. At one time she'd been youngest female corporate credit investigator in San Francisco. She might actually be able to do better by herself than with me, I realized miserably. But I wasn't going to let that happen.

As I stood with the check in my hand, waiting for Mike Rugged to turn around, I studied the man beside him. He was short, barely coming up to Mike Rugged's shoulders. And bald. But somehow when their conversation ended (they'd been discussing different types of diving helmets: they held each one up and passed judgment) and they came around and saw me, I knew instinctively the shorter was the bigger man.

His brown leather airman's jacket looked a size too long, and necessarily so, to accommodate a gorilla chest, herculean shoulders, and arms that made the sleeves look tight, even though he stood relaxed. His face was ugly in a nice kind of way, as if he'd smiled too often and the wrinkles had stayed. He was impressively bald, the forehead simply continuing up onto the top of the bulging skull. I couldn't imagine him putting on a hat or a wig to hide his baldness. His whole expression seemed to say, "That's right, mate, here we are!"

Mike Rugged's eyes flicked first to the check in my hand, then his heavy features fleshed into a smile. "Made your decision, did you? That's what I like to see, a man that knows his own mind!"

"I'd like to ask again about the jobs." I said. "The jobs you said were guaranteed after graduation." Mike Rugged didn't like that, but the little man standing beside him seemed to.

"Top ten graduates, I said, top ten will get jobs!" snapped Mike Rugged, and his eyes showed hard. "But if you're not interested, say so now! I only want dedicated students! Do you want to go ahead? If not . . ." Big Mike made a brushing gesture of his hand, as if dismissing a nondedicated student from consideration for the job in the sea.

I broke. "I'm in," I said, and handed Mike the check. It was gone from my hand in an instant.

"And this is your instructor, Alan Perrano," said Rugged, grudgingly acknowledging the presence of the man. " 'Owjadoo," said Alan Perrano, winking at me as his rough hand closed around mine. "Don't mind that bloke." His grin and wink seemed to say, "You'll be right with me."

"Roight," said Alan Perrano, standing before forty would-be professional divers. "Let's get on wi' it. Any questions 'fore we start?"

"What about the sharks?" First question.

"Aaah, you'll see the fellers in the gray suits now and

again. Give you a proper start, they will. But I never been bit by one." He wrinkled his nose. We all felt better.

"When do we get in the water?"

"Six weeks." A collective groan arose, apparently from every desk but mine. I was thinking that I was good at the books, and I'd better get all the points I could in the scholastic half because I was sure to fall down in the mechanical part. And I had to finish in the top ten.

"Six weeks schoolin', six weeks wi' the gear. Bit of nurse-maidin', maybe, but there it is. Anything else?"

I had a question, but I wasn't sure I wanted to raise it. Oh well, better be straight from the beginning.

I raised my hand, halfway. He noticed, though, unfortunately, and inclined the shining bald spot at me. His eyebrows raised. "Mr. Reed?"

"Uhh—what about seasickness?" The class howled, and I thought my ears would set fire to my hair. But I had to know. I couldn't ride a children's playground swing without getting motion sickness, and the slightest ripple caused a nightmare of nausea in my quaking guts. If I suffered so on top of the water, would I be immune under? "I never got seasick swimming, but—"

"Oh yeah, sometimes," said Perrano when the class would let him be heard. "You'll be hanging in y' suit, twenty feet under, decompressin', and the swell picks you up and down. I remember once I had me a great ruddy dish of strawberry ice cream, just before I went in. Upchucked it bloody all. Did my whole decompress with that stuff clingin' to the faceplate."

At break time I wandered through the converted warehouse, exploring in the shadow of the 20-foot-tall redwood barrels we'd be diving in. Like gigantic rain barrels they looked, but the stuff inside was anything but pure. While one tank did have clear water in it, so that we could visually inspect a model of the oil rigs we would most likely be working on (those of us that got jobs), most of the barrels were full to the brim with a creosote-stinking black muck. "Zero visibility," Mike Rugged had said proudly, "simulates actual harbor conditions. You won't be able to see your hand in front of your face on the job, so we train you to work blind here." Made sense. But it sure did look foul.

A second classroom had a knotboard on one wall: tied and nailed knots we'd be required to duplicate underwater. While wearing a two-finger plastic glove, too. I'd noticed the board before and had begun practicing. Took a piece of rope out of my left Windbreaker jacket pocket, tried to do what I saw on the wall before me. My fingers were clumsy.

"To practice right, you'd need to bind your fingers somehow," said a voice at my elbow. I turned, startled, and saw the man we would come to call "The Swede Who Had Been Everywhere."

We hadn't met, but I'd heard him talking, and every time a famous dive spot was mentioned, the blond, tanned kid would say, "Yes, but you should try the Blue Hole." Or Micronesia. Or Truk Lagoon, or any of the other warm-water places divers hear about and never get to go unless they're rich, or sailors, or incredibly expert hitchhikers.

"Something like this?" I responded, pulling a sock from my other jacket pocket. I had divided the foot of the sock into sewn sections, in a crude approximation of the two-finger glove we'd be using.

"Good, good," The Swede Who Had Been Everywhere smiled, and suddenly I was bursting to talk, to tell somebody of the dreams I'd bottled up inside for years, somebody who would understand.

I told him about the sea being the potential unifier of the world, and how we could multiply its yield many times over, so there'd never be any reason again for hunger, if we'd only farm the ocean instead of hunting it. The old hunt-and-gather boys of long ago had only been able to eke out a bare existence for a tiny number of folks, but when farming began—hey, that was something else altogether! Then people could stay in one spot and grow families and produce enough food for whole nations. The sea was the same way, only we were still harvesting it like blind giants, scooping up whatever we could find, making no provisions for the future, and being surprised when a good fish crop one year was automatically followed by a bad one the next. But if we farmed the sea, why, just sinking car wrecks alone multiplied the fish population by giving the fingerlings a place to hide. Imagine if we really *planned* the sea's productivity! Starvation would be a condition known only to history books, and if the world united in the exploration and development of the oceans, there would be no need for the arms race, and the accompanying inflation of our dollars that the arms race makes mandatory by tying up our nation's value in useless guns and bombs and missiles that are total waste because they produce nothing and are only valuable for blowing up the world. The age of the ocean could make all that unnatural destructive garbage unnecessary. And . . . and . . .

I paused, realizing my fists were clenched before me, and my eyes were staring, and my breath came short. Guess I'd been making a fool of myself. Raving.

Silence for a moment, and then The Swede Who Had Been Everywhere pointed out the door, for I had been walking as I talked, and we had left the knotboard and the classroom.

"See all those people?" he asked, and I looked at the sunshine and the men sprawled in it. Uh-huh, I nodded, having spent my words in the torrent.

"Forty divers in our class, and forty divers with the same dream. We all want to be in on the big move to the ocean, like the gold rush, only with science and technology, and maybe dis time we could even do it *gently*, not wreck the place as we move in. Because we kill the sea—" he shrugged, "we die ourselves. And I tink people know dat now. Yoost things we had to learn, that's all."

I was happily shocked. The dreams, the yearning, the longing for the sea, to live there, inside it, with all the great accompanying changes—I was not unique in these thoughts. I wasn't a freak. I wasn't alone. There were others of my kind.

A door on the trailer classroom opened. Perrano stepped

lightly out, surveyed the crowd. His face was frowning, the kind of frown that said, look, I'm not clownin' now, I'm being serious.

His squinched-up eyes took us all in, then settled on the one who was skipping rope.

The rope skipper had his shirt off, and his stomach muscles were pink with sun and exertion. Soon as class had broken, he'd whipped out a leather rope with handles from his jacket, stripped his T-shirt off, and gotten to it, dancing from one foot to the other, face serene in the exercise of his skill.

Perrano studied him, watched the rope flip lightly round and round, watched the handle grips trade places as the man's hands crossed over and back.

"Yew need some practice, Meester—?" said Perrano at last.

"Can you do better?" snapped the expert, stung.

Perrano snorted. "Them little things? Oi was New Zealand wrestling champion. Almost went to the bloody Holympics, 'cept oi became a diver instead. *Oi can skip rope lyin' on me back!* Now come on. Classes!"

18

Uncle Ugly and the Sharks

Did you ever have an uncle who hated everyone? You know, the guy who never has a good word for any person under any circumstances, and he is so predictable that when he cuts loose with something snotty, everybody just laughs? That's how we felt about Old Uncle Ugly, the electric ray.

A strange-looking creature. A massive circle, flat, dark gray on top and white beneath, and this 4-foot ash pancake was propelled by a wide, powerful tail shaped like the back half of an arrow. As if somebody had shot the ray in the rear with an arrow, and the arrow had stuck and become flexible and alive and a part of the animal, and was now responsibile for transportation. It didn't have to work too hard, though, because the ray liked to rest on the bottom a lot, which was just fine with us divers.

When that strange creature, *Torpedinidae nobilianus*, started cruising, there was no safe place in the tank. Electrocution roulette. One minute you'd be calmly scrubbing the windows, trying not to look self-conscious when people stared at you from 6 inches away; the next, your leg would be in spasm, and you'd fold and dive and try to get away from the clinging, zapping, California electric ray.

But a jolt in the calf muscle wasn't too bad—just a charley horse you'd rub while you mumbled curses about the smug-looking fugitive from a wet monster movie. What *hurt* was to get zapped in the head. Sometimes you could feel it coming, a too-late instant before. Thrumthrum—no! And then?

Below are some heavily censored accounts of what it feels
like when an electric ray swims into the back of your skull.
"I thought the whole reef lit up."
"I saw orange sparks that weren't there."
"Like my own personal lightning bolt."
"Headache which lasted for three days."
Even poor old Chopper, our giant loggerhead turtle, got it
once. My eyes caught the movement of her long, leathery
arms as she pulled downward, but it took me a moment to
realize she was after the dark, edge-rippling mass on the bottom. No, Chop, no, leave it alone! I thought, in the helpless
silence of underwater. I would have interfered, but she was
too far, and the white flash of the inside of her beak showed,
as it opened and closed, on the electric edge of Uncle Ugly.
It must have felt like sticking your tongue in a wall socket.
I never would have thought an old dinosaur like Chopper
could have moved that fast. It looked like about six of her,
going every direction at once.
"With malice toward all and charity toward none," as Mr.
Lincoln didn't say. That could have been the electric ray's
motto. Equal hate for everyone, without regard for race,
creed, or number of fins. Accordingly, we grew quite fond of
him.
Which was why we worried when Uncle Ugly killed a
leopard shark. We didn't see the hunt; all we saw was the
gray-and-black spotted tail protruding from the electric ray's
mouth. A meal that got stuck halfway down? And it could
not be vomited up; the rough sharkhide denticles all point
toward the tail. The shark was firmly lodged. The electric ray
had swallowed gagging death.
If that throat roadblock remained in place, old Uncle Ugly
must surely starve.

Before the nurse shark I sat on, my only shark contact had
been with the timid little leopard sharks, one of whom I lassoed in San Francisco Bay.
Like thousands of fathers and sons before us, my Dad and

I had carried Christmas present fish poles out onto the Berkeley Pier. We'd baited up huge hooks with squid and flung them over, weighted to hang just off the bottom, for I've heard the crabs rise up like armies from the mud of San Francisco Bay, and anything that lands on the floor will soon be pincer-clawed to shreds. We wanted sharks, not shellfish!

I imagined a great white shark, 20 feet long, and teeth like daggers. What would the other fishermen say, when the monster turned belly up at last? "Oh yes, that little boy caught it. Nobody else could have, why—" My rod bent double, and the reel screamed. My thumbs planted down on the diminishing line as I tried to slow the rush. I waited for something hideous and huge, but what emerged was a leopard shark, clean black spots on gray, and no longer than from a man's fingertips to the joint of his elbow. Gorgeous. Neptune could have been no prouder than I was. And what made the catch even more interesting was that my shark had clearly broken away from someone else, for another hook was set in the jaw, and my hook had snared the snarl of the other fisherman's line.

We pulled it up, my father set his boot on the black and gray head and carefully worked the hook out, and we carried the little shark home in triumph tied to the top of our station wagon like a mighty stag.

When we got home, I tossed the hour-and-a-half-dry shark onto the grass. The neighborhood boss cat stepped lightly over to investigate the something new. Cautiously at first, then more and more arrogantly self-assured, the old tom prowled around and around the dead shark. At last a claw-hooking paw reached out and sneeringly desecrated a gill slit. But a chance contraction activated leopard shark muscles, and it leaped forward 6 inches!

That cat shot straight into the air, and came down in the next neighborhood.

Leopard sharks have apparently only attacked a human once in recorded history. The diver developed a nosebleed underwater, and the blood had leaked out of the purge valve in his mask. The 2-foot shark had attacked the source of blood. If it had been a large shark, of course, the situation would have been horribly serious, but as it was, I think the diver was more surprised than anything else, perhaps even a little embarrassed. Like being attacked by a butterfly.

Leopard sharks looked ferocious in the classic monster movie *The Creature from the Black Lagoon*. Remember the scene where the scientists stood before a tankful of enormous black and gray sharks? Must have been a magnifying tank windowpane because the sharks looked 6 to 8 feet long, and leopards don't get much bigger than 3. The 3–D process swam the sharks out into the audience's collective lap, and even though the print was scratched and grainy, and the movie nearly thirty years old, you could still hear gasps and embarrassed laughter. I would dearly love to play the monster if they ever remake *The Creature from the Black Lagoon*.

Our leopard sharks came to the park after the terrible fish kill that wiped out the tropical reef tank. Curator Paul Hoekenga, in practically his last act for the park, organized collecting trip after collecting trip. Men and women stood chest-deep in water, manipulating nets and watching where they stepped as best they could because you never knew what might be down there.

Once everybody jumped and ouched and expressed dissatisfaction in what appeared at first to be a mass attack of epilepsy. That was Uncle Ugly, the electric ray caught in the net and making his displeasure known.

The rods and reels worked well, and it was thus we caught the greater numbers of the little leopard sharks, until we'd collected fifty or sixty that glided and soared, rested and investigated, across the floor of the reef tank. When a diver swam over, the leopard sharks would separate, scattering as the wild game parts before the plane in Africa.

But if the leopard sharks sensibly fled the approach of the vastly larger diver, there were also now two medium-sized sharks of a different kind, and they were not very good at running away.

I had never heard of seven-gills (*Notorynchus maculatus*) until the curator told me I was needed at the reef tank. "Two new sharks," he said tersely as I hustled up my gear. "One of them looks to be in shock. Be careful, they bite." Oh. Now I knew, in theory, what was expected of me. I'd read about shark walking. I'd seen it demonstrated on TV. The diver swims the shark around until the water flooding through the open mouth and out the gill slits revives the animal, and it can swim off on its own. The divers I'd heard talking stressed that it was a long, laborious process. I didn't know that I was about to experience what might be the world's shortest shark walk.

The shark swimming toward me now looked much larger than it was, through the magnification of both the water and my own worry. In actuality, the seven-gill was no more than 5 feet long, or approximately the size of a German shepherd dog, but to me it looked like Godzilla's meaner brother.

While I waited for the shark to turn aside from its present path, which would intersect with mine if it continued, I studied the markings and coloration of the creature. Cocoa-brown on top, with black rosettes like leopard spots and a belly that was dead white. I took note of the heavy underslung jaw, but I could see no teeth. A toothless shark? I would learn, shortly—sooner than I had any idea—that seven-gill teeth lie back when out of action, coming erect only when the mouth flexes open and the jaw moves forward. For use, not display.

The taut-skinned head moved slowly, side to side, in smooth coordination with the long-lobed tail. He seemed in no hurry, maintaining the pace of a person walking slow, but it occurred to me with an uneasy twinge that the space between us was diminishing.

Perhaps, as with the sperm whale, his eye placement was such that he could not see straight ahead. I gave way to my right, and shortly a rounded snout cruised through the area I had just occupied.

I had only moved one double arm-pull away, and I was

amazed at the shark's calm acceptance of my nearness. Was he blind? As his gold-and-black eye passed, I reached my nylon brush out, to see if he would react.

The shark eye disappeared, sucked in out of sight. A white hole showed where the orb had been. And the sharply indented slash of the jaws jerked 2 abrupt inches toward the nylon bristles. Then the eye returned, and the easy motion of the cruiser continued. I had had my warning.

As the gently flicking, high-notched tail eased on by, I remembered the other shark. I had yanked myself around before I recollected that the other seven-gill had been said to be in trouble. In shock, probably.

I found its dark body draped over an intake pipe. Lifting its rough length, I swam forward in the time honored tradition of shark walkers, holding the animal under my arm, left hand guiding the back of the broad tapering head. Feeling extremely official, I swam the circle of the windows several times, pretending to be too busy to notice the people looking in.

Nothing improved. I breathed a little harder, and the shark did not. I was doing all the work, and the seven-gill was ignoring my lifesaving efforts. I was definitely not going to give him mouth-to-mouth resuscitation—but maybe if he got a sudden and deeper rush of water jolting through his gills?

I raised the shark over my head. Easily done, as he weighed only about 80 pounds, and less of course underwater. With a burst of exertion, I flung him forward like a two-hands spear. The results were immediate and spectacular.

The seven-gill sliced through the water, spun around, and attacked me. Shark jaws opened, incredibly wide, dislocatingly wide, white teeth like thorns erect and reaching, crashing shut with an audible BANG! and yawning wide and slamming shut again, my own swim fins before me kicking with maniacal exertion but as if a stranger owned them, a distant uninvolved part of me thinking it's actually happening, I'm being charged by a shark, flashing glimpses down the cavern of shark throat, white slatted vents of gills, the view punctuated by teeth, me on my back and the shark going over, flexing white neck, gills, underside, my knees up and lifting but too late, the shark gone by.

It was over. I watched the seven-gill, *Notorynchus maculatus*, zip off and I wondered: what kind of a wild card animal was this, anyway?

The first seven-gills died, thank goodness. One was too mean, and the other was too dumb.

The stupid one we liked and called Socrates. We thought of the shark as unintelligent not because he didn't live up to human standards of discourse and originality but because he did not appear to understand the most basic rule of primitive-shark behavior: i.e., swim. Which he had to do to breathe.

Not that he was incapable of routine locomotion: he would cruise about the reef normal as you please, but as soon as he would find a hole, he'd swim inside and get stuck. I've never seen a shark do that before or since. Small holes, too—not caves, just broken spots in the reef where the turtles had bitten through—and Socrates would wedge his head in, and because sharks cannot swim backward, there he'd be until we came and got him.

We'd unstick him, gingerly (bright or not, he was still a shark), and he'd swim happily off, looking for another hole.

We plugged up most of the holes he would find, but he would keep on locating new ones, and one day we found him too late. His head was jammed in a crevice on the top of the artificial reef: body vertical but tail bent at a right angle, like a flag at half-mast. We could only lift our hands and shrug. Suicide by stupidity.

The other shark jumped me again, one day when I was scrubbing the top of the fiber glass reef.

It was one of those scorching, sweltering, humid times when the land people sobbed and dragged themselves about. We'd rub it in too, just like they got us in the winter when we suffered from too much cold. We'd tell them how cool the water was now, like a caress, and they'd shake their sweating fists at us when we asked them if it was hot? With our job, we said, we didn't notice things like heat.

I had my jacket off, and the water temperature was like a sigh of relief, though it may have been too hot for the shark. In any event I was making the algae flecks fly when the shadow passed the corners of my vision. It was the seven-gill and moving fast, in straight lines instead of curves. Jerky-motioned, unnecessarily swift. My eyes followed the movement. I had to turn around to do so, and thereby realized I was inside his circle.

I heard the noise my breathing made as I considered the possibilities. Blank, featureless concrete behind me and the bright surface and air above were just empty promises. But the bubble trough, the high-walled open trough that ringed the tank and aerated the water? Too far, and I'd have to flounder a lot to get out. I've read that's where a lot of shipwreck victims get hit, in the last seconds before rescue, when they're being pulled aboard and the shark sees the thrashing legs.

I stood up on the fiber glass reef, which made me feel less like a victim and more like a human being. Then I thought, hey, if I crouch down and slide over the side of the reef, there's a big cave underneath, big enough for even Socrates to turn around in, and I could get in there and kick anything that tried to follow.

The shark took the decision away from me. His circle of motion tightened, in and in until we almost touched and the snout was by my groin.

My fist raised itself without my knowledge or consent, and bashed down hard on the top of the seven-gill's cartilage skull. It was a natural punch, without benefit of skill or science, but I don't think I ever hit anything harder. I think there was a figure eight of brown movement around me after, but I can't be sure. It was too fast. I just knew I was alone again.

We found the shark dead a few weeks later and not a mark on him. But you know I always wondered if he'd had anything to do with those scratches on the side of old Uncle Ugly, the electric ray. Maybe the shark had latched on to Uncle Ugly's fringes, and got his seven-gill peabrain french fried for his trouble.

But Uncle Ugly still had his own difficulty, that leopard shark stuck in his throat, and I figured it had to be a month since he had fed.

I didn't know what else to do, so I got a rake and went swimming. It was our sand-smoothing rake, because we had been experimenting with a couple of inches of large-granuled sand on the floor, to give it a natural ocean bottom look. Clean, it looked lovely, white and smooth, but the algae had a way of mingling the grains together with strands of brown glop, so we had to keep turning it over. The rake was standard garden issue, not meant for saltwater, and was disintegrating. A layer of orange rust would form on the tines, and the sand-turning would scour it off, removing more of the metal each time. A few more weeks, and we'd have mainly a handle. But it was still good enough for what I had in mind.

The electric ray brooded on the white sand bottom. Massive malignancy emanated. "Touch me at your peril," the ray's posture read, for this was no sweet, scared stingray to hold itself immobile—or fly—if potential predators neared. No one messed with Uncle Ugly. He was, if I may be permitted a battery joke, ever ready.

I reached down with the rounded back of the rake.

I had expected some reaction when the metal fingers touched the ray, but I was unprepared for the enthusiasm of it. Afterward I put it together that the ray had reared backward from the floor, but at the moment all I could sense was an explosion of white underside and waves of electricity like heat, while that flabby glabrous agglutination of blubber and muscle heaved itself around the rake I'd thought would be such excellent protection.

I decided to let the ray have the rake and backpedaled, to get the benefit of distance. Uncle Ugly settled hugely on the long-handled garden tool, apparently mistaking it for an extension of me. "Kill that rake, ray!" I shouted in my mind, while Uncle Ugly zapped gleefully. Then the ash-gray pancake slipped off the wood and metal, which had grown still under his furious assault.

It being my intention that the creature should exhaust his charge completely, I lifted the rake handle swiftly. Uncle Ugly turned. Maybe his beady eyes weren't any too good for detail, but I wasn't going to fool him twice. He'd have been on me if I hadn't been so good at retreat. Like an animated mudslide, he chased, and I dodged, now ducking under, now planting the rake and pole-vaulting over, and for perhaps ten minutes we wore down our respective batteries.

But when at last I thought I had not one more dodge or duck or parry in me, the electric ray turned wearily away. That broad flat tail turned upright, and Uncle Ugly fled a whole 5 or 6 feet before lowering back to the floor and turning to face me.

I reached my hand underneath him. As my groping fingers found the rough tail of the leopard shark sticking out of the corner of the electric ray's mouth, the flabby blanket juiced me, to the best of its reduced ability. I remembered where the fillings in my teeth were, and my very tongue seemed to vibrate. I tugged and twisted on the throat-lodged shark.

The ray had no gratitude and did its level best to reduce me to a human crispbread, but I persisted, and at last the rude surgery was done. With one final snarl of voltage, the electric ray broke contact and lumbered away. I did not follow. The reason for our struggle, the throat-blocking leopard shark, lay in my hand.

But such a leopard shark! The incredibly tough sharkskin was almost completely digested away, leaving no more than a few limp, soft, black and gray fragments. The muscle underneath was firm, clean, cooked-looking white meat. I could have eaten it myself.

Apparently I had interrupted old Uncle Ugly in the middle of a month-long meal.

19

And Bury You, Helmet and All

~~~~~~

"Awl of you tyke your little Sudyfeds?" Alan Perrano asked, and the eight of us nodded as one. The instructor had named the most commonly used decongestant tablet, and everyone of us wanted his sinuses operant for what lay ahead this day.

"Right, then, in ye go!" The little bald man in the brown leather jacket slapped me on the shoulder. Leaning over low, I stepped inside the beige-painted decompression chamber.

The decompression chamber was smooth-walled like one of those modern freeway tunnels I can never enter without wondering if maybe this time there won't be any other end to it. There was enough room for the eight members of "yellow" crew (our team designation, referring to paint marks on the equipment and, Not, I hope, to our mental attitude) and for Perrano to squeeze in beside us on one of the two wooden benches. But there was not much space to stretch or move around in here, I reflected uneasily.

A door like the door of a bank vault clanged shut behind us. We heard somebody spinning the wheel which sealed us in.

"Naow, don't nobody go gettin' clauss-trophobia!" said Alan Perrano, and with the labeling of it, our fear subsided. I looked around me at the gauges and the valves and the handles.

We were going to be taking a "bounce dive" today, with a compressor cramming air into the cylindrical chamber as it would if we were on our way down to the bottom in professional "hard-hat" dive gear. A HISSSS! of compressed air started, and Perrano looked anxiously from face to face. We all had our fingers and thumbs on our noses in the old skunk-smell gesture. We were adjusting the pressure inside our heads to the increased air concentration around us by pinching our nostrils together and blowing gently. Normally any practiced diver can equalize pressure by automatically "clicking" his ears internally, but in time of stress or difficulty there's nothing like grabbing the old schnozz and blowing. I heard the sweet click as my ears adjusted.

"Everybody clear?" asked Perrano, and I saw the nods go around, but I kept my fingers up on my nose just in case, and I noticed I was not alone. I had never been down 200 feet, which was where our simulated dive would be taking us today.

The idea was to give us experience breathing the pressure-thickened air we'd be using in professional diving. "If I had moi way," said Perrano conversationally, "I'd bend you all a little bit, give you an idea what to watch out for."

The bends. To go down deep and stay down awhile so that the gases breathed in mixed with the blood, and then to come up too quickly. The nitrogen and oxygen in the bloodstream would come out of solution, foaming like a shaken soda, and the bubbles would get blood clots around them, forming what was called an embolus, and the emboli lodged usually around the joints, blocking the normal flow of blood, sometimes causing paralysis of the limbs. And worse, if one of them shut off the blood flow to the brain, well, you could say good-bye!

Pressures and gases matter greatly to the professional deep-sea diver. The sports divers, of whom there are now nearly three million registered in America alone, need never go below 15, 20, or 30 feet at the most, because the life and beauty of the sea is concentrated mainly at the surface, where the sun's rays reach. At those depths, the diver is far less susceptible to pressure problems, though there are still things one needs to know. (If you'd like to take a skin-diving course, it'll last about ten weeks, usually two nights a week. The best way I know to prejudge the quality of the course is to ask the number of ocean dives included. If they say five, that's excellent. One is insufficient. Anything in between is acceptable.)

I had heard about the group of city officials who got "champagne bent." They'd met in the pressurized air of an underwater tunnel, a trans-bay tube, and had poured champagne to celebrate the near completion of the project. They'd raised their glasses cheerfully (though it was noticed that the "bubbly" was extremely unlively) and drunk toast after toast. When they judged they'd had sufficient of the uneffervescent beverage, an elevator took them to the surface—and a surprise. Solemn dignitarian stomachs rumbled enormously, and bulged. Waistcoat buttons popped, and suddenly expanding gases exited unceremoniously through every available orifice. The champagne bubbles had come out of solution, and the mayor and all his retinue had to be recompressed.

"Gaoin' down," said Alan Perrano again, and again the hiss of compressed air filled the chamber. I felt the push of pressure against my eardrums, but a quick nose-squeeze-and-blow evened it out. A glance at a gauge showed 25 feet, and I knew it would be easy to clear after this. The air pressure was at the concentration it would be if we were 25 feet underwater, and the first 10 were the hardest. If you could adjust your ears to that difference, the rest was easy. Now there were other worries to think about. And dreams.

Someday there'll be cities under the sea. I wondered if I'd be a part of that. Cousteau suggests we will probably not live permanently undersea, but just go there when we need to. We are too much the creatures of the sun and air. So maybe just the houses will stay down there, and the people will rotate their lives between the land and the big blue. Or maybe there will be people who just plain like ocean better than terra firma. The men of Conshelf III, the Red Sea underwater living experiment, were not happy when told they would have to come up. They had lived in a house shaped like a starfish and had gone on swims instead of walks, with fish their neighbors. Initially they had experienced a wrenching shock at leaving land. But then they had felt less and less a part of the dry world, until the voices on the communications radio seemed to have nothing to do with them, like the messages from old Britain to colonial America. The divers had been angry when their month underwater was over, and they had not wanted to return.

Fifty feet, the needle gauge read.

Who were these people, anyway, who wanted to live and work in the sea? The man across from me was someone obviously suited to adventure: dark hair, strong square-cut head softened by humorous brown eyes. Even his name fit: Jon Noble. A longshoreman from New York. He radiated a quiet confidence: just by looking at him, you knew he could handle problems.

But if Jon Noble's shoulders bunched and gathered easily under the coarse work shirt, and his thickly corded forearms showed the muscular accumulations of years of toil, what about the two fellows sitting next to him?

One was almost fat. He had wide shoulders, and the promise of strength was there in his large-knuckled hands, but he looked as though he'd spent too much time before a TV set, with a couple of six-packs by his side. The first time I'd met him, he'd said, "Did you know I was an abalone diver? They told me to dive 6,000 feet down, and I said 'aaa-baloney'!" With a big grin and a handshake and another bad joke. He was an insurance salesman.

The other man beside Jon Noble was thin though it was the kind of leanness that could stand against the wind, with hardness around the limbs. He was pale, intense, with sorrowful eyes behind thick glasses, and he had spent the first half hour of our acquaintance explaining the intricacies of his religion. He was an accountant.

Outside the window, standing around in the shop, I could see a red-faced, blond-haired man I knew had been a farmer—Sidney Bittle, who would later wrestle Ted Pintarelli. We were every kind of person you could pick. The only thing we had in common was the sea.

One hundred feet, the pressure gauge read. At this depth the real sea would most likely be black, or possibly twilight if the visibility was superfine. Oilfield divers worked at this depth, helping with the construction, maintenance, and repair of the oil rigs. Installing blowout preventors, to prevent the pressures underneath the deposits from gushing the poisonous gunk into the sea.

If we kill the sea, everybody dies. Seventy percent of our oxygen comes from the surface of the sea, from the plankton and the algae breathing there.

One hundred fifty feet. I thought about the professional divers who had died in going first, in making the way safe for others. Sometimes hideous deaths—like the squeeze. In the days before the safety-air nonreturn valve was invented, a diver whose air hose was broken, or who fell for any distance underwater, was doomed. The pressure difference would *vacuum* the flesh off his bones. Muscles, fat, eyeballs would mingle in a red mess in the line, "like strawberry jelly," as Jacques Cousteau so succinctly put it. And that wasn't all of it. The enormous unbalanced pressures would "tend to force the diver into his helmet," as the *U.S. Navy Diving Manual* said. If you had been one of those old divers who had been killed by squeeze, the bones of your body would have broken as the tons of pressure squeezed in and crushed you into the unyielding brass. They'd have had to bury you, helmet and all. We stand on the sacrifices of those who have gone before.

One hundred seventy-five feet. The corner of my mouth wanted to turn up. I repressed the smile, pushing my face into what I hoped was alert neutrality. I didn't want Perrano thinking I couldn't control the "rapture of the deep" I could feel beginning. Nitrogen narcosis—when the air is squeezed so close together that the gas becomes concentrated and the now-thick nitrogen can affect divers like too much wine at a wedding.

Divers "narked out" have taken out their mouthpieces and offered air to puzzled fish. The high is pleasurable, but potentially deadly. A diver helping on the construction of an oil rig, for example, might be guiding down metal sections weighing several tons. He'd be working by feel, in total darkness. One slight error and the girder might come down upon his hand and pinch it off.

I could feel the friendly danger seeping into me. I enjoyed the sensations, though I took care not to show it, for this was a test.

My eyes saw with unaccustomed clarity, taking in the detailed roughness of the paint chip on the head of the screw that fastened the bench we sat on to the floor; the pattern of the wood grain—if it had been cut across instead of longitudinally, it would have revealed the age of the tree through the growth rings. (Whales show something similar in the accumulation of hard wax in their inner ears: little rocklike balls of wax which, if dissected, yield an approximation of the animal's age.)

The compressed air tasted like liquid in my mouth. And in truth the gases were closer to breathed water, so densely were they packed together. I fancied I could distinguish between the flavors of the gases in concentration. Nitrogen, sweet. Oxygen, sterile, pure, cold. And the other gases like spice to food because nitrogen is 79 percent of the air we breathe and oxygen 19 percent, which only leaves a percentage point and a half or so to be divided among argon, helium, krypton (haww, krypton: wonder if they can make kryptonite from krypton gas, keep all the Supermans—keep all the supermen away). Ahem. I straightened up, tried to look serious. I was enjoying the nitrogen a little too much.

Perrano handed out some sheets of paper which, I noted irritatedly, had math problems to solve. Arithmetic. I always hated arithmetic. Only one right answer, no room for creativity. Slowly I filled my page with numbers, and I made myself work the questionable ones backward to be sure before adding the sheet to the pile going by.

A cloud of cold steam formed around us. The fog of our own exhalations. A light bulb glowed frostily, and the windows were opaque with mist.

Two hundred feet, the pressure gauge read. From here, in the real sea, began the place of endless night. Darkness. Places never seen by humans. We've mapped the moon but we do not know the sea floor.

In the lightless depths, the fragile 4-inch horrorfish, lanternfish, gulpers, and the like are luminescent. But they are like green-glowing exclamation points and only emphasize the blackness: they cast no shadows on the abyss. Down there the white shark and the giant squid roam, and only the mighty sperm whale (and a puny human, trembling and magnificent in a bathyscaphe) can dive down from above.

"Going up," said Alan Perrano.

20

I Lose My Nerve

~~~~~~~~~~~~~~~~~~~~~~~~~~~~~~~~~~~~~~

The sun shone gold into the tank that day: beams of heaven's
light for a diver or a dolphin to fly through. I had my jacket
off, and I bet Ernestine would have done the same, had the
blubber under her taut gray hide been a removable liner. But
the now-fully-grown female *Tursiops truncatus*, she who had
been consort to Lucky the dolphin king, was in no mood for
any human nonsense.

Catching Ernestine was a challenge under any circumstances. She was no naive, newly caught animal to freeze in
panic at the net's first touch. Nor was she the cooperative,
gentle-minded type who would simply go to the bottom and
wait. Nope, every time we caught Ernestine it was a mountain climb. The longest dolphin catch I ever burned out on
was with Ernestine. It took us two hours that time, with Ernestine alternately nosing up the bottom of the net to scoot
under and blithely leaping over the top, just ahead of our
reaching fingers. I had fallen into a kind of nightmare trance
then, swimming without mind or sight or consciousness of
anything except that net to be pushed across the bottom, and
another gasping breath to take at the top and go back under.
Even so would I swim if I were pushed out of a plane into
deep ocean, swim until I died or found land. It might take
days. My muscles felt like oil, and when finally Ernestine
miscalculated, or took pity on us, and my strengthless arms
collapsed around her, there was no energy for exultation left
in me, only a dim awareness that the pain was to end now.

But this time Ernestine didn't run. She raced, violent rushes of blurry speed, swerves like the wings of a plane, but she made no attempt to escape. She just warned. With the hunching of her torso, and sideward slashes of her eighty-eight white needle teeth, she threatened. Jaw snaps KLONK!ed through the conductive medium, loudly: for sound, like sight, is magnified underwater.

The rawest novice could not have misinterpreted her mood.

Once more Ernestine served notice. Eyes locked on mine, she tail-kicked violently twice, once downward, once to the side, ZWOOSH! ZWOOSH! The sound was like the sound a jet plane makes when it passes over very low. I wondered at the power that could drive those wide tail flukes so resistlessly through the water.

I did so love to be the one who made the grab, who rose casually to the surface with the three hundred pounds of muscle and beauty in his arms, and, with luck, heard somebody say, "Good catch!" I sculled forward, head just beneath the surface, so I could snorkel-breathe and watch Ernestine at the same time.

The dolphin did something peculiar, a move I had never seen before. A kind of somersaulting forward roll underwater, gray head down and torso following, a front flip that turned into a half twist as her tail moved across and around and up—the movement seemed almost slow in its grace.

An impact like a car crash lifted me half my body's length into the air. Rivulets of water streamed off my face, and my mouth was open.

As I sank back down and the coolness closed again around me, I heard a whistling SEESEESEESEE in my left ear. The walls rotated as my equilibrium left, and Ernestine seemed to have multiplied into half a dozen buzzing, shrieking dolphins shooting around me. Pain, as if somebody had shoved a sharpened pencil into my ear.

Following the wall upward, my fingers grasped the top and yanked. I sat on the edge and took my fins off. The hot air felt cloudy, as though there were a mist. The people's voices made no sense.

Now, when a diver feels an unrightness in the ear, his automatic response is to equalize. I raised my knuckles to my nose, pinched, and blew gently. Normally this would cause a short hissing rush of air which would stop when it filled and bulged the eardrum. This time the air hissed right on through. There was a hole in the resonating drum.

If I'd had a cigar, I could have blown smoke out my ear.

In three to six weeks, the doctor said, the eardrum would heal. A thread of scar tissue would draw the edges of the rip together. The scar tissue would not be as resilient as the original membrane, so there might be some hearing loss. Also, the wound would be a weakness. If it broke again, I could go deaf in that ear.

But there was also something wrong with me that scarring could not cover, nor the doctor heal. For, if a diver has lost his nerve . . . ?

Before Ernestine cracked my eardrum, I had thought I was almost immortal underwater. Nothing could hurt me there. I was safe, I always figured, as long as I could just get wet.

On land, I've always tended to walk into stationary objects. Otherwise inanimate furniture reaches out and kicks me in the shins as I go by, and I can never seem to bend over without first finding something to bang my head on. But toss me in a lake, and I'm not clumsy anymore.

And if in everyday life I had difficulty getting along with people, always seeming to be saying the wrong thing and getting into trouble, well, that was no problem in the sea, where conversations are necessarily limited.

What, then? I had no negotiable skills. Mechanically I was inept. I could write, but I had almost no proof of that except rejection slips. Everybody thinks he or she can write. The only universally accepted method of judging quality is sales, and I hadn't had any for years.

I couldn't even talk to Jeannie about it, because I knew

what she would say. Go back to school, become a teacher. Which was nice, a noble profession and what she and my family had wanted for me for years. It just wasn't my dream. I had to dive and here. I wanted to and I needed to. This was my path. I had chosen it. I must stick with it.

But every time I walked past that section of the park where the dolphin training tanks were, where Ernestine was, I remembered that helpless feeling when her flukes came up so swift and terrible. Why hadn't I been able to block that blow? Was I getting old? No, couldn't be, I was only twenty-eight, but still, isn't that the age when boxers begin to slow down, when they have to consciously make their bodies do what had been reflex before, and when the big, fat, easy-to-dodge punches come crashing through their guard?

I was afraid. Not my normal prerisk jitters either, but a gnawing, ratlike dread that ate at me, invading my sleep with ugly dreams, shaking my confidence in everything I did. Was my nerve gone? How could I call myself head diver if I could not lead the dolphin catch?

What if I showed yellow before my friends?

The cutshack, where I would be working for the next month and a half while my eardrum healed, is probably the most important and least acknowledged department in the park. Everything hinges on what happens here, for the cutshack is where the food is prepared.

Mackerel, herring, silver smelt, squid—boxes to wrestle off a truck, cardboard and plastic wrap to rip apart, blocks of frozen food to dump in sinks under running water in the afternoons. And in the morning, the real work begins.

My hands thrust into the freezing water of the deep sink and came out with a pile of pink-and-white squid, surprisingly unslimy. I flopped it on the cutting board beside me, picked up one individual squid, squeezed the body with my thumb. The guts came out, and I brushed them aside, my fingers darting back to the tiny carcass to pluck out the cartilaginous quill pen type object that must serve as a kind of backbone to the squid. I tossed the limp white-and-pink carcass into the next bucket. One squid cleaned. Two thousand to go.

J.B., the round faced, wide-shouldered Guamanian beside me, worked swiftly and smiled as he talked. His hands were red from the inky, ice-crusted water. He finished his sink full of squid before mine was well begun. Pulling the drain plug, he moved to the next job, his broad back bending as his hands disappeared. They came up full of herring, separated from the semithawed blocks we'd put under the running water. He pitched the fish into a gray plastic bucket. His hands were red from the cold. But though the knuckles looked stiff as rusted hinges and the fingers looked stuck in an arthritic position, still they darted swiftly, snatching up here and there a broken fish to toss to Ygor, the giant garbage disposal.

J.B. worked 70 or 80 hours a week, often months without a Sunday off, and since he had been put on salary, that meant he got no overtime.

At first I had thought he was an Eskimo, with his smiling face that would have looked so natural framed in a parka and eyes that seemed forever squinting against the midnight sun. He was built like a walrus, blubber all over, but with great slabs of muscle too, which showed itself in the nonchalant way he slung those 40-pound buckets around.

But his outstanding characteristic was his love for the creatures he cared for. In a park full of animal lovers, J.B. stood out. It wasn't just that he was almost continually working, looking for ways to better the lives of the voiceless ones: more than that. He gave of himself. Once when a seal mother died, J.B. spent the night in the wet wooden travel cage. Why? Because of the baby. The seal pup, deprived of its mother for the first time in his or her short life, had been whining and crying, and J.B. worried the little one might be cold. There was a heat lamp shining red light into the pen, but still, it was a baby, and the first night without its mother. They found J.B. shivering in the morning, curled up on the plywood, with a snug infant sea lion in the circle of his warmth.

I finished the squid as fast as I could, which meant slowly, and J.B. pilled the mackerel, inserting blue chalky vitamin tablets through the red gills into the body cavity, seven or eight pills to the fish. Laying the special food on top of partially filled buckets with names of animals on them (Coco, Patches, Cyrus, Mother), the huge Guamanian weighed the buckets so he'd know exactly how much was eaten by whom (he'd record the information in a notebook later). J.B. carried the buckets out to a waiting electric golf cart.

"Come and help me feed Seal Compound!" he said.

Seals? Seals? I do not like seals, or sea lions either. (The species are different, of course, in ears, flippers, and the composition of their coats. Seals are wearable, sea lions are not; the former has fur, the latter hair. But both share a nasty, treacherous disposition that is totally at odds with their appearance.) I am prejudiced against the tribe, and I have my reasons.

First and foremost was Nero, the biter. A performing sea lion who weighed about 350 pounds, with a snakelike neck. I remember with an absolute clarity the first (and only) time I cleaned his pen while he was at home.

YARKYARKYARKYARK the monotonous racket had greeted me that day, as I dropped my coiled hose before the door of Nero's pen. The door was green, open-mesh fencing—open so Nero could see and insult the other sea lions and any available humans. He took full advantage of it. I could see him in the shadow on the redwood deck, smooth and glowing from a thousand seal oil rubbings as the elder *Zalophus californianus* entered and exited from his individual swimming pool beneath.

"I'm going to clean your house!" I said brightly, on the theory that he would be less likely to eat me if he knew what I was up to. The trainers had warned me Nero was a biter, but I felt sure that a calm, rational approach would prevail.

Besides, I reasoned, animals almost always liked me because they knew I liked them.

As I dressed, fastening shoulder harness straps, snugging up the weight belt and plugging in my air hose, Nero watched and seemed to smile, with his large, round, Walt Disney eyes.

The door opened inward. I expected the semipanicked response a sea lion in the wild would give, diving off rocks into the water below, in a frenzied rush when danger neared. Nero didn't bother. The opened door touched his smooth flank. One side of a whiskery lip pulled back. His frontal canines were broken off, probably from fighting, but his side teeth were plaque brown and ugly and capable.

"Uhh—'scuse me?" I increased pressure on the door. Nero grudgingly flopped off into the pool but surfaced immediately, 6 inches from the edge of the deck. It was disconcerting to put my feet in the water with the seal that close. I considered asking him to move but decided against it—something about the unintimidated way the animal, who was larger up close than he appeared in the shows, was studying me.

As soon as I entered the water, I knew I had made a mistake. The blue panes of underwater light seemed filled with buzzing Neroes, and he gave my territory no respect at all. He snuffled at my swim fins as I tried to scrub, and then SNORT! he put nose/mouth/teeth on my bare arm and roared bubbles. No bite but the noise and the sight of his teeth in juxtaposition with my limb put my pulse into overdrive. He did not look cute anymore.

I held up my brush, but the sea lion had become a brown bullet again, leaving me shaken on the floor. And I still had my tank to scrub. He had made his point: this was his home, and I was an intruder. Believe me, sir, I share your sentiments, and I will be out of your way just as quickly as I possibly—

Nero snatched me off the floor by my butt. I felt the clamp of jaws, and I was raised and shaken as if I weighed nothing.

It's funny now, but it wasn't then. Has anyone ever picked you up off the ground and shaken you? Somebody who did not wish you well? Remember the empty disorientation as your feet lost their grip on the earth? Imagine then my feelings of fright and helpless rage as that *thing* ripped me back and forth through the water, like a dog with its teeth on the neck of a cat.

With a contemptuous toss of his neck, Nero flung me aside. A cold gush of water rushed into the split where the back of my pants had been.

My eyes felt big as my mask as I rolled on my back and scooted into a corner, scrub brush up. Then I felt the skin on my face tighten. And when that miserable low-down, no-account excuse for an animal came near me, I jumped up with my scrub brush. I cursed and punched at and chased that creature, and if results matched intent, I'd have carried him home for a rug. Fortunately for me, I did not catch up with him.

The frenzied charge did, however, gain me a *little* respect, space and time enough to do my work: to scrub the algae off the walls and git.

YARKYARKYARKYARK Nero called sarcastically, as I shuffled close-leggedly away.

I was not, therefore, overjoyed when J.B. invited me to help feed the residents of Seal Compound.

The enclosure did not threaten at first. There were no gloomy walls, no skulls of former visitors, just a roomy corner of the park surrounded and divided by the same kind of open-mesh fencing that housed the performing animals at Oceana, where Nero lived. Open-roofed rooms, with different species of water mammals. Asian river otters here, yearling sea lions there, Mother and Lou the bulbous elephant seals over there, beside the main swimming pool.

But in the center of the pool was a large, long, sleek brown head, with eyes the size of the base of my clenched fist. The outline and extent of the body attached were obscured by the muddy, roiled water. "We're gonna have to pen Cyrus and clean that pond pretty quick," said John Benner, nodding at the thing in the pool.

"Hi, Mother!" smiled the happy Guamanian and raised a fish like a toast to one of the strangest creatures I have ever seen.

Only a blindly rutting male sea elephant could a find a female sea elephant attractive—and that's at her best—but moulting? From the bulging, snot-dripping proboscis which gave the elephant seal its name, down the one-ton blubberous body to the tip of her massive folded flippers, Mother's hide hung in rags and tatters, as if she'd slept in her clothes so long they'd rotted. "Hi, Mother," said J.B. again, softly, seeing beauty where I could not. Mother reared her pendulous nose back and belched. Benner dropped a mackerel down the open pipe of throat before him. I heard a splash.

J.B. fed for a while, then remembered something. "You finish feeding Mother," he said. "I'll be right back. See you in a little while," he added, more to Mother than to me, and off he clumped in his white rubber boots, silver buckets swinging by his side. The head in the water turned and watched him leave.

Mother burped again, a signal of irritation. "Oh, okay, Mother." I pinched thumb and forefinger around a blue-skinned mackerel, poised it over the wide pink mouth, and released. The mackerel arrowed cleanly down the yawning throat, not even touching the sides. I heard a splash as the fish landed in a dark pool of stomach acid.

Mother moved. The ripple began as a bulge near her tail and progressed heavily along her body like a wave. Shhlump. She had gained 6 inches. Shhlump. Twelve. Elephant seals do not saunter casually. I almost panted with her, so obvious was the effort it took to move her one-ton bulk.

"AOURRR!" An enormous shadow rose behind me. I glimpsed it, something erupting from the pool, heard the hissing scrape as it slid for the place where I stood. I did not wait to identify it.

There was a fence in my way, a 10-foot chain link fence. I believe I touched it on the way over, but I am not sure. As I halted, panting on the other side, the roar sounded again, and this time there was a triumphant note mixed in it. The bull Stellar sea lion reared back his mighty head. Red-rimmed eyes caught mine. His bulging neck was bigger than a big man's chest, and his chest was vast. He looked like a grizzly bear with the fur slicked down. He vocalized again, the guttural utterance like a slow, raucous, belch.

The narrow head shot downward, burying itself in the bucket of mackerel I had so precipitously abandoned. One of the enormous black flippers adjusted the container. Huge scapular "wing" muscles rippled in the shiny black-brown upper back.

"You bad boy, Cyrus!" came a chubby voice of authority. J.B. was frowning over the other fence. It appeared to take real effort for him to force the corners of his mouth down. He looked about as ferocious as a pouting infant.

But the gargantuan sea lion immediately turned and flung himself into the water, sending waves over the edges of the pool. "Don't let him bully you," said J.B. as I clambered awkwardly over the barrier I had cleared so lightly just a moment ago. "He's only a big baby." Big Baby leered at me from behind J.B.'s back. "Shake your broom at him, if he tries to steal Mother's food again—but don't hurt him!" he added hastily. "Now come and help feed the otters, and scrub out their pen."

Otters! Brown-furred fun. Bright, happy eyes and inquisitive strong fingers that plucked at the edges of a pant leg, puzzled over the lacing of a work shoe, or tested the smoothness of a cutshack waterproof boot. Sharp little clean teeth, showing white as they delicately chewed a whitebait, CHKCHKCHKCHK, starting at the head and sometimes the fish skull popped—SNAP! Perpetual motion, chirring contentedly at a world that obviously needs to be taken apart and examined, piece by piece.

One pulled my pant cuff out of my boot. I sat down to

play, or rather to be played with. The otter climbed right up my chest and onto my shoulders, as if we'd known each other always, sniffed inquisitively in my ear, rummaged thoughtfully through the roots of my hair, in case there was something valuable and overlooked. I felt like hugging, but of course I did not. I just sat still and enjoyed her pungent smell and her otter nearness.

I've read that Asian otters very much like ours, only larger, attack and kill *crocodiles*. My source for this is the great naturalist and hunter Colonel James J. Corbett, who grew up in the Indian jungle and loved it as a friend. According to Colonel Corbett, the 50-pound cousins to the weasel work in pairs, leaping in at the crocodile's neck from opposite sides, giving the giant reptile no rest, evading the big, crushing jaws until their smaller but effective ones can open a wound, and the crocodile dies or vacates the territory.

So swift, these small fellas. Once we'd had to catch an otter in his pen, and he'd gone to ground under a fiber glass "rock." I pushed the fork of a stick against his out-thrust chest, but he braced with gripping paws, and I was making scant progress when suddenly my finger sprang a leak. Blood fairly popped out at the knuckle. I knew the otter had done it because there was nobody else around, but hanged if I saw it happen. I saw the before, and the afterward, but the in-between escaped me.

"Clean their floor real good, okay?" and J.B. left to bring food and attention to somebody else. A heavy black hose hanging over the fence shot a crystal pipe of water to the concrete floor.

I like to watch water. It makes me ache sometimes, it is so beautiful. The clarity, the grace of its fall, the tiny blobs that spring up one instant and then are gone, flattening into wetness on the floor.

My broom and me scrubbed the manure up, and the good clean water sluiced the mess away, chasing it down a concrete channel which led to a drain. The otters were here only temporarily, until construction people built them a little island to live on.

I called to J.B. to turn off the water. Nothing answered but a sea gull and a small stealthy ripple in the center of the main swimming pool, like the ripple a crocodile might make when it sneaks up softly behind its prey.

The water gushed from the black hose. Might as well get a drink, I thought, but the pressure was too great, and the water bounced out of my mouth before I could swallow.

"J.B.?" I called again. My eyes followed the path of the black hose, over the mesh fence, along the floor, past the occupied pool. There was the faucet, by the murky-brown pool with its inhabitant. One hundred feet, no more. I had only to open one door, walk past Cyrus one step at a time, and turn off the water. Few adventures have ever appealed to me less.

J.B.! In the electric cart, its back all loaded down with shining buckets full of food, coming to rescue me! The need for nerve subsided. J.B. would swing by, stride boldly into the compound, and I would accompany him out.

The electric cart, springs sagging under the burden of food, disappeared over the hill and was gone. J.B.! You forgot your poor, lonesome helper. Got to thinking about your animals, and your human friend completely slipped your mind.

The water continued to flow.

I considered alternatives. Leave the water running? Or, I could climb out the back way from this enclosure, over the fence, around the whole compound, and poke my fingers or a stick through the open squares of meshing and manipulate the faucet in safety.

Cyrus in the pool lifted his head and made an impolite noise in my direction. I felt my underlip start to stick out, the way it had used to do when I was a kid and my mother told me not to talk back. I picked up the broom and gave it a shake.

And I opened the door to the main compound.

Cyrus boomed up onto the swimming pool edge. "ORRRR!" I answered him, shouting, "HEYYY!" and charged up the short slope like the U.S. Marines. The head of the broom slammed into his belly. The giant sea lion fell back and disappeared in a welter of foam. I couldn't believe it. That simple! I turned off the water with a flourish and stalked in elbow-swinging triumph past the pool where my former fear lay hiding. Hmmpf! Guess I showed him a thing or three about humans.

"ROARRK!" towered over me. His jaws were wide, and giant brown dog teeth showed, as long as my little finger. My body flamed hot/cold all over, and I shook my broom so hard by his face that its bristle block flew off.

Cyrus and I watched the long brush head soar through the air, turning end over end and landing CLUNK FLOPFLOP on the opposite side of the pool. The handle I held was like a pool cue. I'd heard of somebody trying to stop a Steller's charge with a broomstick like this, whacking it across the broad chest. Had to get a new broom and, I think, maybe a new attendant. I recoiled, ready to poke or prod off half a ton of . . .

Cyrus came unhinged. This had never happened before—the huge form whirled and floundered, heaved itself off the edge into the pool, and the water divided and fairly boiled with the little harbor seals flung out of the way of his mad rush.

This time I had the good sense to shout insults after him, so the "big baby" would think it was me and not the flying broomhead he was afraid of. I insulted his character, family, ancestors, and the entire flipper-foot clan. I ran through my stock of profane character aspersions, improvised, borrowed, and reduplicated. He may have missed some of the subtler language, but I think the emotion carried.

"And you remember that!" I shouted to his nose, which was sticking out from the far end of the pool. Then the rush of adrenaline eased, and my knees began to shake again. I tried to strut as I left the compound, but I am not sure I was entirely convincing.

o o o

I took it rather well, I thought, when the girl from the vet clinic called. "Zsa-Zsa . . . and Ernestine," I heard myself repeat, and my voice did not even quaver when I named the dolphin who had broken my ear.

My lungs and tongue and lips went on working, pumping up air and shaping it into the vibrations that communicate, talking about the catch to come. But my insides were in another place entirely, a place I'd wish no friend of mine to ever go. A place of snakes and corners and darknesses, of small rooms, and fire, and rats' eyes. Incoherence, incompetence, impotence, fear. Where everything is lost . . .

I watched my bootees trading places, down the steps, a pause at the equipment locker, across asphalt, gravel . . . stopping at a concrete tankside.

My ear felt bright red, as if someone had painted a target on it, and the bull's-eye was the just-healed eardrum, which now throbbed, reminding me.

I heard my voice mumbling the usual things about getting the net in close to the wall before we went over, and the man beside me answered softly, as he always spoke. This was Keith Worcester, a heavy-shouldered man, blue eyes and a youthful, mildly pink face, the owner of two of the quickest hands that ever locked around a dolphin. I wasn't talking to tell him anything he didn't already know, but more to reassure myself, by taking refuge in the familiar.

My options had vanished. I had no more choices. I could not quit in fear. I would not let them see me cry. I slipped my hips off the side of the tank and left the dry world behind.

Holding my breath, I bent through the blue, pulling with polar bear strokes for the bottom. Sometimes we had to set lead weight belts on the net fringe, but this net had a chain fringe, so I had only to take a double handful of it, and swim forward. Ernestine's shape showed through the squares of the nylon net. At another time the free-swimming conformation would have aroused my admiration, but now she appeared cruel, like a weapon. She snapped her jaws, as in a declaration of war.

But as I went up and breathed and dived again, I was delighted to note that the fear had lifted away from me, like the bubbles from my snorkel. Another couple of pushes and the net was in place, and Keith and I pulled ourselves over the bobbing floats, into the area the dolphins held.

Ernestine showed me her teeth. I paused, backed away. Not because I was afraid, but because it was right. I was listening to her mood and trying to coordinate my movements to it. My lungs itched, and I rose, to blow out the snorkel pipe full of water and catch another breath or two.

Keith's white shoulder flashed before me. What? I yanked my head out of the water, and that is how I got one of the cleanest, most gorgeous memories of my life.

Keith had a body grab on Zsa-Zsa, and she was leaping up into the sun with such force that she dragged the diver with her, completely out of the water. Man and dolphin, together in the air. With an example like that, what else could I do?

Keith caught the first dolphin. I got the second.

21

Upside Down

~~~~~~~~~~~~~~~~~~~~~~~~~~~~~~~~~~~~~

"Missster Perrano." The rope skipper almost hissed, his muscular upper body pink and glowing from exertion and the summer sun. Our leather-jacketed instructor paused in the doorway. "Wotcher want?"

"Show us what you can do, if you're so good," the rope skipper said, and tossed the handled strand to the man who would be teaching us to dive commercially. Perrano looked puzzled at the challenge and let the coils almost hit him before reaching up and taking the rope from the air.

"Show us how you can skip rope layin' down," said the lazy-smiling youth. Suddenly I could hear the freeway noise in the distance. All the students, all of us who had read the brochure and listened to Mike Rugged and now were wondering—we all turned our eyes on the short man from New Zealand. Come on, Alan Perrano. Please be real.

"We don't have no bleedin' mat around here. Think I'm gonna break my head on the concrete?" It was hot. I hoped that was the reason for the sweat on Alan's forehead.

"Just skip standing up. You can do that, can't you?" The younger man folded his arms, ignoring the rope Perrano was thrusting back toward him.

"Yeah, come on, Mr. Perrano, do it!" said some voices in the crowd."

Then Alan Perrano smiled, and it was like the sun breaking through a clouded day.

"Awl right. I'll play your silly fuckin' game—but just this

once, I ain't no bloody *hen*tertainer! Back up, give me some room."

He gave a little hop and a skip off the porch and suddenly that rope came alive, and the man was dancing! I don't know what he did, but it was musical: rhythms of pattering TAPTAP-TAP and the feet skipping up and the rope alive and loving him, whispering tricks and calling the tune, in a way its original owner never knew.

" 'Course I am a bit rusty," said Alan Perrano, stopping all at once. "Noice little rope, though." He tossed it back. "Naow *if* you don't mind, we do have some classes to attend to?" The rope skipper put his shirt on before coming into the classroom, and I don't remember hearing that instantly recognizable TAPTAPTAP anymore the rest of our school session.

I had expected to do well on the written test after the six weeks of classroom lectures. I had studied regularly, and the night before the exam I sat all night at the kitchen table with the massive navy manual before me until the morning light came in the windows.

But when the test results came back, I stood only nineteenth in the class of forty, which was disaster. The top ten, Mike Rugged had promised, would get jobs.

Now the mechanical portion of the course was before us. I had hoped to build up a strong lead in the book part, because I knew my weakness in mechanics, which was what the practical section dealt with. Because diving is really only how a commercial diver gets down to the job. It's what he can do when he gets there that matters. If I'd finished fourth or fifth in the written exam, it wouldn't matter getting knocked down a rung or two by my ignorance of nuts and bolts, but nineteenth? I don't think I mentioned to Jeannie what the standings on the written test were.

The first few days we spent patching. The rough canvas diving suits were masses of repairs, and we added another couple of layers to the efforts of the students before us, gluing squares of twill to whatever looked like a leak.

At last it was time to don the gear. I was crew chief, which meant I got to climb into the stiff gray suit first. It had feet attached, like the sleeper pajamas little kids wear, and rubberized cuffs and collars. I had to smear my hands with liquid soap before I could thrust my wrists through the cuffholes. They had to be tight, and they were. My hands turned faintly blue and seemed to belong to someone else.

A massive copper breastplate was put over· my head and worked under the rubber collar with difficulty. Holes in the rubber collar matched up with studs sticking up from the breastplate. Lead weight belts crossed my chest and looped around my waist. A leather belt, appropriately dubbed the jock strap, went between my legs, and a strong man yanked violently as I leaned forward, and the belt tightened further as I straightened. My face went cold, and my gonads seemed to be somewhere in the vicinity of my navel. "Does it 'urt, Mr. Reed?" yelled Alan Perrano, our semibeloved instructor. "Like *Hell*, Mr. Perrano!" I yelled back above the hubbub of the four crews dressing their divers. "That's good!" he said, grinning sadistically. "Otherwise your helmet will lift off your shoulders!"

The helmet. The Mark Five helmet. The single most identifiable piece of deep-sea diver equipment. It looked almost magical. If you've ever seen a deep-sea diving movie, this is the helmet they almost certainly wore. The reason commercial divers call themselves "hard-hat divers."

The enormous brass helmet lowered slowly. A quarter-turn onto brass threads: SHHHUNNK! Locked. I had a last glimpse of the deck and my teammates, and the top of the redwood barrel I would be diving into on this first, exploratory dive.

Sound stopped. A wave of claustrophobia swept over me— it was small in here! Bars crisscrossed the faceplates before me. I could see almost nothing through the four small panes. I caught flashes of fingers moving as the two tenders adjusted wing nuts, and then SMOCK, SMOCK, echoed hollowly. Stand up, the two head taps meant.

As I leaned forward and rose, I knew what it was to weigh

400 pounds. The shoes alone weighed 35, and when I raised one foot, it was like weight lifting. CLUNK. I felt it settle down. Like a blind robot, I half-stumbled forward.

A crew-cut head loomed at my side window. Jon Noble, the assistant crew chief, and his lips were moving. I couldn't hear a word he was saying, but it was reassuring to know there were still people out there. He must be wanting me to turn around. I'm probably at the edge of the redwood barrel-tank.

Reaching my hand out, I fumbled until somebody connected my fingers to a ladder. Yep. Here I was. I stepped and turned and was climbing down, just as if I knew what I was doing. Ignoring the part of me that wanted to go home, I clambered backward, step by step. My feet were surrounded by cold, and I felt the wetness climb. We had patched the suits a lot, but they still weren't watertight.

My hand on the rung of the ladder, the yellow-painted ladder. That was the last thing I saw as the level of murky water rose past my window. I pulled back up once, just to be sure everything was still there, and disappeared.

There were no more rungs underneath my shoes. I let go of the ladder and dropped. The yellow surface light vanished, and I fell into blackness.

Ever been in a cave where the guide turned off all the lights? No matter how your eyes strained to adjust, you could see nothing, and that's how it was for me too as I flailed in slow motion and fell to the floor—was lowered actually, because one of the best features of hard-hat diving is you have a friend on the other end of an air and lifeline connecting you to the surface.

I landed in a crouch, knees bent, arms out, as if I was about to catch somebody. Couldn't see a thing, and at first it was scary, but then it got to be fun. I did all the things Perrano had suggested, deep knee bends, push-ups, standing on one foot, and then I got creative.

I'll turn upside down, I thought to myself. What a good idea! It worked neatly too, because as soon as my helmet got below the level of my knees and my hips lifted, all the air rushed from the top half of my suit, ballooning out the legs. The jacket flattened against my chest from water pressure without opposing air, and my feet were yanked straight up. I was absolutely vertical. My helmet bounced gently on the floor.

The water that had entered the patchwork on my legs poured down my thighs and underwear and chest and over my face. I snorted and spluttered it out of my nose. There was now a pool of cold water sloshing around the top of my head. This began to be not quite so much fun.

I tried to kick my legs over, but the air had lifted the shoes slightly off my feet, and I couldn't muster enough leverage to overcome the upward force. I stayed upside down, pinned there by the weight and jacket leads pulling down, and the lift of the air in my puffed-out legs tugging up. A headache began to nag me as well, pulsing in the veins by my temples.

I made a serious effort to sit up, straining with my abdomen muscles, and moved perhaps 20 degrees from the perpendicular, which I then lost immediately as I ceased to struggle. I tried to swing up, without result except for a slight dizziness.

Then I thought of the little exhaust valve inside the helmet next to my jaw. I'd push the button with my chin, let some air out, collapse the suit, sink to the bottom, and stand up triumphant. I pushed.

A gush of black water smashed me in the face. It took only an instant to release the chin button, but the level of liquid in the helmet was now at my forehead, and if I moved, the ripples came near my eyes.

Apparently exhaust valves worked backward, upside down.

The air seemed to yield me less strength. What was that Perrano had said about working on your back under ship hulls? Something about a pool of carbon dioxide from your own exhalations collecting in your helmet, and you got a terrific splitting headache? If I was upside down too long, breathing my own exhaust, might I conceivably *die*? I would be down here an hour unless I signaled topside sooner.

Better give four pulls on the lifeline, let them pull me up.

Embarrassing, but that's how a fellow learns, right? I rehearsed some excuses to use, while I fumbled for the line. But in this position, the lifeline was awkwardly angled, and I could not get hold of it.

My head hurt quite definitely now, whether from the blood-rush of being upside down, or CO_2 buildup, or my own worries. Think, think! I lectured myself. There has to be a way out; there is always a way.

The answer was under my hand all the time. Two inches from my palm was the wrist exhaust valve. I had only to cross my hands, turn the knob like a faucet, and wait. HISSS. The bulge of air around my lower legs grew, the puff spreading down to my thighs and belly, and then I was going up, ascending. Too fast (do this from depth, and I'd get the bends), but my feet and legs broke the surface, and I floundered a bit before the amazed eyes of my teammates before turning over and heading back down the right way.

Then, of course, I had to try it again because I couldn't accept that there wasn't a way to turn back over. And, of course, I got pinned again and couldn't break out and had to rescue myself in the same ridiculously undignified manner. Two feet-first ascents in a row.

I'm not even going to tell you what Perrano had to say.

22

Rick Pool and the Golden Summer

～～～～～～～～～～～～～～～～～～～～～

The early morning sunshine lay softly across my desk. I leaned forward into its gentle glow. And as I closed my eyes and propped my chin, I thought: never again, no matter where I go or what I do, will I have as much pure fun as I have had this summer.

It was the crew—we were all of an age and an attitude, and life was an adventure to be both played and paid for. We would work hard, hurling ourselves against the tasks, and then we'd play. Nobody shirked; everyone worked to the limits of his ability, and that gave us the base of innocence: the clean conscience that is necessary for play to be totally enjoyed. Then it seemed natural to have contests to see who could spend the greatest number of hours underwater working, and though four hours is an exhausting underwater day, we pushed the record up to twelve, although that did cripple the three-way title holders for a day or two. We would try experiments to see how many wire-brush scrub strokes we could make on the floor before changing hands. It was an amazing lesson in the endurance of the human body. Because it was always the will that gave way first; I could never honestly say there was not one more push left in me. Normally, I would scrub eight wire-brush pushes before switching hands, but in the game I did, once, one hundred shoves. I'd tell myself, that's it, just one more push, and the shoulder and arm won't try again. But there was always one more.

Out the window I could see Sarge, the water buffalo,

119

scratching his enormous rear on the fence. Dust lifted off the black hair and hide, and the nailed logs trembled. As well they might. Sarge had leaned too heavily against the fence once before, and it had been unable to accommodate his thousand pounds and collapsed. A faint look of surprise had crossed his placid face. He'd considered the new opening in the fence. Water buffalo are not flighty: they like to think things out. Sarge pondered. His great nostriled snout tested the fallen logs, snufflingly investigating the limits and potentialities of the change. He even turned his back on the break once, chewing his cud, giving the new situation a chance to go away. When it did not, Sarge ambled out into the world.

With considerable disturbance of the ice plant around his enclosure, Sarge half-stepped, half-slid down the slope to the lagoon behind the dive shack. He was, after all, a *water* buffalo and he contentedly navigated the shallow watercourse for perhaps a quarter of a mile before exiting up the bank on the far side of the waterway. If he had noticed, he would not have understood the consternation he aroused. Sarge was no threat to anyone, unless he should happen to step on a foot. He would even talk, though his conversations were terse and to the point. He had a one-word vocabulary, and if a visitor greeted the water buffalo, he would respond, "Hi," in a *profundo* bass. When Mary Rose, the red-haired birds-of-prey lady, found Sarge wandering, she led him home.

Footsteps and laughter disturbed my reverie. Two men, and two sets of feet, differing in their impact upon the decking of the porch outside the dive locker door. One made the boards rattle with the furious enthusiasm of his walk. The other trod gently, with control, as though his feet were paws. His name was Bill Beardsley, and the stomper was Rick Pool.

The door burst open, the knob slamming into the wall. As Pool hurled himself into a chair, rocking it back onto two legs and balancing precariously, I was struck again by the man's refusal to accept the limitations of his body.

If you heard the man's emotion-swept voice and saw his

great brown beard and heavy eyebrows and dark eyes as full of energy as the ball of ink beneath an exclamation point, you would think, this man is a lumberjack. The mackinaw jacket he wore didn't get in the way of the image either, and in fact Rick had played the part of a mining camp extra in the movie *Paint Your Wagon*. With his head-back approach to life, and face like the spirit of the North, it was natural to assume his frame would have the muscular covering of a giant.

But in actuality, the limbs beneath the jacket were pale-fleshed, flabby-looking, and weak. And clumsy?! If there was a banana peel anywhere in the neighborhood, you could depend on Rick Pool's foot to find it. We'd hear a crash— "there's Rick," we'd say.

His spectacular lack of coordination, coupled with a diver's natural penchant for play, almost cost him his life the second day he worked here.

One of our favorite games was the divers' slide. Officially it was the reef tank's tarp covering, but, when wet, that plastic-coated canvas achieved a degree of glasslike slickness that seemed especially designed for a crazy diver. We'd climb up the spiraling reef-tank wall, poise for an instant against the sky, and plunge down the presoaked surface, fast as a hawk when it folds its wings and falls. For a hundred feet the slide continued, from high to low edge of the circle-walled tank. The only drawback was what could happen at the bottom.

You had to plan your slide stop because if you went off the lower edge you'd land in pipes and red metal barrels and sharp-cornered angle irons: filtration equipment. So a thoughtful diver either turned sideways and stopped on the projecting square iron planes of the tarp fastenings or caught them with his feet or persuaded friends to pile up at the edge and catch his hurtling, down-rushing body. Rick chose none of the above.

When he crouched at the upper edge of the diver slide tarp, the slipperiness took him before he had either a chance to dive or to sit completely down. He resembled a skiier schussing down the tarp face. He may have wished to stop, but the momentum was immediate and without reserve. For perhaps four seconds Rick Pool looked terrific, rocketing down, faster than any diver had gone before.

"I saw what was going to happen," said Keith Worcester afterward, "and I dived down the tarp to try to catch up. But he disappeared over the edge." There was a silence from the pit. "I braked my descent on the fastenings. 'Rick, are you all right?' "

"I don't know," came the unsteady answer. Blood trickled from forehead to mustache, nose to beard. But the man was getting up, even as he spoke, and that too was important about Rick Pool. As in W. E. Henley's poem "Invictus," Rick might be bloody and he might be battered, but he was by God unbowed. He'd always get up.

Bill Beardsley's foot shot out to the back of Rick Pool's toppling chair. Rick's chairborne weight teetered, sagged, and grudgingly settled back into balance.

"That floor's kind of treacherous right there," said Bill.

Bill Beardsley, a stocky block of relaxed and graceful musculature, was one of the most gentle and considerate men I've ever known. Also one of the most potentially ferocious. His eyes were lynx green, but the light in them was gentle. It could flare up and dance, as we shall see, but never accidentally. Bill had achieved the unselfconsciousness of an animal. So completely confident was he that he could wear ugly clothes, including a pair of the most ridiculous looking Bermuda shorts, bagging and flapping above bare, muscular calves. He could have worn a pink ribbon taped to his nose, and it would not have excited comment. When he entered a room, shutting the door behind him softly so as not to interrupt whoever was talking, every eye turned to him and was glad. Because whether he had met you once or a hundred times or never, Bill was always glad to see you.

And more. When Bill looked at people, he saw through the underbrush of their awkwardness or bad moods to the light of their best self within. He expected the best from people, and they usually gave it to him. When they got off the track, he would say so, but in such a manner that the door was always open for an honorable reconciliation.

I envied Bill's easy grace with people, contrasting that with my own too-frequent aloneness. Socially, I was as disaster prone as Rick Pool on the tarp. I could not seem to converse. I could monologue, talking too loudly or too long, or I could withdraw completely. I could perform, I could be totally at home on stage before people or with a microphone before me; then I knew what was expected of me. I could concentrate totally, sharing with people, reaching out. I was okay, then. But in the uncharted shoals of everyday getting along with people, of give-and-take unplanned conversation, that was and is the hardest part of life for me.

I didn't mind when Bill taught us karate. That was just generosity on his part. He had studied under a legendary great of the martial arts, Joe Lewis. Tremendous innovator.

"Joe Lewis took an art form thousands of years old, and said, 'they might be wrong,' " said Bill. "For instance, the punch. The old masters said, 'Move the bigger, slower muscle groups first. Hips, legs, back. Then, shoot out the clenched fist.' But Lewis said, 'No, let the hand go out *first*, with as little big muscle movement as possible, and only at the last bring the power groups in for impact.' The reason for that is—well, let me show you."

I crouched in my wide-legged beginner safety stance. Bill took up an identical front "horse" (as if riding one) posture. "Okay, I'm going to punch you in the chest. Not hard, but you try and block it." This was no challenge, a demonstration only, but I felt my competitive instincts rise, and I was completely "Ready?" Yes.

THUMP. I saw the fist as it retracted. "Try that again," I said. THUMP!

Study his body as I might, I could detect no warning signals. There was no windup, no beforehand lean back, no anticipatory flinch of shoulder muscle, no head or neck movement—nothing. I could see the hip rotation only as I felt the impact (substantial enough to jar, but not hurt) but not in time to do anything preventative.

"When Lewis introduced that movement in the karate circuit, virtually no one could block it," he explained. He could strike at will. Here's how it works.

"Imagine there's an invisible *string* tied through a hole drilled in the third knuckle of your hand. Really visualize that string. Now. Standing completely relaxed, let that string pull your fist out, almost all the way, and only at the very last instant before it hits, let the hips rotate and the legs drive. Ready?"

I nodded, and BANG! that fist came in, reddening the exact same spot it had hit before.

Bill had a scar on his chin, an unanswered question. I had to ask, and that's how I heard about the fella with the pool cue. To get Bill mad, as I say, you practically had to hit him with a stick, and that's what the man had done.

"We'd been shooting pool, and this dude with a blue chin and curly hair was trying to hustle me. You know, playing badly at first, faking, lying low till the money comes out? Only when he went to turn on the steam, he wasn't as good as he gave himself credit for, or maybe he was having a bad day. In any case I was able to take his money. I guess that made him mad because when I left the table and bent down to pick up my motorcycle helmet, he said "hey" real soft, like he wanted to play some more. I looked up and he was swinging the pool cue like a baseball bat. It broke on my chin."

Bill's eyes looked different.

"Then what happened?" I asked, envisioning flying high kicks, knee lifts, screaming kiai's, or the slash of a stiffened, knife-edged hand.

"I was holding my helmet by its strap, so I swung it, beat him down. He went to sleep, and his friend wasn't interested in discussing the matter further," Bill shrugged, "and that was the end of it." Adaptability.

I practiced religiously, doing thousands of the special punches, trying for that magical speed of fist or foot Bill could so routinely summon up, and eventually I did learn the difference between a punch and a shove. I could never approach Bill's ability, but the knowledge did stick, and it came in very handy later on in the glorious summer.

"Hi, guys!" A kinky-haired, almond-eyed head poked around the door, openmouthed and wide-smiling. "Oh, no. Just when things were peaceful for a change!" we greeted Sunshine John.

I forget if it was that day or another that I nearly drowned John Patterson. I only remember how it started. And ended.

We had been wire-brushing the grotto, which was supposed to be blue-white, instead of the hard green which disgraced it—and us—now. We fought the tight-clinging algae for hours until our arms vibrated with fatigue. But as the work began to finish at last, I could feel the other guys begin to look around, for mischief. Personally, I did not have to search for such childishness. I had mine planned. I knew just exactly who was going to be the beneficiary of my malice. As my arms moved in that sweet caressing blue coolness, I gloated over what I was going to do to John Patterson.

URRRK! My eyes were flooded with saltwater. Fingers grabbed at my stomach. Had I not folded immediately and clutched my gut, the weight belt would have fallen and my wet-suited body bobbed right to the surface. But I had been thinking of something just along these lines, and so was able to keep my belt. One hand glued to the buckle, I glowered through the blur until a black blotch proved to be my mask. I tugged the straps around my head, pulling out some hair as I always did, and exhaled through my nose. As the level of saltwater lowered like a curtain of invisibility, I saw the muscular Irish-Japanese on the floor, clutching his lean belly with one hand, pointing at me with the other. Laugh, John Patterson, laugh. Your hour is nearly upon you.

I waved to him sweetly and turned back to my scrubbing.

Disgusting kid anyway. Body by Michelangelo. As if his maker had doubled up on the muscle and forgotten the fat. Keith Worcester and I, whose bodies supported approximately equal layers of pudge, used to take turns hating John. We'd be starving ourselves, either fasting completely or suffering on some soulless diet, and there would be John, buried to the eyes in an extra-large pizza. Worcester and I would exercise daily, lifting weights, karate kicking, running until our pink faces flushed out wells of sweat, and the best we could look was not too fat; John might yawningly help himself to a handful of chin-ups, easy as taking dates from a dish, or ripple through some handstand push-ups, or a couple THUNK!ing kicks on the heavy bag, and his muscles would stand out like a leopard under stress. We would never have admitted it to him, but John was beautiful.

Sunshine John. Always verbalizing, never still. Some mornings in the preceding winter had been so chill and gray and miserable that the rest of us would sit and glare at everything and each other, waiting for Sunshine John to come and perk things up, like a cup of coffee. Too much coffee, of course, jangles the nerves, and there were times when Patterson's incessant chatter made me want to cover my ears. He had a fine voice for singing, I was told. I just wish he hadn't used it for talking quite so much. I didn't know I was almost to silence him permanently.

Pretending to pretend to pay attention to my scrubbing, I let the suspense build for John. Knowing he'd be suspicious if I didn't try something, I made myself appear to be sneakily coiling my energies, then dove suddenly in a strong but spurious attempt on his mask. His swifter reflexes blocked my hands, as I knew they would—as I intended they would. I chased him vigorously a few seconds to make it look real, then shook my fist. "You're just too fast for me, John," I sent out the false vibration.

Then I made my real move. He had just picked up his brush and was eyeing a likely-looking spot to work when I hit him in the gut with one hand and raked up his face with the other, yanking his belt and his mask in one move. His hands fought for control, but there was no chance. Blind and helpless, he belched out bubbles and was flung toward the surface by the lift of his suit. Not a good game, really, for if he'd held his breath, he'd have embolized and died or burst his lungs. We were fooling around with death, like kids on the freeway with too fast cars.

Worse was to come. For, unbeknownst to me, when I had swept my hand up his face to yank his mask, I had also pulled the regulator out of his mouthpiece. He exhaled, still feeling the rubber grip between his teeth, but he breathed in warm water.

How funny it would be, I thought, snagging his air line as it shot by, if I didn't let him get to the surface. . . . I held the line and watched him flail, 3 feet from the air. Keith Worcester, who had got out a moment before to get another wire brush, spotted the distortion of the struggling diver. At first he didn't understand, but when he put his face into the water and saw John's bulging eyes and clawing limbs, he knew. Keith reached down and out. Couldn't reach. So he turned, hung by his knees from the stage, and extended his hands. Desperate John grabbed a hold and pulled Keith off the stage.

"I had forgot I was wearing two heavy belts to keep me down. John's pull and the belts dragged me off the stage, and I didn't have air on. I went right to the floor," said Keith Worcester later.

I was congratulating myself. I don't clown around too often, but when I do it's a corker! I'll have to do this more often, I thought, watching John's frenzy. When Keith's descent brought him to me, he pointed repeatedly to the surface and John and the hose I held. I nodded gleefully. Yes, isn't it a good joke, I agreed, misunderstanding Keith completely. Keith, having told me, sprang upward, commencing the difficult task of surfacing with two weight belts on. Like climbing a ladder with somebody on your shoulders.

A faint uneasiness touched me. It was a fine joke, but

. . . I watched John's weakening struggles, clutching for the air I didn't know I was denying him. I thought he had his regulator in his mouth as always. But maybe he would get mad if I teased him too long. Better let him go. I released the air line, watched him weakly clutch and grab and vanish from the green. Guess I'll go up, see how he liked it, I thought.

He was face down on the stage, gasping. "You nearly drowned me, Reed. You nearly drowned me," he kept repeating, in between fits of coughing and near vomiting.

That was too heavy for me to accept, so I told him it was his fault. Why didn't he undo the chest straps? Or search for the regulator? Or pull himself back down the hose to me and make the out-of-air gesture?

But a man drowning doesn't always think calmly and logically and analytically.

"You almost drowned me, Reed," moaned John Patterson, unanswerably.

A pall began to descend upon the golden summer. As if a powerful witch had cursed us, ill luck seemed determined to blight our happiness.

Ernestine got sick. Not just any usual dolphin sickness, either. No moderate skip-food-for-a-few-days-and-back-to-normal, either, no: no. Erysipelas. The dreaded scourge of dolphins.

Ernestine. She who had been the great love of Lucky's life. Ernestine. Unscarred, unmarked, no deformations of any kind. Clean and sweet and perfect. Ernestine, she who had taken part of my hearing. Her mark was on me. I would carry the scar on my eardrum till I died. Ernestine. Like the wind made water and the water made flesh and the flesh granted beautiful life.

Holes developed in her side. She had to be removed from the company of the other show dolphins and placed in the flume with another called Annie, who was also ill and under constant medication. Annie died. They found her in the morning, stiff underwater. When they raised her, a bubble escaped from her mouth: noxious, nauseous gas, as if her intestines or their contents had rotted. Ernestine grew worse, and she was alone.

To be alone, for a dolphin, is the worst thing. They are so social, these gray flyers of the sea, that to be denied companionship is almost to be denied life. I am convinced that Opo, the famous dolphin of Oppononi who adopted a beach town, making the people her family, was a dolphin separated from her herd.

The dolphins in the next tank communicated with Ernestine. I say this because when we would come in the morning to give her her shots, we would sometimes find her lined up perpendicular to the wall. And on the opposite side of the thick concrete, their heads pointed directly toward the dolphin they could not see, were the others. Visiting her just as surely as kinfolks at a hospital.

But Ernestine came apart in our hands. We had to force-feed her, ramming that ugly but necessary plastic tube down her throat. As the vet poured the ground fish slurry into her, Ernestine would naturally wriggle, and pieces of her rotting flesh would break off in our grips. Like wrestling with the living corpse of a dolphin we had loved.

The usually relaxed atmosphere grew tense. The divers quarreled. Foolishly, over inconsequential issues. Keith liked to imagine accidents, like falling down bleachers. What exactly would happen? How should a person fall to minimize breakage? What kind of first aid would be required? Patterson thought this was terribly morbid and stopped speaking to Keith for a while, avoiding him.

I grew jealous of Bill Beardsley's easy way with people. I imagined he was trying to take control of the dive locker away from me. The natural friendly acts he performed for others began to seem political, as though he were trying to make me look bad. I withdrew and brooded.

Keith lost his backflip. He used to grip the edge of the tarp with his toes, balance, spring, and do a neat, dignified flip into the water below. But now it went away. He'd poise himself, spring, and . . . he couldn't nerve himself to bring the knees up as he hurled himself backward. He would just jump and enter the green water feet first and frustrated.

A mania for competitive pushing-in developed. No one could stand safely on the edge of a tank. We played too fiercely now, with almost an edge of desperation, trying to bring back something we had lost. As though by manic exertion we could undo Ernestine's hurts and our own.

Sometimes it worked. Once I was coiling my air hose on the edge of the grotto. We had been talking and soaking up sun after work, and my hide was baking, and the warmth was just beginning to penetrate my chilled innards. I had my jacket top down, and I was talking some foolishness to the dolphins below me, in the pool. I don't know how I could have been so careless. A two-year-old could have pushed me in from that delicate juncture of balance, as I bent and traced the yellow circles of hose and mumbled to the gray players. I didn't see Rick Pool nudge Keith and point to me.

The rushing tread of footsteps triggered in me the need for some response, and I straightened. "Pardon?" I said, as Rick's body went flying by. "NOOOOO!" he screamed just before the water closed over his head. He had missed! An 8-foot run at a stationary, 220-pound target, and he had run right past. Amazing.

Then there was the time somebody shoved Rick into the water. When he surfaced, and climbed out, looking for revenge, he did not notice at first that his *weights* had been pushed in also. He scratched his head, looked down, and saw them. Down at the bottom of the million-gallon pool.

Now swimming down with a neoprene rubber suit but no weight belt is a challenge. The rubber has tiny gas bubbles trapped inside, and the flotation power these generate is really extraordinary. One of our most treasured pleasures was to lie, fully suited but with no weights, on the surface of Oceana's pool, where Rick was now. The rubber lifted and supported us. Arms spread, we would watch the sky, so endlessly blue. No muscle tensed in the quiet. We felt so light it almost would have been no surprise if we'd lifted up and drifted away . . . but swimming *down* sans weight belt was another matter altogether.

Poor Rick. When he dived off the side and got stuck halfway down, it must have been as if the sea rejected him. His upper body, head to hips, went under—his swim-finned feet scissored radically—but he could not get down. The flotation lift pushed back too hard. He was stuck on the surface like a fly on gelatin.

Now many—probably most—divers cannot pull themselves to the bottom against the buoyancy of a full wet suit. Most would probably have to do what Rick did, which was to try several times, surface diving, head down and tail up, kicking and pulling. When that didn't work, R. P. removed his jacket, which halved his floatability. It was still a struggle to get down: a violent exertion which was comical to watch, for like all comedy it had suffering at its core.

With the casual cruelty of friends everywhere, we arranged that Rick's weights should take up permanent residence on the bottom of the tank. At least once a day there would be a splash and a soft, delayed klunk as the weights settled down and stopped on the nearly unreachable floor.

It wasn't quite so comical to Rick. Once I saw his eyes before laughter clouded them over, when he heard the splash of his belt going in for the third time that day. His eyelids pulled back exposing more white and the total brown of the cornea. He inhaled through his nose, and he almost shook. Then he controlled and laughed.

Emotionalism, false and real, tensed us all. And one morning, I exploded at Bill Beardsley. In front of everybody. All the divers. I shouted. I knew what he was doing being so nice to everybody! He was trying to make me look bad. Disloyal! Some friend he was! I even, inexcusably, picked up a heavy tape dispenser and tossed it to him roughly, not throwing it at him, not actually, but close and the tape-cutting edge poked into his hand. "That was an aggressive action, Bill!" The more I made a fool of myself, the more I talked.

The witch's curse had my lips and was flapping them to my utter disadvantage. Even as the words bellowed out, I knew they were untrue. But I couldn't stop.

"What are you trying to be, head diver?!!"

The explosion ceased. The room was still and shocked. "Where did this come from?" asked Bill. He had been nice, helpful without hope of profit, and now this? Maybe there was a logical explanation, his posture read. He leaned forward, elbow on knees.

The truth was, I envied Bill. But, of course, I couldn't say that. I could only retreat into emotionalism, substituting volume for accuracy, ranting and raving. "You're disloyal!" was probably my most coherent statement.

"No," said Bill. "I have always supported you. And I will continue to do so." Even then I didn't know how to stop so I went on yelling.

"So what do we do now?" asked Bill, spreading out his hands moderately. "Freestyle?" meaning fight. As if to say, you see how ridiculous this is?

I knew that friends should fight, and I also was fairly certain I would get busted up if we tangled. He was too fast and strong. A great heaviness descended on my limbs. But the only thing I could think of to say was "all right."

Then Bill Beardsley stood up. Energy poured off him like flame. Green eyes scanned the inside of my brain, and I knew in that moment what that fellow with the pool cue had felt like. There was no way on earth I could defeat this man, except at the cost of my own life.

Bill spoke, in a curious, half-whispering voice that riveted attention. "You are behaving badly," he said. "You know what I am going to do? I am going to walk into the next room, and I won't come back until *you* return." Meaning the real me, I suppose.

He had his hand on the doorknob when I said no, I was going out, and shouldered past him. As I jumped off the porch, not even wanting to take time to use the steps, Waldo across the water lifted his muzzle and said "Hi." But I ig-

ABOVE: Flying with Stormy. Dolphins appear to enjoy playing almost as much as we do. They are also distinctly individual personalities, and, at least in captivity, capable of violence against humans. (Photo by Dave DiFiore)

LEFT: Carrying a nurse shark from a Steinhart Aquarium truck to our tank. Although this shark is almost completely harmless, it is struggling quite convincingly and my arms were numb before we could get it into the water. Note the tiny teeth, and the mustachelike barbels that the bottom-feeding shark uses to locate food. (Photo by Steve Castillo)

BELOW: Face to face. This is the everyday reality of working in a tank with sharks. This eight-foot seven-gill is making his rounds as I scrub the floor. Only about once or twice a year do we experience actual aggression from them. (Photo by Dave DiFiore)

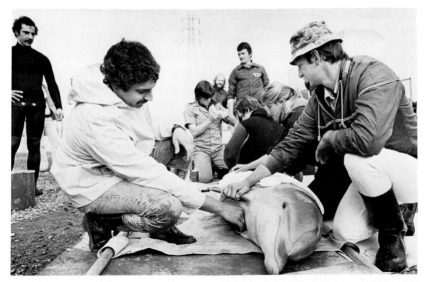

ABOVE: Dondi gets medical attention. Left to right around the small female dolphin are: Chris Pavlos, diver and whale sculptor; Dave De Nardo, now curator of fish; Ron Swallow, veterinarian technical assistant; unidentified bystander; Sonny Allen, director of marine mammal training; author in wetsuit; Deirdre Ballou, trainer; Patrick "Bucko" Turley, trainer. (Photo by Steve Castillo)

BELOW: And back you go! With great relief for all concerned, Dondi splashes back into the water. Our favorite part of the dolphin catch. Left to right: Eric Hurst, then curator of fish; author; John Racanelli, diver; Kevin Walsh, trainer; Dave De Nardo; Ron Swallow; Jim Mullen, head dolphin trainer; and trainer Bill Winhall. (Photo by Steve Castillo)

Before we began having trouble with the killer whales, we used to clean their tanks with the animals in them. This is Yaka, a very sweet-natured female, swimming upside down. (Photo by Dave DiFiore)

RIGHT: Even a shark can be beautiful. That gold-black eye can be sucked back into the skull if the seven-gill feels threatened. (Photo by Dave DiFore)

BELOW: Things are getting a bit too rough in this shark-feeding show, and I am about to bonk this seven-gill, to make him back up a little bit. The sheepshead at right appears to be watching with interest. (Photo by Dave DiFiore)

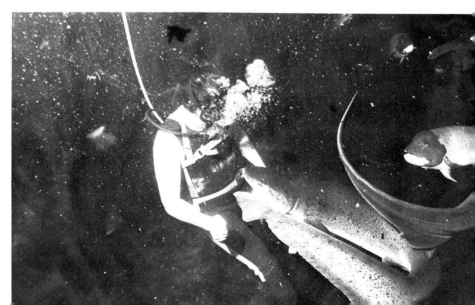

When this large sergeant major started spending time with me, I thought we were pals. But, as I found out when he helped himself to two large chunks of my elbow, he only wanted me for my body. (Photo by Dave DiFiore)

ABOVE: Top jaw-bottom jaw, a game dolphins seem to enjoy, partially recreates the fish-catching movement. I yank my hand down as fast as I can, and Stormy effortlessly catches it—gently. (Photo by Dave DiFiore)

LEFT: Nepo and Yaka, killer-whale couple, leaping. Nepo, on right, can be distinguished by his unusually large pectoral fins. (Photo by Steve Castillo)

LEFT: The groupers in our wall tank like to rub the sand aside until they expose the floor. Their eyes can move independently. (Photo by Dave DiFiore)

BELOW: Author with giant loggerhead turtle Chopper. Chopper mistook my hand for food once, and I felt the bones bending in before I could make her let go. (Photo by Dave DiFiore)

ABOVE: Author with white shark. Notice the clean lines of this immature (two years old, 350 pounds) female. (Photo by Lindy Mitchell-Cook)

Roman Jason Patrick Reed, five, waving at Dad through the window, has already done his first professional dive job, earning a quarter for scrubbing the walls of a swimming pool. (Photo by Steve Castillo)

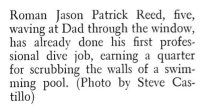

RIGHT: Lindy Mitchell-Cook with white shark. (Photo by Ken Silverman)

A rowdy crew: Left to right: Dave De Nardo, Chris Pavlos, John Racanelli, author, Lindy Mitchell-Cook, Reid Dennis.

BELOW: Trying to adjust twenty feet of semicooperative Kianu in the stretcher. Vet Jay Sweeney tries to calm her down. (Photo by Pat Foster-Turley)

TOP: In the stretcher. (Photo by Pat Foster-Turley)

CENTER: Trying to cinch up and adjust her. (Photo by Pat Foster-Turley)

LEFT: Comfortable—we hope—in her stretcher, Kianu is hoisted out of the tank. She will be lowered into a specially constructed cradle and packed in foam rubber and ice to keep her from overheating on the long trip to Osaka, Japan. (Photo by Pat Foster-Turley)

George and Ellie, Steller's sea lions. George, left, who may weigh 2000 pounds when fully grown (he's roughly 1200 here), once pulled himself over a ten-foot fence to be with Ellie. (Photo by Dave DiFiore)

Moray eels sometimes like to cluster up. Despite their evil reputations, they are sensible, good-natured fish, biting only when in feeding frenzy or when they feel their lives threatened. In hundreds of dives with these spooky-looking creatures, I have only been bitten four times, and each bite was a quick snap-and-let-go, none of the hang-on-till-death-do-you-part stuff. But I still get nervous, every time, before I go into their tank. (Photo by Lindy Mitchell-Cook)

BELOW: Desireé Reed goes in with Shiloh dolphin, who treats her with great courtesy, totally ignoring nervous father. (Photo by Jeannie Reed)

nored the talking water buffalo, scuffing up the path and across the bridge.

The summer was ruined. I had nearly drowned John Patterson, Ernestine dolphin was dying, and I had just made a complete ass of myself, insulted probably the nicest guy in the park. I kicked a post on the bridge and the fact that it didn't hurt because I remembered to curl my toes back was the only positive factor in the whole miserable morning.

I looked up at the reef top, the spiraling reef-top wall. Half of it was covered by the slanting tarp, but half wasn't. All summer we had been jumping down into the water from the halfway point, trying to gradually nerve ourselves up to the topmost point. Now that topmost pinnacle mocked me. Its silent presence sneered. You don't have the guts, it seemed to say.

I had to go back and face Bill.

I paused by the window. Patterson had just said something, and Bill was answering him. "Drowning's not so bad," he said. "I almost got snuffed once that way. Ran out of air suddenly at 70 feet. My J–valve reserve didn't function. Took me too long to get up, and I wanted to breathe so bad. I finally accepted that I was dead and let the warm water enter my lungs. There was no pain. I blacked out, and a friend rescued me."

I opened the first door and the second. Everybody looked away except Bill. He looked up, and his eyes were guileless and clear, as though nothing had happened.

My body was pins and needles all over, like a foot that's gone to sleep. But I had to say it.

"I was wrong. I apologize." Voice came out lumpy, like separate chunks of gravel. If he'd said the wrong thing, we would have fought because I would have punched him, consequences or no. But all he said was: "Thank you."

As though I had done him a favor.

The next morning was strangely cold. As I drove my little vehicle by the rolling hills of Redwood City, I saw billows of low, whipped-cream clouds pouring over the slopes. Overflow of white fog in the chill morning. It looked like surf, like a tidal wave building out of the sky.

It was to be a day things happened.

Early. I had an excitement and a need to get my wet suit on quickly, before the others arrived. I dressed, shivering as the wet wet suit, clammy as the inside of an oyster, slapped onto my skin. But it warmed as I walked toward the reef tank.

I set my feet on the spiraling wall of the reef tank and climbed, edging sideways, skyward, and the necessary slowness of the ascent added to the chill mist I felt on my face. Up, up, feeling the wobble internally as my feet misplaced slightly, shuffling upward. Gravity sucked at my will, calling me to yield and fall.

From the halfway point on I had to move slower. The walkway was no narrower, but each sideward edging step was now over my height. And at each step was the urge to jump prematurely, to get it over with before the spiral rose another inch. The last 2 feet were the very hardest. I don't know why, only a few inches different heightwise, but it was terrifically difficult to force my right foot out and clutch the highest corner of the wall.

Mist rose off the water, 30 feet below. Thirty feet is nothing to a platform diver, maybe, or to those folks who fall like swans from the cliffs at Acapulco. But I am no cliff diver. It looked like I'd never reach the water, but only fall and fall, and disappear into the screaming distance.

A wind whistled around me, and I overreacted, correcting against a force that wasn't there. I nearly toppled backward, to the bleachers far below. I had to progress downward in precisely one direction. Too far forward, and I'd hit the tarp. To the right, and I would break on the hard fiber glass of the filtration trough. I leaned—no! Backed off, trembling. A turtle had surfaced just below. All urge to jump had now left me. I wanted only to go home.

Go for it! The transfer of weight, the shove of unwilling leg muscles, and I had committed to the void. I immediately regretted it.

Gravity clutched my guts. It had me! Out of control, I wanted to reverse and scrabble back up the air to the ledge— but then my warrior side stiffened my legs and my pride, and I was glad I no longer had the opportunity to chicken out. The tarp was hurtling up at me: I could not believe I was going so fast . . .

WHOOSHSHSH! Safe! The water had me, cushioning my fall with bubbles. I was underwater, cool surrounded me, my knees bent as I impacted the top of the reef but there was no hurt. All over but the exultation.

I went to hunt up somebody to tell, and the first people I ran into were Keith and Patterson, jabbering as though they'd never quarreled. "Hi, Reeeed!" said Sunshine John as he punched me in the shoulder. "Gonna drown me again today?" "I'll do my best," I answered as he hit me again.

But it was underwater that the best of that day waited. Beardsley and I had been asked to take a new divelight down and test it, in the dark interiors of the structured reefs. We crawled in through a hole in the side of the smaller hollow reef. I shoved in first. Not much room in here. Be hard to get out quick if the air failed. I switched on the flashlight. We hadn't known beforehand that there was a moray eel inside.

The beam did not illuminate the eel until it was in motion. I saw the yellow-brown flash of body and a glimpse of the lining of the open mouth. Flashing past me, flying at Bill's face.

As though pulled by a string, my hand shot out, and the scrub brush in it deflected the eel's path around Bill's head. The moray, obviously bent only on escape, kept right on going, weaving out the hole and into the openness.

When the walls were around us no more, and we had glided up until the water broke and became air, Bill turned to me and said: "You saved my life." Which was a gross exaggeration. I had at most defended his nose or more likely just his mask lens, but the compliment so flustered me that I vocalized the first stray words that made themselves available. "Thank you," I said to Bill.

The spell was broken. The golden summer was ours again. I saw Rick Pool, when he thought he was alone and unobserved, pick up his weight belt and deliberately drop it into an unoccupied training tank, to practice swimming down, against the pull of the floatable wet suit. The wet suit won that time, but eventually there came a day when the scissoring fin tips coordinated, and Rick Pool slipped downward, steadily. Strongly. With polar bear pulls of his forearms. He barely limped at all when he walked away from the tank that day. Even Keith got his backflip back again.

And Ernestine? She had been "one day away from dying," as Keith Worcester put it, and the breath from her blowhole stank of rottenness within. We expected her to convulse and vomit, heave the contents of her stomach in a pink gushing flood, for that is the last thing a dolphin does. Everyone assumed that she was gone, that one morning we'd find her stiff and stark in the flume, as we had found Annie. But Ernestine ignored the universal assumption.

She began to eat again, of her own free will, without the need for that ghastly stomach tube. And she fought us when we went to catch her. Which made me want to cry. She was herself again. The holes in her side healed over. The scalloped scoops gone from her dorsal and pectoral fins could not grow back, of course, but that did not interfere with anything. She was Ernestine once more. And she was beautiful.

A party at my house would be a farewell to Sunshine John Patterson and Rick Pool. John was going to go into professional singing, and Rick was resuming his formal education. We drank some beer and engulfed good Mexican enchiladas, courtesy of Jeannie, and I even read a poem. It was unprintably mushy, and most of it made sense to the occasion only, but one line referred to Rick's struggle, how at first he was so out of shape and clumsy, and how he made himself strong, through exercise and work, until he could dive easily, like the dolphin dives. When I read the last line, "Go sing your songs, John Patterson; go learn the world, Rick Pool," Rick rubbed his palm on the side of his neck where the scar was.

"You know why I was so clumsy?" he asked. "I was into racing cars, and I flipped over a Corvette. Broke my neck. Before that I was big, husky; lifted weights, played football. After, I was paralyzed from the neck down. Like being in a black, sensationless pool with only my head sticking out. What usually happens in cases like that is the body wastes away from lack of exercise, and the person dies. But I wouldn't! I told myself I was going to be physical again, I was going to connect up the fibers again, or straighten them out or whatever I had to do to make my body obey my brain. I imagined energy, light, trafficking back and forth, connecting up the tissues and the nerve endings.

"One day I screamed! The nurse ran in and she asked what happened, and I said, 'I moved my big toe!' I was crying, and she was crying, and I knew I was going to make it back.

"And I have!" he said fiercely, pounding his fist on his knee, "I've earned my living at a *physical* job!"

"Oh, Rick, you should have told us!" said John, plainly remembering the pushings-in and the dumping of weight belts. "Why, if we'd known you were handic—"

"It wouldn't have made the slightest difference," said Bill Beardsley.

"I wouldn't have wanted it to," said Rick Pool.

23

Thumbing to the Sea

~~~~~~

The car broke down in New Mexico—the car and my carefully made plans. I was to have shared gas costs with the insurance salesman from my dive class, and the two of us were going to look for work in Morgan City, Louisiana, the industrial diving center of America. There, we were sure, we would find work.

We had not been discouraged when our 212 letters of job application brought no response. Well, one response. The state of New York was accepting applications for sewer divers. "Shit divers?" the word went around in class, for we all had access to the same list of dive companies and got back an identical lack of response. "Yeah, you crawl down the sewer pipes and unclog blockages, like a human enema in the intestines of New York. You wear a dry suit, covers you head to toe, but I wouldn't do it," said a New York diver, "Besides, there's *alligators* down there. People buy little gators as pets and then get bored and flush 'em down the toilet. Alligator holds his breath, comes up in the sewer. Can you imagine that? Workin' in the black, knowin' what that mud around you really is, and then a big ol' alligator shows up?" I didn't believe the part about the alligators, but I still didn't fill out the application for sewer diver.

And as for the 211 "no" responses, well, that was understandable, we told ourselves. Who would want to hire a man from a letter? But if we were there, in Morgan City, Louisiana, where almost all the dive companies were, they'd know we were serious, we said.

138

So I'd kissed my wife on her sweet lips and on her tummy where our baby was and headed for Louisiana, to make my fortune.

When our vehicle, an ancient, fat, black Ford, began to explode internally, making noises like a giant with a sledge-hammer who hated engine blocks—BONG, BONG, BONG—the fella in the garage patted her hood like a horse that would have to be shot. "Yuh thrun a rod," he said companionably, "cost y' five hunnert dollars." "That's more than I paid for the car!" gasped the former insurance salesman. The man in the overalls shrugged. "I'll take her off y' hands," said Hiram of Hiram's Junk and Auto Parts. "Throw in some cash money for it too." "How much?" "Sixty-five dollars." "Get a second opinion!" I advised my friend. We weren't suckers to be taken advantage of! "Uh, where is another wrecking yard?" Hiram spit expertly sideward into an as yet unused section of sawdust on the floor. "There's my brother William's, down the road." We checked in a phone book just before driving off, BONGBONGBONG, but it was no use. Hiram and William had that burgh sewed up tight. Hiram was on the phone when we left. William was hanging up when we arrived.

"Hello, boys." said William.

Sixty-five dollars later, the insurance salesman and I were shaking hands at the Greyhound bus depot. "I'm going back to Winnetka, think things over," he said. "I hope our paths will cross again," I told him, and we both knew they proba-bly never would. "Listen, let me buy you a ticket to Morgan City," he said, "I got some extra money." But I knew he didn't have much. I'd seen how carefully he studied the menus of the shabby little diners we'd eaten at, and besides, I'd seen his shoes. He was offering me, probably, all he had left. "Thanks, but I got plenty," I lied right back. HAAAAP, the rubber-edged bus door divided behind him. "See you, pardner," I said. "Good luck!" he almost shouted, before the rubber doors closed between us.

As my only friend within a thousand miles pulled away, I

slung up my duffel bag and looked for a likely crossroads. A place where people would naturally slow down, have time to check a hitchhiker out, decide if he looked like a monster or not. I was glad I'd had a haircut just before leaving home. It was cut collar length, which I'd figured cannily, would be acceptable to both old and young employers. "Hey, hippeeee!" yelled a truckful of crew-cut New Mexico teenagers. Well, so much for protective camouflage. It wasn't the movies, so I didn't yell anything back. Had no intention of getting beat up for nothing.

A couple of rides and hours later, I found myself beside a big sign in Albuquerque, New Mexico. The sign informed me that hitchhiking was illegal and that even to pick up a rider was to court a fifty dollar fine. I didn't stay long by the sign, but I stood eight hours in Albuquerque, New Mexico. As I stood and walked and watched the comfortable cars whizz by, I realized the sunburnlike sensation of not being wanted. I had almost no money. And to my baking brain it seemed that everybody knew this, as though there were a sign pinned on me: he has no money.

I saw a police car cruising slow: Were the eyes behind the sunglasses studying me? *Keep moving*, was the message the reflecting lenses projected. A phrase like an evil song ran through my mind; "shun him, run him, turn him from the town!" I had no money and no job and I was therefore in need of the stuff of daily subsistence. How would I get it? If I could find no job? I would have to go on welfare or unemployment. And then? I wouldn't steal, I didn't think, but if I was broke too long? No city would want me, a drain on the public treasury. I shuffled faster, as if by motion I could blur the folks around me and make it be as if I was alone. I'm on my way, I'm going somewhere, I'm going to find a job. "Shun, him, run him, turn him from the town!" Keep moving.

For eight hours the traffic passed me. Eight hours is a long time.

But all things end except the story of the stars, and at last a dilapidated truck pulled over. That truck was so old, the color was no longer discernible. It made a horrendous racket and leaked steam. But it was the limousine of luxury to me. And the man inside, a wrinkled Mexican who smiled and shoved some junk off the seat for me—well, I'd have hugged him if it wouldn't have looked weird. The fifty-dollar fine for picking up hitchhikers would have ruined him, but he risked it, for a stranger.

The old man drove me to the edge of town and the night. I watched the single red taillight and dented bumpers recede into the shadows, and I was alone.

Now New Mexico is a beautiful state, with many scenic wonders, but there are certain places in it where you'd better not be caught out of doors in the night. Not that the coyote howling will hurt you, of course: he's just marking off his territory with a song. And the shadows of the cactus growing longer in the dark do not really forbode ill luck. They just make you feel alone.

But the wind! The day clung your shirt to your body with sweat, but the night wind would flap it loose. And a California boy with little notion of cold weather, who thought that he would travel light and have no need for winter clothes, was soon persuaded of his mistake.

Chilled to the bone, and with the sudden silence of the highway beside me, I could think of nothing better than to walk. And walk and walk and try to dwell upon remembered triumphs, to ease the pain in the shoulder where the duffel strap cut in, and the cold, and the endless exertion of breathing.

I had placed tenth in my class at Mike Rugged's school of deep-sea diving. Tenth, in a dead-even tie with Jon Noble! Tenth, which I had to be, to be eligible for the promised job help. "We'll be in touch," Mike Rugged had so sincerely said, and my wife was waiting by the phone. There would be no call. Not now, not ever. Mike Rugged's promise was empty as the wind.

But I tried to not think about that—I thought instead

about the days when I had found out that I could make it underwater.

The swimming test. For scuba certification the first test was four laps of a small pool, underwater on one breath. It was steamy hot in that enclosed room, and we were relaxed and loose, standing in our swimming suits and looking good. Made me proud to look around and think: these are ocean people.

Perrano, in his swim trunks, looked like a hairy-chested pocket Hercules. His biceps were huge, grossly swollen, almost threateningly powerful, as though they and the heavy, work-hardened hands could twist a man's head off. But the instructor's eyes were the same as always, wry and humorous, an inch away from a wink.

Forty dripping bodies wet-footed it into line. Behind me. I was first. Well, that is my pleasure. I felt the quiet grow. The length of blue water stretched before me.

"Awl right, Mr. Reed, show us 'ow it's done," said Perrano, and I realized he wanted me to make it. And everybody else did too! To have a good omen to start the test with. For if we failed in this scuba course, we'd fail in the school.

I knew I wasn't going to let them down. Their energy flowed into mine. I took four deep breaths and dived. Nothing fancy, just straight-arrow in and glide through the blue element. My legs and arms opened in the sensual, powerful breaststroke, and as my legs closed, my arms were reaching, and the strength flowed through me. I felt as if I could be lazy, take my time about it, that the need to breathe would never come again. But I knew this for the illusion it was and wasted no second but kicked and glided and turned.

When my knees touched my chest the third time, I turned and pushed off for the home lap: I felt an inexplicable urge to fail. The burning itch to breathe was only beginning in my chest, so there was no reason to rise and admit defeat. Something told me to quit, to give up—I don't know why— but I ignored it.

When my hand touched the wall and I raised up my head to breathe, a ripple of applause greeted me. Everybody was glad to see the first trier make it. "Well, at least you can swim, Mr. Reed! Awl right, let's go, next!" said Alan Perrano.

But I had known and trusted my swimming ability all along. What still worried me then was my almost absolute lack of mechanical ability. How could I fix things underwater if I couldn't on land? This was the other hurdle I'd had to overcome.

I liked the Mark Five helmet and stiff canvas suit. They made me feel like a walking tank on land, but once in the water the dress was perfect for certain projects. Stability and protection.

Once the strangeness of the underwater blindness had passed, I got used to depending on my fingers for information. The touch of even numb fingers sends information to the brain, and pictures of objects I had never seen. Sometimes little cartoon characters too—when the mind is denied stimulation, it will apparently entertain itself.

But there was no time to spend in play. We had sixty minutes to a dive. They passed like a finger snap because even the simplest project is complicated underwater. Some things stopped me cold, like the wood and the drills and the vise. A block of thick plywood needed three holes drilled in it. There was a vise on the floor in the dark, and the object was to find the vise, clamp the wood, and drill three holes. Simple, right? Except that you needed three hands to do it. When I pushed the drill against the vise-held wood, the reaction shoved me away. I vented out most of the air in my suit so as to be heavy on the floor and leaned my stomach against the butt of the drill. Locking my left hand around the vise, I turned the crank with my right. It was a good system. Using it, I was able to drill one hole in the board in an hour. One. The drill bit would slip off, couldn't get bite. At least I had company in that failure. Nobody in the class could do much better—except The Swede Who Had Been Everywhere, who brought down a second drill he'd brought in from home. The second drill had a small, thin bit, which went in easy and by making a little hole first, The Swede Who Had Been Everywhere was able to get purchase for the second, bigger wood excavation. Perrano praised him as an example of how divers got the work done in the field. "Be creative! Use y' brains!"

The next project had made me think I had none. It was pipe cutting, and it looked easy at first. Jon Noble handed me the cutter, which looked like a C–clamp with a blade and had a handle which increased the pressure of the cutting edge. "Turn the handle to get the blade in," advised the crew-cut assistant team leader, who was acquainted with my mechanical inability. "Got it," I said, thinking that I understood.

I found the vise on the floor of the tank almost right away, which was a tremendous advantage. If you had to wander, you might get tangled up in somebody else's line. Then your tenders would have to pull you up and sort you out, a loss of precious minutes. It was also possible to miss something by six inches and never find it at all in the dark.

The pipe I was to make five of nestled in one numb hand. I slowly plopped it into the vise, secured it, took the pipe cutter, and cupped it around the length of pipe. Now turn the handle at the top, I thought. Nobody told me anything about spinning the whole kit and caboodle around. I understood that the handle attached to the blade kept right on turning around till the knife sliced through—wrong.

My hands were not exceptionally strong, I knew, because I had met some people before who did have mitts with real gripping power. Folks who could bend nails with their fingers and compress old-fashioned thick-walled beer cans into indistinguishable scrap—I wished I could borrow some of their hand strength for a moment, to work this pipe cutter. I couldn't turn the handle at the top of the C any tighter. Could my grip be that much weaker than the other divers'?

Come on now, move this thing! Okay, get ready; do it right. I stopped what I was doing, let my hands fall to my sides, shut my eyes (though it wasn't necessary in the absolute black). Letting my mind clear of thoughts and my energies gather, relaxing, so that body and mind could act as one. When my eyes opened, there were no distractions. Whatever I had was present now.

I bent to the short wooden handle; wrapped the base of my right hand and the top of my left around it. Set myself, adjusting the position of my legs on the floor, and turned. I exerted myself as if my whole future depended on it. The handle budged, turned, perhaps another 30 degrees from where it had stuck before.

But that was the limit. Not the whole mass of my concentrated will could make that pipe cutter work the way I was trying.

The time was running out. I pulled my line four times, and my tender responded to the signal, hauling me up by the lifeline that linked us. "I can't make the damn thing work!" I shouted, hoping they could hear me. Jon Noble took the pipe and the pipe cutter from me, looked at it strangely, then held it before the foggy front port window of my helmet. I could dimly see that the pipe was collapsed inward like a squeezed straw. Handing it back to me, Jon cupped his hands together around his mouth, leaned close to the helmet and said: "*Spin* it." He stepped back and made a twirling motion with his finger. Ohhh.

I took the mess back down, backed the handle off, reset it higher on the pipe, tightened the blade handle slightly, and shoved the apparatus around in an inward cutting circle. A few easy turns and the device fell off in my hand, its mission accomplished. I felt the edge of the newborn pipe end, clean and sharp. Five minutes later I had five sections of new pipe lengths crowding my hand. So much for brute strength versus technology.

Tools, I had become convinced, were just extensions of the hands and senses, guided by the brain. I didn't have to be afraid of tools. They just had to be learned. Machinery was there to make things easy.

And so it had proved, the rest of my time at the school. I had even taken welding classes. I loved welding. To play with lightning and make a puddle out of iron. Prometheus, who stole fire from the Olympian gods and gave it to humans, could have been no prouder. I just pulled the cover of my welding helmet down, held the clamped, electrified rod in my heavy gloved hand, and sparked my arc. When the charged rod touched metal, a spark leaped, and I played with that fire, melting metal, shaping the pool of molten steel in circles along the line of the two metal plates I was joining together. When I broke the contact and set the grippers and the rod aside, the silvery liquid cooled immediately, turning gray as the slag or useless metal rose to the surface. I tapped the gray bubble with a hammer, and the slag broke. Wire-brush off the crumbled gray, and underneath was something shining and beautiful, like a stack of new dimes, the welder's bead.

I could only learn the most basic beginnings of the welder's art in the six weeks of evening classes, enough to clamp together two perpendicular plates of metal with the elementary "T-joint," but I knew what a flat bead was and how to "throw" it evenly by moving the tip of the electrified rod in backward half circles. Few things in life have been so satisfying as that working with fire and steel.

Welding underwater, though, was apparently not something a person could learn in the one hour the school provided. When I clutched the handled rod in my mitt and went down, I was hoping to achieve the most elementary task in welding: to cut. The rod tip would touch the metal sheet, an arch would explode and murkily brighten the gloom for a flash, and then the rod would have poked through the other side. Flame so hot the water couldn't extinguish it but broke it down instead into its original gaseous elements so that bubbles were created by the heat. When we pulled the sheet up, there were pencil-size holes through it but no continuous cutting.

Still and all, there was the sea, and, magical mystical moment, the scuba test in the real ocean. Lovers' Point, Monterey. Every scuba diver in California knows that name, for here is where the classes test, and thousands (at least, there are now nearly three million certified scuba divers) break their oceanic virginity.

We had joked as we hit the beaches below the famous stairs, below the wind-twisted trees and the weathered rocks, but when we looked out upon gray Mother Sea, the foolishness died from our lips. She was too vast and great and of too many ages. It was humbling.

Staggering under the weight of the tanks, we waded out, and not without misgivings. Just once I turned and looked back toward the shore. One poor student was sitting brooding on the beach. His fingers locked defensively around his shins; his eyes were down, and he was not coming with us.

I saw purple fish, and shadows and a crab scooting under a rock. And the light intermingling with the waves. When at last the dive was over and our chilled limbs turned back toward the land, there had been a bag of homemade cookies waiting for me on the shore. And Jeannie, the lady I loved most in all the world. . . .

A flatbed truck pulled over, out of the cold New Mexico night. With a shout I shouldered my gear and ran for the ride.

On my way again!

24

Lindy, Shiloh, and the Moray Eels

~~~~~~

"If ever I can't do my share, my fair share of the work, I'll quit, and you won't have to ask me," Lindy Mitchell had said her first day on the job at Marine World. Her promise. Her commitment.

I remembered the first time I'd seen her face danger. It had been in the tank of the giant sea bass, or groupers. "Watch the spines," I had told her as she spit in her mask and tugged on her fins. "If he gets mad, those lying-down blades on his back will stand up like knives. They're weapons." Even a little bass can rear back and sink its slimy and infectious spine deep into a grabbing hand. A fish as big as this one could drive a hole in your chest. (As had in fact happened, at another marine park like ours. A netted grouper had stabbed back at the diver transporting it, and one of the gray-green blades had penetrated the man's breastbone.)

"I'll be watching from up here," I told Lindy for the psychological value of it. "If the grouper swallows you, I'll come down and pull its gills, poke it in the eye or something, maybe tickle it. Make it spit you out."

The fish Lindy would be facing had dive-bombed me once, as I'd been rearranging the sand over a repair job on the floor. I had heard the booming sound of warning and spun on my back with the scrub brush in front of my head. My eyes could scarcely credit what they saw. The jaws of the

148

grouper were yawning, and that oval pit was lowering slowly down onto my face. *Slowly.* More like a threat than an actual attack, but still I whipped my brush up and pushed it cross-wise against the projecting jaws. My brush, 26 inches long, barely reached from lip to lip of the mouth pressed against it. But the grouper either hadn't been serious or changed its mind because it backed away.

Now, crouching on the divider above the warm water tank where the groupers and the nurse sharks lived, I could see Lindy moving through the glass-clear water. She was to clean the windows, the four windows of the double-sectioned tank. The first two were no problem. The heavy-bodied nurse sharks swirled off the bottom when the diver approached. Lindy swiped her brush across the algaed windows without incident and pulled herself around the divider into the second half of the grouper tank.

The mild-natured brown sharks settled on the sand, gills working in an occasional, rhythmic flex. The two giant sea bass held their favorite position by the fourth window, facing the intruder. Bubbles rose from Lindy's regulator as she edged along the wall. As she reached the first of the last two windows and attached her suction cup to the glass, one of the two sea bass shifted suddenly, and Lindy swayed with the movement of water as the fish swam away. The other sea bass settled itself more comfortably, fanning the sand from the floor so it could nestle its cavernous belly on the smooth filtration grid beneath. With a final whisk of the nylon brush bristles, the algae film on the third window was gone.

Now the test of Lindy's courage and judgment was upon her. She must impose her will on a creature equipped to swallow her, literally to bite her head off or drive the spear-spines on its back through her body. Lindy had to scrub that fourth window, where the grouper was secure in its favorite position which it might choose to defend. And more was at stake here than the cleaning of one window. I had to know if Lindy could handle the danger the other divers accepted: the danger that might one day happen when she was alone.

Could she protect herself and at the same time get the job done?

Confrontation. I could see, plainly through the glassy water, the opposing figures. The blue-clad diver looked small and fragile against the granite-gray of the huge fish. Lindy moved forward 6 inches, slowly, in her bid to drive the grouper off his favorite spot, to budge him from his throne. Then what I had been dreading happened.

A blur of motion distorted the water by the grouper's gills. KACHOOOONK! was the sound I knew Lindy heard. The warning boom of the giant bass. Watch out: I can kill you, the reverberating thud seemed to say.

I had my hand on Lindy's air line. I almost hauled her out of there. But no, the deal had to be played out. Besides, any movement now, whether interpreted as attack or retreat, might trigger aggression.

She neither charged nor fled. She did exactly what she should have done for that instant, which was to do nothing. Lindy held, in space and time. Then—did the upraised spines relax just a hair?—she advanced, hugging tight against the wall, scrub brush up before her face, toward the giant head of the waiting grouper. The bulging opaque eyes did not flinch. The creature was not going to budge.

They were head to head, and the cruel mouth was as wide across as Lindy's shoulders. Lindy stopped. They thought about it for a while. Looking elsewhere about the tank, the two forms let themselves grow accustomed to each other.

Then Lindy did what the nurse sharks did. She wriggled slowly but determinedly in between the grouper and the wall, shouldering gently where she wanted to go. The grouper accepted. Their bodies touched, shoulder to tail, swim fin to giant head. Lindy pressed her suction cup on that crucial window and cleaned it thoroughly, as though she were going to sign her work.

Then she rose, her task completed. The grouper rolled an eye upward, following the diver as she left.

It was typical of Lindy that when I shouted with pride and

slapped her shoulder in a congratulatory cuff, she immediately said: "Thank you so much for being up here the first time. It gave me confidence knowing you were there," turning the compliment back on me, as though it was I who had accomplished something significant.

It was also typical of her to hunt up a long piece of wooden dowel and secure it to the scrub brush, so that the next time she cleaned the grouper tank windows, she could reach alongside Mr. G. and not have to disturb him in his favorite resting place.

Although Lindy wasn't as strong as the rest of us divers, we knew we could count on her to find a way to do her fair share of the work. On the walls, with the light nylon brush, she could leave me behind, which was both a pride and an embarrassment. She learned a different brush stroke, one that involved her leg and total body strength, rather than just arm and shoulder power. Instead of working down the wall, swipe swipe swipe, she would attach a suction cup, pull with one hand and kick with both legs and fling herself along the wall, the brush biting in as she went. She would finesse the algae off and then come down and help me finish up my half. I studied her technique but could never quite adapt it to my build.

The dive locker seemed special now since Lindy's femininity had made it an oasis of freshness after years of nothing but men. There had been, of course, some adjustments to be made.

Immediately the word went around that the divers had a woman among their number and there was some nudging and eyebrow lifting. "Where does she shower? And with whom?" There was only one shower, and to get to that she had to walk through the men's room.

But a lady is a lady, even in the men's room. Lindy would just knock, and say "Excuse me?" and whoever was inside would say, "Wait a minute," or, "Okay, come on through," and Lindy would walk past, unembarrassed and unembarrassing, and shut the shower door behind her. At first she hung out a cardboard sign, on which I had written, "Occupied," but by the time the sign disintegrated, everybody knew that we had to knock now.

And while she was neither our maid nor our mother, we did learn to live a bit cleaner than we had before. Flowers started appearing in pots and odd places, and dark corners brightened. One day, when I'd knocked on the shower door and she'd said okay, I entered to find her in a wet suit and pushing a broom. "Look at that!" she said, flicking something white out from under a cabinet. "Underpants, underpants, underpants!" she snapped, and I saw that there was indeed a pile of men's shorts that had somehow accumulated over the years. We had gotten somewhat casual about our housekeeping, but with Lindy around it became worthwhile to pick up after ourselves.

She was strong and had muscles, genuine unashamed hard-work biceps. Once we had to move some 100-pound sacks of sand, 10,000 pounds' worth, lifting them from a forklift pallet. The sacks had to be transported up a patch of sloping ground, wobbly steps, and along an enclosed hallway before having their sandy contents dumped into an unoccupied tank. Stooping and heaving the heavy sacks up required the brute strength of the heavier divers, but at the top of the steps stood Lindy. Her arms wouldn't let her toss the sacks around like we could, but she could and did balance the burden on her shoulder and carry it down the long hallway. The strong supportive column of a person's legs and back can carry quite a bit with some effort. And Lindy always tried.

Many reasons have been advanced to explain the dolphins' peculiar aggressiveness that summer. Part of it was unquestionably the heat. The sun's rays penetrated the tank, making the water warm instead of cool. Dolphins cannot, of course, shed their layer of blubber though they do what they can to thin it down by eating less. In the ocean they can dive deep or migrate to escape the heat; here it must be like an overcoat they can't take off. If you want to see dolphins or killer whales at their best and brightest, come in the winter, on the coldest, grayest, gloomiest day you can find. Then you'll see some leaps!

But now, the sun beat down. The dolphins picked at the food the trainers offered, and only the stimulus of the crowd and the trainers' personalities kept the shows on track. Even then, every performance was a question mark, at the peak of the heat of that summer.

As is only natural, the dolphins looked for something to take their irritation out on. Like the divers.

The show animals had always used us as toys and sex objects, but now the play took on an edge of meanness. Now it wasn't enough for three dolphins to surround a diver and shove their groins against him, pushing violently while he tried not to get too tangled up amongst their bulks. Now, they would hit.

They were so strong and blubber-padded themselves that maybe they didn't realize they were hurting us. But whether they meant it or not, when that terrible beak came thunking down on a diver's braincase, or buried itself in his or her ribs, the result made the intentions irrelevant.

Rick Pool even returned to try a project to diminish the dolphin aggression. By increasing the playtime with the animals, he felt, we would decrease their tendencies to violence. Before this, we would play with the dolphins only on a casual basis, when the trainers weren't looking.

Sometimes we would lie on our backs and blow rings upward, to delight the dolphins, who were experts at it. Our rings of air were clouds of many bubbles; theirs were pure loops, one bubble per ring, and they seemed to hold light, lovely and luminous. The rings would lift, and the dolphins would watch, or follow, to bite the bubble just before it hit the surface, breaking it into thousands. Or two dolphins might flex their blowholes in unison, that two rings would rise together and join into one. I once saw a dolphin approach a rising bubble ring, and, with incredible delicacy, set the ring of air to spinning, without breaking it. The wobbly circle of light and air kept its integrity all the way up, save for the one edge where the dolphin's beak had touched it.

Sometimes Spock, the big male with a hole in his right pectoral fin, would shove his beak into your hand. This was an invitation, and the desired response was for you to push, gliding back his 350 pounds as if on rollers. He would enjoy the glide for 15 or 20 feet and then kick and shoot back for more. Fun, but strenuous for the diver.

The best, of course, was to ride. To experience for a brief moment the thrill of oceanic speed. To cup a right hand around the dorsal fin and, if Spock was in the mood for it, hang on. Because once that bull dolphin felt you were securely aboard, he would take off at speeds that would yank your mask away unless you looked straight, straight ahead, into the onrushing current. Such power! The masses of muscle and the perfect mastery of the element would send him rocketing around at a speed that was almost frightening, and you were a part of it.

There were other diver/dolphin games we played, like top jaw, bottom jaw, in which the diver set his fingers lightly on top of the beak and then whipped the fingers swift as possible down to the underside of the lower jaw, before the dolphin could catch the fleeing fishlike object in the points of needle teeth. The delicacy with which needle teeth could catch but not tear human fingers was a delight to behold. Fluidly the jaws whipped up and down in the fish-catching motion that had ended the lives of many frantic flee'ers; but they'd never forget and bite us too hard. Occasionally a tooth might accidentally slip beneath a fingernail, but that was all.

Dolphins supposedly have no facial expressions, lacking the musculature to alter their features, but their eyes and their motions reveal their moods. There was one particularly all-encompassing, penetrating blaze of a look, coupled with a sharp head nod, that read quite clearly: "You will play with me *nowww*." We had learned which dolphin invitations could be safely declined.

Rick wanted us to offer games to the dolphins as soon as
we entered their domain and at any slightest hint of interest
on their part. Our constant availability, he hypothesized,
would lessen their aggressiveness. If we would just give them
what they wanted right away, Rick thought, they would have
no reason to beat us up, and they might even ease up on the
sex-based rubbing.

It almost worked. The first few days we offered to play as
soon as we broke into the water. We'd jump off the bottom,
arch, and circle back down to land on one finger, swim with
hands alongside and legs undulating in a crude imitation of
their jointless dolphin kick and stand the center drain grate
on end so a gray beak could nudge it over. Sometimes they
would invent games themselves, as when Spock shoved the
stainless steel mesh grate along the floor until it dropped into
its square-cut slot with a satisfying clunk. My part was to
remove the grate and disarrange it so the dolphin would have
to push the square of metal and mesh from different angles
until it would fall, clunk, onto the concrete shelf.

But presently the dolphins drew back and would have none
of us. I don't know if we'd worn out our welcome or violated
too frequently some dolphin etiquette, but whatever we had
done, the mood in the tank changed.

Then the threats began and escalated. We would try to
approach, and they would furiously warn us off. Violent
head nods, jaw snaps and rusty-squeak shrieking, EE-EE-
EEEE! were only the beginning. Speed runs, like a jet veering
low, hurtling at you. If they hit you, your spine would snap
or your internal organs rupture. They would alter course
SNAP! half a foot short with murder 6 inches away. Or a
cruelly casual backhanded flipper would smack at your mask,
to drive it onto your nose or smash the glass.

Lindy went to the hospital with cracked ribs from a half-
speed dolphin ram. Half-speed because full would have killed
her. She came back with a body brace, like a wide Ace band-
age. She wore the constricting thing for a few days and then
threw it away.

We began to hate the dolphin tank.

One cause of the problem was Shiloh and the unsettled social pyramid in the tank. If the dominant male, Delbert, had not had the dolphin equivalent of asthma—which made his breathing like a strangled wheeze and denied him the wind for long fights—he could have controlled the female with the scar on the back of her neck. If Mr. Spock, the bulky, easygoing biggest bull dolphin, had been just a little bit aggressive, he could have smacked Shiloh good and proper and established peace in the tank. But Spock was not like Lucky. He wasn't one to lay down the law. Spock liked the sun in the center of the tank and gentle cruises, promenades, and a little lovemaking with Shiloh now and then. And she beat him unmercifully. Whack, she'd tail-smack him on the side of the head, and he'd shrug to one side. But only rarely could he work up the energy to rake her sides in a chase that raised waves, and even if he did, he never tamed her. Vernon, the fourth dolphin, was too nervous to even think of giving Shiloh trouble, and if she looked at him crossways, he'd dash to the lowest status position in the tank, the corner by the inlet pipe, where a dolphin had to swim constantly against a current and could never relax, and he'd stay there until it was safe to come out.

Shiloh was the instigator. She'd start fights with us, snapping her sassy jaws the instant we entered her territory, and we'd work fast, hoping to get done and out before we got hit. Rarely did that succeed. If we went in, we would almost certainly get hit. And for some reason, she picked out Lindy as the target for the worst of her unresolved ambition. Shiloh wanted to run that tank, but she wasn't physically big enough. Delbert she couldn't dominate at all; Spock only some; Vernon totally. She couldn't find peace with her semi-vice-presidency in the dolphin power structure, and so she made life miserable for everybody, human or dolphin, that got within reach of her beak. And the smallest got it worst.

Rick Pool's project was discontinued, and Rick left the park again. Although he was not disheartened (you'd have had to shoot Rick at least twice to really discourage him) he felt badly that his project had not solved all the problems between dolphins and humans, but he shouldn't have. He'd sacrificed his savings and his time trying to bridge a gap of misunderstanding between two species.

The problem, however, remained with us, and it was growing worse. When I entered the dolphin tank now, I was on my side, edging along the wall, nervous, fidgety and jumping at anything as I worked reluctantly out from the comparative safety of the wall, which at least sheltered a person's spine. Shiloh had a cute trick now of swimming over a diver and slamming into his head, so that his neck cracked and popped from the sudden stretching of vertebrae. I'd look up and curse as she turned, whipping her tail around, popping her jaws, smiling her smug dolphin smile: "You want to try something?"

One day I definitely did.

WHONK! The sound of the blow carried loud underwater: loud and ugly, like the back of an ax against oak.

My eyes scanned swiftly, seeking the source of disturbance. Were the dolphins fighting? That noise had meant impact, and if the combat was a serious duel, the divers had better group together, in case the loser wanted a punching bag to take out his or her frustrations on. But I saw no swerve of returning dolphins, no motion of the oceanic royalty lining up to fight again.

Only Shiloh, her terrible rostrum beak just above the neck of the small figure on the floor. The brush was idle in Lindy's hand, as though she had tired and taken a nap. The short length of regulator hose stretched out beside her cheek, and the mouthpiece dribbled a fat bubble of air, uselessly, six inches from the open mouth.

Even as I rushed to her, the stunned diver was attempting to regain awareness and control. Her blind fingers fumbled for and found the mouthpiece, stuffed it back into position, pushed the purge valve to roar out the water from the length of line and let her breathe. I saw the bubbles lift from her and knew she was alive.

When I reached her, she was tilting back her head, slowly, in stages, as if the mechanism had rusted. The mask had been knocked half off her face by the force of the downward blow, and she was snorting bubbles into it, to clear the water out.

And as I made the questioning "Okay?" signal with thumb and forefinger circled and Lindy gave it back, Shiloh shrieked and shot around us, in the terrifying disorienting spin which is the dolphin prelude to attack. You crud, I thought, you want to hit her again?!

Automatically, we sought the wall, to put it behind us and protect our backs. Shiloh screamed at us in a frequency we could hear and slashed savagely back and forth with her teeth, like "This is what I'm going to do to you!" Her dolphin smile was no longer beautiful, and her shape was like a shark's.

"You okay?" I asked as Lindy pulled herself out on the stage before me, and Shiloh gave a wham to the bottom of my foot, bending it back, and I floundered quickly onto the red-painted decking. "Yes. I am all right," said Lindy, sounding very stiff and formal. "You want to go to the hospital?" "No. But I think I would like to rest for a little," she said. I could see the tiny pink veins in her eyes. "Oh, yeah, sure, fine, wonderful," I said, redundant in my relief.

"Listen, there's something I forgot underwater. I'll be right back. You sure you're okay?" She nodded but said nothing. I slipped off the edge of the stage. The heavy leaden weight belt carried me down. The wire brush projected from the heel of my right hand. Even so, I had clenched it before, for the thousands of punchlike repetitions of floor scrubbing.

But now as Shiloh rushed toward me, issuing her dolphin challenge in voice and speed and bodily posture, I did something I had never done before. I challenged *back*. Removing the mouthpiece from my lips, I thrust my head forward, nodded sharply, and snapped *my* teeth. Shiloh braked sharply, thrusting down her tail, fanning out her pectoral fins, and I repeated my gesture, in as close an approximation of the dolphin threat as I could muster. I even banged the bottom of the brush on the floor, that there be no misunderstanding. Later on, I hoped, we could be friends again, which would mean a need for trust between us. So now I signaled my intent to fight. She had crossed the line of acceptable roughness. A few more pounds' pressure from that underhooking lump of ramming bone and gristle, and Lindy's neck could have broken. I wanted to get at least one good sock at Shiloh to let her know my feelings.

With a shriek, a buzz, and a spray of sonar clicks the heavy-muscled dolphin virtually disappeared, flashing into the high-speed dash of encirclement. This tactic of racing around a potential victim is apparently intended to frighten him or her into helplessness. Nothing but a killer whale or another dolphin could hope to match that maneuverability. At its height, all the diver can see is an occasional gray outline zipping past. The only way to keep the dolphin in sight is to fling yourself on your back and rotate on the weight belt, spinning like a human propeller. And when the frantic flutter kick exhausts you, and you give up trying to face the animal—BONK!

But I had been in that circle before and knew what it meant and what was to come. This time I would not react defensively.

As Shiloh shot around me in the blinding circle speed, I made no attempt to keep up but only crouched, and timed the encircling clockwise rushes. ZIPZIPZIP, I waited, and struck! Counterclockwise, pivoting at the hips, left knee bent and right foot back, in the strongest punching positions humans have. The shark-killing rostrum met the wire brush in my right hand. If I had punched with my fist, it would have broken. As it was, my whole braced body shook with the impact. I had gotten my one punch in.

Then there was nothing but retreat. I wouldn't let myself creep along the floor and up the wall but swam in a straight diagonal line toward the stage, making myself strong against the punches and kicks I knew Shiloh would be throwing. She did, too, striking me perhaps once for every foot I traveled while I pretended to ignore her, as if there was no way she could hurt me. Funny thing, though, I had been hit by her before, when she intended results, and this time her heart wasn't in it. She slammed her fluke kicks and rostrum knocks into me, but nothing serious. As though she only wanted to let me know I still had to respect her, but that she also knew she was in the wrong.

Lindy was slinging her coiled air line around her shoulder. "I gave Shiloh a good sock!" I said, and she nodded, silent. She walked off, very straight and by herself, which was unusual.

Shiloh poked her head up from the water. Her eyes sought mine.

"No, you big stupid, I am not going to play with you! I am furious with you. You could have broke Lindy's neck! I am not going to play with you anymore, ever, today!" Later on we would make our peace, but right now I was worried about Lindy.

I hung my gear in the equipment locker, and walked around the park for a few minutes, to give Lindy time to shower and dress.

I went through the swinging door to the men's room and paused at the shower room entrance. Raising my fist to knock, I hesitated, and said instead: "Lindy? You decent?" The reply was a little while in coming.

"Yes. Come in."

She was sitting on the bench, her back to me. She had her surface work clothes on, an old pink-and-gray long-sleeved shirt and faded jeans. She sat very straight. But she did not turn around, and when she breathed, her shoulders shook just the tiniest bit, traitors to her will.

I washed my hands, which weren't dirty.

"You okay?"

"Yeah."

Draping my wet-suit jacket over the shower stall, I fumbled for something helpful to say. But my tongue seemed stapled down. I wanted to comfort her, but . . . that would embarrass her. Wouldn't it be like saying, "You're weak; you can't take it"? Lindy reached down for her shoe. I noticed that she kept her head tilted back as she leaned for the footwear. I better get out.

"Uh, see you later," I said, one hand on the door.

"With the tide, Clyde," her voice came, faint but strong. She laced up the shoe, still without looking down at it. She appeared to be staring fixedly at the painting of the killer whale on the wall. Lindy had painted that orca there, I remembered.

As I stepped out into the men's room and the door swung slowly shut behind me, I listened, shifting from foot to foot, but no sound followed me out. I was sure I was doing the right thing, wasn't I—letting her take the pain and fearfulness of animal attack in the cold of solitude?

I U-turned and burst through the shower-room door, walked fast to her and picked her up by the shoulders, turned her around, and pulled her to me.

"That's my favorite tank," she said.

"I don't want Lindy back in that tank," glared Dave De Nardo when we were alone. Dave was a sullen-eyed, heavy eyebrowed San Francisco Italian who usually seemed to be mad at something. Just now he was glaring at me, as though I was the one who had hit Lindy. He leaned forward, his wide shoulders hunching together.

"If you or I get hurt," he said, his voice hissing softly, as though he was personally menacing me, "We're big—we can take it. But Lindy? She's already been to the hospital once, with cracked ribs; next time it could be her spine. Do you want that?"

"Well no, of course not, but—"

"And it's not like we're babying her because there's plenty of other, valuable, necessary work for her to be doing—right?"

"Yeah, uh-huh, but—"

"So tell her, but *delicately*. Don't blow it!"
"I got to think about it, David," I said.

I took Lindy back in with Shiloh a couple of times more, both in the hope that Shiloh might straighten out and to let Lindy know I knew she wouldn't run. It didn't work. Shiloh had apparently made up her cetacean mind to pick on the smallest diver, and I had to practically hover over Lindy the whole time, both dives. I could not relax or get any work done.

One day I walked into the dive shack and found Lindy there, waiting for me. She pushed her long straight hair off her shoulders. She had a brown sweater on, her eyes were blue as the ocean, but pink veins were flexing in the whites. "I've got something to tell you," she said, very loud. Lindy's voice is never loud.

"I know, me too" I said very fast. "I don't want you going back in that tank with Shiloh anymore. You could get—"

"I know, I've already made up my mind and I have to—"

"I've got a deal to offer you!" I blurted.

"WHAT?"

"I'll make you a deal," I said, "You know how scared I am of the moray eels—right?"

"No, I did not know that," said Lindy slowly, looking at me sideways, "This is the first I have ever heard of it."

"They give me the cold willies," I said, and it was perfectly true. Quavery flesh, yellow skin with spots, and eyes of madman blue. And teeth, so many teeth, splinters of crystal, and on the top jaw—three rows. All pointing inward, so the eel could keep what it caught. It used to be thought that once an eel bit down, the jaws locked forever, till death did them part. I knew the truth of that belief from personal experience.

One day I had been cleaning the moray eel tank by myself—a particularly ugly job because as the brushed-off algae went into suspension in the water, the visibility lessened.

Some of the eels' heads looked big as horses' skulls. That's just the magnification of water, I'd reminded myself. There's no eel here much over 5 feet long, although one was as thick as a big man's thigh. But moray eels are very gentle, very gentle. Unless threatened, cornered, or in frenzy.

The decreasing visibility had affected me like claustrophobia, as though the walls were closing in. The range of sight had grown less and less, until I could see only the plastic lens of my faceplate, and rubber lining around it, and the bridge of my nose, and the little bit of water that raced back and forth inside my mask when I turned my head.

There were forty-some eels in the small tank, and I couldn't tell where they were unless my mask came flat up against one, or, as happened then, a piece of swimming wet velvet slid across my hand. I'd known something was going to happen: I could almost hear that noise of screaming tension—SNAP! The noise and pain had been like a wolf trap shutting on my finger, and I'd shaken it violently, feeling the whole eel whipping up and down, the pain hot, sharp, and then gone, and finally relief that it had happened and was over and I didn't have to anticipate it anymore.

As I'd climbed out and coiled my hose, red drops had fallen on the yellow rubber. My right ring finger was a beautiful bright crimson. Brushing aside the blood, I could see only tiny holes ("a classic avulsion fracture!" said the doctor, proud as if he had done it himself), and I let them bleed unhindered, to clean out the gunk left by the eel's presumably unbrushed teeth.

"So the deal I got to offer you is this," I told Lindy. "I'll *trade* you eel tank for dolphin tank, danger for danger. You make the wall tanks your territory, so I don't have to go in with those creeps—ever again, I hope—and we'll make the dolphin tank our responsibility, so you won't have to go in with Shiloh anymore.

"What do you think? Is that fair? Is that a deal?" I held my breath as I shoved my hand through the air across the top of the desk. Her hand met mine, and we shook on it.

"*Now*," I said, leaning back and putting my feet up, "What was it you wanted to see me about?"

"It slipped my mind," said Lindy Mitchell.

25

Jobless in Louisiana

Normally, a storm is for me an omen of good luck, or at least something to sooth the nerves. So long as no one's hurt, I love it all: the black clouds gathering; the first flung drops, a scattered warning of what is to come; maybe even some lightning, real lightning, not the powder-flash FOOF!s of the West Coast, but the jagged, raw-edged bolts of the Midwest and the East, ripping up the guts of the sky: and then the roaring, pouring, *torrents*—then I like to go out in it, exploring, never minding the wetness which is no more than swimming anyway. The emotion is a grand one, like organ music growling low, adventure all around and all things strange: then I can become, temporarily, a skin-soaked tiger, prowling, in the rain.

Just now, however, I did not watch the leadening sky with any joy. Rain now would just be an intensification of the humidity; the only difference between it and sweat would be the salt content. A walking, hungry, and unemployed man cannot be expected to have quite the same appreciation for nature as he did when he had a comfortable house to retreat to. And whatever happened now, weatherwise, would happen on my last clean clothes.

Nor could I afford to launder the interview clothes that covered me now. I had squandered a dollar fifty of my last two dollars when I had reached Morgan City early this morning. My scant resources had bought me a shower (oh, what bliss to soap and scrub away the grease excrescences and dust and grit of travel: to feel the skin squeak clean again beneath the sudsing washcloth) but now that luxury was done. Remaining was one paid-for night at the Sailor's Rest, a canvas cot in a group-filled room, and after that I didn't know.

I hadn't eaten properly in—what. Three days? Two? I wasn't sure. My own fault, really: my wife had given me more money than we could afford for the trip, but there had been this little bookstore in New Mexico. . . . I did have some cookies, dried apricots, and vitamins in my green duffel bag back at the Sailor's Rest, but I was saving that for supper.

I kept thinking about cheeseburgers and chocolate milk. I knew exactly how I wanted both. The cheeseburgers would be double-pattied so they could support three slices of American cheese, and butter would be used on the grill instead of oil, and the buns would be toasted, not slapped on after. No salad, tomatoes, or onions: just tasteful slatherings of catsup, mustard and relish, extra pickles. About three of these would satisfy the cravings of my appetite, with a fourth thrown in for fat and gluttony.

The chocolate milk. A rare California brand I had discovered in a drive-in theater. How well I remembered it—the waxed container slick but textured under my fingers. Even as my thumbs pressed in and back, spreading the white cardboard lips and remoulding them into the pour-spout, I had known I was onto something special. With mounting anticipation I'd raised the pint to my lips, sipped delicately—chocolate. Milk. The perfect mixture of rich, delicious, bittersweet cacao, and cow juice. A quart would do nicely now, I thought, perhaps two.

How many gallons of chocolate milk had carelessly gone down my gullet; how many cheeseburgers had I engulfed? What wouldn't I give to have a few of them back right now!

Or, better yet, a job, from which all milk and cheeseburgers flow. But apparently I had picked a bad time to seek work as a diver. Because while I had only been in eight companies so far, the words I heard were not reassuring. So far I had gotten exactly the same answer my 212 mailed-out résumés had received.

Worse. "Ah wish there was some hope to offer you," the pleasantly sophisticated secretary in the cool, dehumidified office had said.

"But there's really no po-int," she made the word two syllables, "in yoh even fillin' out an application," though she let me do it anyway, "because look heah." She held up a bulging file folder with both hands. "These are all experienced divers, on call from ouah office. They are not working. When the envi-onmental re-strictions ease up, and moah oil rigs ah allowed to go on line, then—" She paused while the obvious sunk in, then concluded charitably. "If yoh stay in the a-rea, do check back with us in two or three months. But until then—well ah *am* sorry." She was, too.

But not half as sorry as I was for myself, walking back out into the muggy heat of that sweating, empty-stomached day. My inner thighs chafed, the outer layer of skin removed from the friction of the sweat-soaked cloth and the elastic of my underwear. The doors of Morgan City are very far apart for a man on foot, and I kept getting lost.

Getting lost is easy for me, a skill I developed over long years of practice. A certain natural inattention and serious inclination to daydream, limited vision and a determination to avoid the practical details of life combined to make me a champion of the art of getting lost. I was in that state of directionlessness right now, as a matter of fact. I did know my destination, a salvage shop which rumor had it hired divers "sometimes," but there were conflicting opinions on how to arrive there.

"Cross the Long-Allen Bridge," people said on both sides, "and turn left." I was crossing the bridge for the third time when I reflected there was really no reason to hurry. I had already turned both left and right on both sides of the bridge, my upper thighs were in pain, and my belly was about to digest my backbone. I had no job, no money, and no clean clothes. The heated rain had begun, falling almost unnoticeably, but soaking through fabric just as effectively as if there had been some fun in it.

I sat down on the walkway of the unoccupied bridge. Everybody else was smart enough to get in out of the rain, I reflected sourly. I looked down at the river. I missed my wife and the new person growing within her. Jeannie said she had dreamed of a baby girl. I knew who she was already, a little. I knew her name.

Désirée. I had carried her name with me since the eighth grade, when I'd seen it on the cover of a book by Annemarie Selinko, *Désirée.* Napoleon Bonaparte's first great love. I had almost seemed to recognize that name, the most beautiful woman's name in the world, and I mustn't forget it. I hadn't, and I knew the boy's name too: *Roman,* after a weight lifter friend, Roman Mielec, 132-pound champion of America. "Roman," or "Desireé," I thought, you could have picked a better prospect for a father.

I rocked back and forth on my haunches, moaning softly, holding my head in my hands. A child? I couldn't support a wife! I couldn't support *myself* right now—no job, no experience, no mechanical aptitude—and scars in my lungs from boyhood bronchitis. If I dived deep, nitrogen would accumulate in those scars, and I'd be much more prone to get the bends. But even that, even the wracking agony of the bends, would be better than this, to have no job.

Unemployed. What a sickening shiver that word shot through me. "Dishonorable." "Lazy." "Shiftless." "Bum." "But it's not my fault! I want to work, really!" "Shut up, bum." "We know your kind," the imaginary chorus hissed. "You're just no good."

Below me rolled the Atchafalaya River. Six hundred and twenty-eight feet wide at this point the guide book said, "and very deep." A cargo ship boomed mournfully through the drizzling mists. There must be people on that boat, I thought, and every one of them has a job. A trick of sound carried a voice to me. No discernible words, just a hum of somebody calling something to somebody, and when it passed, it left me unutterably lonely.

Wonder how far down it is, I thought idly, just by way of speculation. No great distance to fall, but if a person belly flopped, the shock would surely knock him out. And then he'd either float or not. In my case, not.

No. No. I don't like the way my thoughts are drifting. I am of value. I am somebody, and somewhere there's a place I can fit in. Just have to keep on trying, that's all.

Then, way down the river, something small but spectacular happened. The clouds cracked open, and a beam of purest sunlight struck the Atchafalaya with such force it seemed as if the water must steam. The column of light broadened, expanded, raced up the river toward the bridge. And me.

As that white track advanced, faster than a man could run, I knew I had to do something to match the moment. Self-pity backflipped from my shoulders; feverish energy filled me. I sprang into the crossbeams of that Louisiana bridge and climbed. The gray sky, the cargo steamers, my personal pack of troubles—everything vanished except the crosshatched woven thick strips of metal, and my hands and feet trading places, as I moved up the framework.

I was halfway to the top when the flood of sun broke on me. The heat wrapped my shoulders like the arm of a friend.

One elbow crooked firmly round a flat-edged girder, both feet ensconced in the notches of iron grillwork, I pivoted away from the dull gray metal, and with one arm wide received the sun. My eyes shut against the blinding, my face grew warm, and the light penetrated to my soggy soul.

Not two hours later, the convict's brother found me.

26

Judy, The Water-Skiing Elephant

The light over the arena was at that delicate, early-morning stage when everything is clearly seen: but gently, without sharp corners. Nothing harsh. An artist might wait an entire lifetime for such a magical illumination; a movie studio might spend millions on lighting and camera angles and not achieve the detail-revealing quality of the light that fell so softly, and for free, on Judy, the elephant that water-skiied.

As I considered stepping over the electrified wire that encircled the small arena, I remembered the first time I had seen Judy in action.

"LADEEEZ AND GENTLEMEN," the amplified announcer boomed, "HOW WOULD YOU LIKE TO SEE . . . A WATER-SKIING ELEPHANT?"

"YEAH, YEAH!" we shouted in our thousands in the show stands. This was gonna be great, we nudged each other, only how was such a thing possible?

A painted *wooden* silhouette of an elephant on fake skis was towed into view. A hush fell over the bleachers. Had we been cheated? "Phoneyyyy!" yelled one of the more vocal elements, expressing our common sentiment. "WHAT? YOU DON'T LIKE OUR ELEPHANT?" rumbled the announcer in mock-shocked tones. "NO-O, BOOO, BOOOO!" we answered.

"THEN HOW ABOUT THIS! LADIES AND GENTLEMEN, FOR YOUR ENTERTAINMENT AND EDIFICATION, JUDY! THE WORLD'S ONLY! BABY! WATER-SKIING! *ELEPHANT!*"

And there she was, a genuine, certifiable, flap-eared baby elephant on long yellow "ski" pontoons. Ploughing dignifiedly across the ski lagoon, Judy raised her trunk to the audience.

Once, I had heard, Judy had gotten suddenly nervous or angry in the middle of a show and tipped the pontoons over. Her feet were chained to the hollow yellow cylinders to prevent her falling off, and her body swung directly underneath. Upside down, in the green water of the lagoon. Her head was underwater, and she could not get upright! The audience had sucked in a collective breath, and a woman had screamed. The man at the wheel of the towing motorboat gunned it for shore. Skiers dived in, and curses and contradictory commands filled the air.

The only calm one had been Judy, who came from a long line of competent swimmers. A favorite elephant pastime, in fact, is to tiptoe lightly across the bottoms of cool, shallow rivers. The gigantic quadrupeds thrust their tunks up the surface and breathe as through a snorkel tube, which was precisely what Judy had done then. The pink tunnel of her long upper lip and nostrils (for such the trunk really is) poked calmly up between the pontoons, and Judy was quite fine, thank you (though inconvenienced) until the humans got their act together.

"Be okay if I got close to her?" I asked the trainer that gentle morning.

"I think so. She's in a pretty good mood today, aren't you girl," said the trainer affectionately, smiling on the no longer quite so babyish elephant. The reddish sprigs of infant hair were nearly gone, replaced or darkening into occasional sparse clumps of black wire, and her back rose taller than the top of my head. Her flat skull lowered as I lifted my thigh over the wire charged with alternating current. Her trunk, ridged and wrinkled like an arrested lava flow, twitched and curled by the straw-covered floor.

And lifted up. "She wants to check you out, see if you've

got any apples or carrots in your pockets," said the trainer. "Did you know they can pick up a ton of logs with their trunks? Or a wisp of straw." The top of the tip of Judy's trunk, I noted hypnotically as the thing reached forward like a martian investigatory tool, had a fingerlike projection which was quite dextrous. With a moist, sucking fumble, the trunk tip searched me.

I had forgotten to mention—and the trainer could not have seen—the rubber diver shoes, or bootees, I carried tucked in my armpit. But Judy found them.

The trunk snatched. My armpit pinched air. Judy chawed. "Hey, elephant, don't eat my shoes!" Judy obliged. PTOO, she spat out the inedible object. Her ears fanned. Her long, lustrous eyelashes framed no friendly eye. She thinks I tried to poison her, I thought in an infinitesimal fragment of time. "Judy, no!" the trainer tried to dominate, but what happened next took place too swiftly to prevent.

No time to think, act, run, the gray rough forehead filled my vision, lifted, and shot me flying backward through the air.

I landed on the electrified wire. The jolt shook me, and then my falling weight broke the wire and the current. Judy shuffled over, ignoring the trainer's shouts and hook. I rolled and replaced the wire so she'd think it was still operating, and she stopped.

I rested for a bit. The ground can be quite comfortable sometimes. The trainer explained my mistake and apologized for Judy's misunderstanding. After a while we rescued my bootees with a rake, and I went my way.

But it was a long time before I could properly appreciate elephants again.

27

Grover, the Storm, and the Birth of a Water Person

~~~~~~~~~~~~~~~~~~~~~~~~~~~~~~~~~~~~~

We had met walking down the same lonely Louisiana road, and had gotten to talking. Before I knew it, I was telling my story to this little fella, and he was listening, nodding, as interested as if he had known my family.

He was too young to stoop, but it was as if he were bowed under by some unnamed burden. His large blue eyes were beautiful but scared, and seemed to be seeking something. The tousled head was never still. Now he peered back down the road between the trees; now he stared as far ahead as the encroaching forest would allow. As though he anticipated the arrival of something wicked.

"I know where there's *work*," he'd said, and I shivered all over.

"Not diver work, but deckhanding. Take care of a crewboat, cook, clean up, easy! You eat good, and you get to go out to the oil rigs, take supplies and work crews back and forth, and you'd meet the divers, *and be where the dive jobs are.*" I wanted to grasp him by the arm and hang on, lest he prove ephemeral and vanish, like the mists which rose now from the cypress and water oak in the swamp around us.

"Got a place to stay?" the thin teenager asked, and when I'd told him where my duffel bag was, he said, "Don't stay there—you got to pay them. Spend the night at my place. In the morning I'll point you the road to Coastal Marine, where the work is." Just for a moment his frame relaxed, and the slack shirt filled, in pride that he had a house to share. I had been just dee-lighted to accept.

Now, having picked up my duffel from the Sailor's Rest hotel (and got my dollar fifty back, which swelled my resources to two bucks again) we walked in twilight from the edge of town, where the last ride had left us off. Mosquitoes zeee-ed by our faces, and we slapped at them, the smack of fingers on faces carrying in the gathering dark.

The house was white, or had been, once. Now the paint was mostly blisters and flaked off, and gray wood showed through underneath. No lights showed. My newfound friend opened the creaking screen door to the front porch, and we left the mosquitoes outside. Then the knob to the wood door turned in his hand, and a blast of faintly vomitous heat, the stale dead air of a closed-in place, greeted us.

The door opened directly into the kitchen, and beyond in a larger room I saw a mattress and a blanket on the floor. I began to wish for the mosquitoes and the swamp. But no, this was his home. I quelled the strange nervousness this house roused in me and sat down at the oilcloth-covered table. An air conditioner crouched in a window. Grover reached his skinny fingers for the knob, and with a whir and a groan the fan started up. An insect carcass flipped out and landed on the red checkered oilcloth.

Grover opened the refrigerator door with a flourish and left it open. I half-expected it to be dead or inoperant, but no, sweet coolness emanated and caressed us. What delight a change in temperature can bring.

And standing on the shelf in a cardboard case—beer. Four blessed brown glass bottles, beads of condensation showing on them. My host handed me one and opened another for himself.

"Got to leave the last two for my brother," he said. "He's coming home tonight."

I drank the beer slowly, savoring its coolness as long as I could, loving the feel of the cold bottle in my hands. I ran the wet glass across my forehead like James Dean did in that movie *Rebel Without a Cause*, I think it was. Felt nice.

"I'd almost go with you tomorrow," said Grover, wistfully. "There's a couple openings, I hear, and it's a good life, deck-handing. Someday, be pilot. I'd—I'd like that." His eyes grew dreamy and faraway. "The river," he said, "and the sea . . ." Then he sighed, and scratched his head.

"Why don't you come along tomorrow?" I said.

Grover looked around the room. His nervous blue eyes blinked repeatedly.

"Do it," I encouraged. His eyes flicked to me and away.

"My brother's kind of rowdy," said Grover, apparently changing the subject. I sipped the water we were finishing my cookies with. "Want a vitamin pill?" I asked him. He shook his head.

"He's been in jail, my brother," said Grover as I ate another health-food cookie and tried not to look inquisitive.

"Some asshole pushed a fight on him. Wasn't his fault what happened, but my brother, he—"

Grover was interrupted. Footsteps sounded on the walk outside. The screen door rattled. "Open this goddam door!"

Grover flung himself from the chair. I heard him in the dark at the door, apologizing. The voice that answered him sounded positively evil. "I found me some work as a roustabout," it said. "Roughneckin' on a rig. Don't know if they'll have a job for a shittin' fool like you, but—"

The lean, hard man paused in midspeech, lips parted like a snarl. Acne-scarred face and weasel's eyes glared in my direction. Then his look lashed back to Grover. "What's *this*?" he hissed, indicating me with a thumb. "Oh, that's my friend," pleaded the younger brother. "He's looking for work, and I told him he could stay here tonight."

"Ain't runnin' no goddam hotel," said the elder brother, and kicked the refrigerator door. It shut with a crash. "You wanna sleep here, you got to pay. Cost ya . . ." his glance raked swiftly from my shirt to the worn but well-made work boots. "Fifteen bucks."

I stood up, quite frightened and not knowing what to do.

He aggressed over to me, pushing his ugly eyes close to mine. He was skinny but . . . A mental picture of him with a broken beer bottle, ruining somebody's face, flashed into my mind. I wanted neither to challenge him (he might be insane) nor to enflame his tendency to violence by appearing afraid. I did nothing, said nothing, kept my face resolutely neutral.

He completely misread me. He did not detect my shaking spine and quaking guts; he only saw my still face and large frame, and shockingly his entire appearance altered.

He stepped back a yard, and his body twisted in a cringe. Incredibly his hands came up before his face to ward off a blow I had no intention of throwing, and his voice whined: "Course, you know I'm only jokin'! You can stay here tonight, long as you want, don't have to pay nothin', no, nothin'—Suthrun Hospitality!"

I knew enough to press my advantage. Without altering the expressionlessness that had worked for me so far, I stepped forward as if to walk right over him. You little punk, I thought, what did you do to make your brother be so afraid of you. He leaned back against the table, and I walked through the space he had occupied, out the door onto the porch, and to the couch where I intended to sleep.

"Can I get you something fo' yo' haid?" he asked. "We don't have no pillows, but I got a old blanket you could fold up and—"

"No. No thanks," I told him, and at last he left me.

In my pack was an old shoemaker's awl, a short leather punch with a ball handle. I had picked it up on the road somewhere, and it had looked so substantial I kept it. I put the round base in my palm and closed my fist so that the spike struck out from between my knuckles, and rehearsed how I would fight with it. Would the brothers come against me? I had nothing worth stealing, but they might not believe that.

That night I kept all my clothes on, even my shoes. I wanted to sleep uncomfortably, so that I would wake lightly. I heard them whispering late into the night.

o o o

At the first creak of the boards in the morning I was awake and on my feet. I held the awl inconspicuously in my fist.

It was the younger brother.

"I'm sorry about last night," he breathed, quiet against the snores emanating from the room behind him. "That's okay." I shrugged and pocketed the awl. "I wanted to tell you how to get to Coastal Marine," he said.

"Come with me!" I urged, "Go to work on the river like you talked about."

"I can't," he said, his blue eyes scared and trapped. But there was something else there too.

"He *is* my family," the convict's brother said.

Four weeks later radio static crackled in the night, and Morris cursed and climbed out of his sleeping bag. I opened one eye from the upper bunk and dimly noted the older man's pajama-clad progress across the cabin floor. "I'm comin', I'm comin'," snapped the strongly built Louisiana pilot, "Don't get your bowels in an uproar." I closed my eyes again and listened while the boat rocked softly in the harbor. "Uh-huh. Yeah. All right," I heard. Then:

"Cast off the lines, will you, honey," said Morris, using the term that to Southerners means no more than "pal" or "friend" did back home. "We goin' out."

"To the rig?" I sat up suddenly. Swinging my legs off the mattress, I landed on the deck in a crouch, shed the baglike trousers, hustled into my jeans.

"Yeah, they got a machine part somebody wonts in a hurry," Morris's voice followed me out onto the top deck as I ran to untie the *Island Princess*. A wind whipped my shirtless upper body, and the lights of the boats around me moved.

Putpuputputputputterputputputput . . . I had never been out of the harbor before. I who could get seasick on a playground swing. But this didn't feel too bad, I thought, only faintly queasy as Morris threaded our boat expertly through the harbor lanes.

But the sheltered cove was like a parking lot, and the freeway was the sea. As soon as we left the encirclement of land, the waves began. WHUMP! the bow lifted up and whacked down, on water that was no longer soft.

WONK! I stumbled back against the wheelhouse wall, sat down on the padded bench. Outside the windshield-wiping glass I could see only blackness and waves that towered before they crashed against us. "We in a storm, Morris?" "This?" said Morris, his old hawk's face quizzical. "Oh, no, honey, this is just a little breeze building up. A storm, now, that's something different." Could have fooled me, I thought to myself, trying not to think about the greasy cheeseburgers I had fixed for supper.

Morris, easy as a commuter in his pilot's chair, laid his lit cigarette in the sand-bottomed ashtray. The boat lurched, and the ashtray slid away. Morris didn't even reach for it. He just waited, and presently the boat shook and lifted again, and the ashtray returned to him. The curl of smoke lifted into the room.

My forehead turned cold, and I could feel the sweat beads popping out on it. At every wave my head thumped back against the wall. I felt a reverse peristalsis in my guts beginning, as food that was gradually supposed to move downward through the digestive tract changed direction. Lumpy burger, cheese, milk and suddenly loathsome chocolate chip cookies began to force their way out of the stomach wall prison. They knew the route and were coming up. " 'Scuse me, Morris, I got to take a leak," I lied.

"You goin' be okay, honey?" asked Morris.

"Yeah, I'm fine, I'm fine." Don't start talking now, Morris, I don't have time. He might still have been talking when I closed the door behind his crew-cut head.

I had to kneel beside the toilet because the floor was lifting and falling five and six feet at a time. The whole boat seemed alive and straining at the seams. I was grossly heavy one second, the floor squashing up; the next it dropped away, and my stomach hung unsupported—ugggh. I gripped the toilet with both hands so that I would not miss.

A moment later I felt somewhat relieved. But when I went back to be with Morris, the cabin was filled with smoke.

"Morris," I said hollowly, holding the door open very wide, "I'm kind of sleepy still. Do you mind if I go lay down?"

"Sho', honey, but don't lay on the bunk—you'll bounce right out. Just lean on one of them card tables. Rest good now, we'll be busy when we hit that rig."

I wondered vaguely what he meant by "busy." They were just going to lower down some little part to us, weren't they? But nausea still gripped me, and I staggered back to the anchored card tables, throwing myself down on the padded bench beside.

The back of the boat leaped less. By the simple expedient of wedging my shoulder under the anchored table, I could keep my head more or less in contact with my folded hands and the foam-rubber bench cover.

Wouldn't be able to sleep, I thought, but anything was better than that unsupported nightmare up front.

I daydreamed, remembering how I'd almost lost this job a scant week after I had walked into the aluminum barn marked Coastal Marine.

Men in work clothes had been waiting in the shade of the factorylike building. They looked up as the intruder entered their domain. "Hi!" I said brightly, with a confidence I did not feel, "I'm looking for work!"

"You are, huh?" said a hefty bald fellow with no discernible teeth. "Well sweep out this place then. It's sho' in need of it!" His joke brought a laugh, but I pretended to think he had meant it. "Great!" I said, "but when will the boss be back?"

"Maybe not for a long time," said a large man with a very direct stare. "Wonderful!" I said, determined to be Mr. Sunshine at all costs right now. I picked up a broom and went to work, ignoring the unwelcoming vibrations. When I came to a pile of old machine parts with oil underneath, and dust and grass on the surface of the oil, I asked one of the people for rags and solvent. He hesitated, but he gave them to me. I soaked the rags, instead of pouring the solvent wastefully on the floor, so they'd see I was thrifty. Then me and the solvent and the rags and the broom—we cleaned *up* that place!

"Honey?" said a rough voice, and I blinked at being called that, for the first time by a man. His face was reassuring, though, beneath the black, brush-cut hair. Eyes obsidian black, broad forehead, big Roman nose, weather-wrinkled skin, and a mouth that looked like it woke up smiling. "How'd you like to work on a real nahs boat?"

"I'd like that a lot, sir," I said.

"I *lahk* the way you clean that floh. We goin' get along real *good.*" He walked away, talking with his friends.

"Yew *lucky,*" said the man whose joke had given me the excuse to pick up a broom. "That was Moh-ris," said the chubby old guy, settling himself on an empty oil drum, "best damn pahlot you evuh gonna meet."

When the boss's son showed up, neat and clean and educated, Morris called across the room, "Ah wont him for *mah* boat," and I thought I had it made.

Trouble was, Morris's boat was dry-docked for repairs. They had to find something for me to do meanwhile and apprenticed me to Bobby (I never knew his last name) as a mechanic's helper.

Ever know a man who can make a motor sit up and beg? That man is royalty around the shop, and such a man was Bobby. Bobby was the man you listened to. His rank extended to all areas. If anybody else was talking, and Bobby cleared his throat, Bobby got the floor. He had good opinions, too, a commonsense approach to everything. But it was with machines that his genius revealed itself.

When other mechanics had a problem they couldn't handle, they would bring the offending mass of nuts and bolts to Bobby, who did not fail. He would examine the patient without saying a word while he was told the symptoms. Then Bobby would either say "Junk it," at which point you threw it away without further comment, or else Bobby fixed it. It was as if the motors were afraid to not get better, when Bobby put his hands on them. Sometimes he would seem just to touch something, jiggle it a little, and the pieces would align, jumping into place to please him.

Even grease seemed to stay away from Bobby, who always appeared neat, no matter how dirty the job. His gray-striped work shirt with the sleeves rolled precisely three-quarters of the way down muscular forearms was clean and pressed each morning. Bobby was pride.

And the man they assigned to help this king of mechanics? Uh-huh.

"Hand me a spanner," said Bobby from underneath the chain-suspended motor. A spanner? I opened the neat green toolbox, hoping there would be labels inside. There were not, of course. As the massive metal sides parted, an arranged assortment of well-maintained equipment met my gaze. The careful accumulation of years of watching for just the right tool, for the champion mechanic.

"Uh . . . Bobby?" I had to say.

"Yeah?" came a grunt.

"I don't know what a spanner is."

He looked at me flat for a moment and then rolled swiftly out from under the motor. And took a *wrench* out from the toolbox. Drat, one of the ones I knew! The whole morning went like that, with me squatting on my haunches, trying desperately to be helpful and mainly succeeding in getting in the way. At lunch I heard Bobby tell one of the other mechanics, "They give me a helper what don't know nothin' about machines." I should have kept quiet, but I ran over quick and said, "A man can't know about something until, until, he knows about it!" Which made a lot of sense. Bobby shook his head.

In the afternoon I was assigned to help somebody else.

As my footsteps sounded on the deck of the large boat (the back of Coastal Marine is a bayou), a noise of great activity came from its engine room below deck. Whistling and the sound of rubbing and—was that the creak of chair legs?

As I looked down into the dark of the hold, a face as pink and oblong as a ham glanced up. Eyes as dark as raisins winked at me. "Why, I didn't hear you coming!" he said. "But who are you?" I told him, and he smiled a smile of sheer content. "Of course, you are, dear boy," he said. "And I"—here he resumed his seat—"am your supervisor."

He was, too, and probably the best supervisor I've ever had. He did not stifle my creativity in the slightest but merely directed me to the red industrial rags and the barrel of solvent. I soaked the limp rags and turned to the mighty wall of engine, rising above my head, looking like acres of grease and hot metal and burnt carbon. Slightly appalled at the magnitude of the chore, I turned back to my companion. He was raising a brown paper sack to his lips. "You don't indulge, of course, my son?" he stated, and before I could say "yes, definitely," he answered his own sentence. "Naturally you do not, and wise you are to pursue the course of temperance! Ahh, out of the mouths of babes!" he said as I tried to interrupt. "My son, I wish I had your wisdom!" I wished I had his whiskey.

As my new friend supervised, sometimes so diligently that grunts (presumably) of fatigue escaped from under his pulled-down cap, I applied the acidy solution to a black-encrusted cylinder head. Rubbing hard, I made a spot of clean appear. It didn't look much different from the grunge-coated engine around it, but it felt smooth. I compared the silver-dollar-sized scrubbed area with the vastness of the unclean-motor, stretching beyond my sight in the lightless hold.

When dark fell, I assumed we would discontinue our labors, but, no, my companion hunted up a length of extension cord and a light which turned everything into stark black and greasy white. Mosquitoes buzzed around us, stirring my companion to a frenzy of activity.

"Yes, my boy," he said, actually sitting up. "Someday these bayous will resound once more with the roars of mating alligators. Why, when I fence off the desired allocation of swampland, and populate it with a predetermined enumeration of reptiles (too many and they will devour each other, you understand), their natural reproductory propensity will assert itself, and the result will be—progeny! Miniature alligator handbags, needing only harvest. Ah, my son, to be young again, and to have before me the possibilities that lie at the feet of—oh, one such as you, for instance. Why for just that small accumulation of capital you probably have rotting away in a bank somewhere, daily losing ground to inflation, why . . ." And on, and on, and on. He sighed and settled back.

At eight o'clock he raised himself, reluctantly. "Well. The dragon calls. You're not married, I trust? You are? Then you understand. Good night, dear boy. I shall leave this source of illumination, against the likely possibility of your wishing to continue your labors. Perseverance, my boy, perseverance!" He raised a finger, admonishing, and disappeared into the night.

Immediately I dashed for the can of waterless soap and plunged my hands into the green-tinged white glop. Ten minutes later I could stand to touch myself, and the flashlight led me to the sleeping bag on the next boat over. Although the night was swelteringly muggy, I stripped and got in the sleeping bag, pulling the top over my head. Inside, the mosquitoes could not reach me, and I could write to my wife in peace.

As the days passed, the motor was gradually uncovered. I kept to myself, which was not difficult, as a small cloud of silence seemed to hover around me wherever I went. Conversations would stop when I approached and not resume until I left.

One loose-limbed young giant named Jimmy spent some time telling me how much he enjoyed "kicking ass on big dudes, especially Yankees," arc-ing his fists through the still air, "WHOHM! WHAM! BIP! BAP!" he showed me how he had laid them away.

I think he was about an inch away from a flat challenge when I thought to ask, "How come you want to go hurting all these people, anyway?" And for some reason it was exactly the right thing to say because he grinned and said, "You're

right, I got to work on that. Where'd you say you was from?"
We had a few minutes of nice talk before he went away, off
on a boat again.

I was alone and lonely, tired of the endless labor and tired
of being ignored, when a spider brought the tension to a
head.

It was just a common ordinary spider, gray and business-
like with its small body and neat silky arms, but the web it
was building—I'd never really noticed a spiderweb before,
how marvelously it was constructed: each segment delicately
balanced, in subtle juxtaposition to every other portion of the
almost invisible web.

I was admiring the arachnid's labors when: "Quit starin' at
that spider will ya? I don't like spiders, all creepy crawly the
way they are. They make me nervous." "*Yankees* make *me*
nervous," somebody else said, softly, but loud enough to
make the others laugh.

I heard a strange, high-pitched buzzing as of blood circulating through my ears. My skin was of a sudden cold as if a
thin layer of refrigeration separated it from the muggy air.
My breath came hard.

"I *like* spiders," I said, making my stand. "They're like a
master mechanic. Their webs are architectural marvels. Hur-
ricanes have blown buildings down but left the spiderwebs
beside them untouched. Spiders are *tough!*" I said, sticking
my chin out at the group. Then I stopped and waited, for
whatever came next.

"What's going on here?" snapped the boss's son. Oh, no.
I could almost hear it. "We don't want troublemakers around
here," the boss's son would say, and I'd have lost my job.
Somebody started up, to tattle. "This *Yankee*—"

Then Bobby spoke, and as usual everybody else shut up.
"We was all looking at this spider," he said. "Did you know
spiders was natural mechanics? Look how good that web's
put together." I held my breath.

"Spiders, huh?" said the boss's son and smiled as he
walked back to his office.

"Who's the new guy?" I heard somebody ask Bobby.

"A hawrd werkuh," said the master mechanic.

" 'A hard worker,' Bobby said I was!" I wrote my wife that night, and everything was okay.

"Wake up, honey; we're here!" A voice shook me out of my jouncing lowered awareness. Couldn't call it sleep with my head jolting up and down to the crash of the boat through the waves.

Don't get up, my stomach warned me.

I rose. Nausea and the boat's pitch swayyyyed me. I felt very tall, with limbs of rubber over which a stranger ruled. I watched my hand reach for a counter and miss, saw myself falling, foot twisting, ankle folding, slamming onto my side without sound, and the floor went from vertical to horizontal to vertical in opposite directions and I slid like wreckage across the padded room. I'd almost rather have been dead than there.

My fingers locked around something. The door to the cabin. Brace yourself kid. I knew the smoke behind it would—aaagh, ropy coils of thickness . . .

Through the smoke and the rain-smeared window, I saw the rig. Talismanic yellow, lights flooding down, in total contrast to the black rain. Morris was saying: "You be careful out there on that deck now, honey, because it's awash, and I don't want to lose you. Watch them gears when they lowerdown, too—they're heavy. Don't get mashed, hear?"

He wants me to go *out* there? On that deck that's turning vertical with the sea? He must think I am insane!

But there was no help for it. The only choice: to do it or go hide. Against my will, I fought into a yellow rain slicker and opened the back door.

Unbelievable the shock of rain and wind—I skidded out and grasped the rail and tried not to go over. "Here you go!" came a voice very faintly from above. My fingers were locked unreleasably, and I looked up and saw what looked like my own rain slicker high up the side of the rig, which was the only stationary point. Or was it moving and were we stationary?

Something like a braided boa constrictor shot down, becoming larger before crashing in stiff coils on the deck. Unwilling to risk my grip on the railing, I reached across the foaming deck with my feet, got the noose, pulled it back and hooked it around the cleats at the stern. Morris gunned the motor, the rope stretched—I had a momentary vision of a boat hanging upside down from the oil rig—the deck still, rocked, but the rope-motor tension kept us in approximately the same position among the heaving waves.

We waited. Presently a huge wooden crate, like a piano box, began to lower. That's a *gear*?! I thought, just as my stomach served notice.

I had to be sick again. The unmistakable signs asserted themselves, the freezing forehead, bubbling belly, and the itching in the trigger at the back of the throat. I looked wildly around for a place to get rid of it without being seen. This final indignity was too much. I won't let you bastards see me draped across the rail!

The box in the cargo net was growing huger: no time to run inside. I did the only thing I could do. My tortured guts spewed up; my cheeks bulged out, and I swallowed the vomit back down again.

And then felt fine. Dizzy, almost weightless on my feet, but I could work. The netted box drew near, I leaped and caught the ropes, swung an instant, and the corner touched down. Then the weight of the box gave us both stability. The net dropped down around the box, and I rocked it corner by corner off the mesh, and waved and shouted, no, roared "GOT IT!" through the wind and the black rain.

All the rest was Morris, piloting us back to shore, the boat like an obedient eagle, under his powerful, ocean man's hands.

Six weeks later I stood beside my wife in the delivery room and helped her struggle in that most strenuous of all athletic events, the birthing of a child.

The highest moment of my life. I had been so afraid that something would go wrong, that my sins would be punished by awfulness visited upon my child, but it was not so. For as my wife's forehead sweat, and she groaned in muscular exertion, not a scream but the noise of vital effort: our Desireé, our Desireé Don, middlenamed after me, entered the world. Her head popped through. The doctor reached and lifted; the shoulders emerged. The doctor held a baby. My baby. Our baby. He made some snips and gentle wipes and handed her to me.

She was perfect. Red and wet and without flaw. Her eyes were open, undimmed by the drugs her mother hadn't had. Her first sight on Earth was me. Her large brown eyes contacted mine, and she smiled. Don't tell me gas, don't tell me accidental muscular contraction: she saw me, and she smiled, and I loved her more than I love life. Then her eyes flicked to her hand that she had never seen before. She closed her tiny fingers in the littlest of fists.

I was supposed to be counting her fingers and toes because I had promised Jeannie I would do that first thing, but my daughter was so beautiful my eyes misted up and overflowed, and I could only get to three or four, and then I'd lose track and have to start over again. My wife saw her husband's tears and thought something was wrong because it took me so long.

Then the doctor took Desireé away from me, and I almost growled, but it was necessary. He had to give her some eye drops, I think. Still, I was pleased when he turned back and said: "Mr. Reed, your daughter just urinated on me!" I laughed out loud and said: "That, Doctor, is the beginning of a lifelong lack of respect for established authority!"

We tried to feed Jeannie some gelatin, but she was too tired to chew. All she had strength for was one look and a cheek snuggle with Desireé ("She's byoo-ful") and sleep.

Then the nurses chased me into the hallway where I grabbed my mother-in-law and threw her up in the air again and again while she screamed and laughed "Stop! Stop!" and I shouted, "My baby is born! My baby is born!"

And, oh yes, I got the job. As diver at Marine World. Jon

Noble, my old friend from dive school, had heard about the opening but had had to pass it up because it did not pay enough to support his family. So before he went back to New Jersey to be a longshoreman, he called up Jeannie, and she went down to the office of Ted Pintarelli, the head diver. She got the interview, I came home and took a physical.

It was all over but the handshake.

Now the great adventures would begin.

28

A Movie as
a Preview of Our Lives?

"Just don't scream in my ear, *Melinda*," said Dave De Nardo as we stood in line to see *Jaws*, the first week of its nationwide release.

"David, really!" said Lindy Mitchell, "I have my pride. How dare you suggest that I would scream?"

"Maybe because I've been to a scary movie with you before," sighed the heavy-eyebrowed Italian wearily.

"Boy I can't wait to see how you're going to be when the white shark shows up on the screen!" said Gary Trevisan, our summer replacement diver, to me. "I bet you're going to be thinking up all kinds of ways to catch it or kill it!" Little did he know.

I had some hope that the knowledge of white sharks I had accumulated over the years would protect me from the terror. I liked to point out shark inaccuracies in movies, like the painted teeth on the famous *Jaws* poster, where the 6-acre mouth ploughs up to feed on the 2-inch naked girl. Not only were the proportions wrong (the shark looked about 60 feet long), but the teeth were those of a mako shark, not a great white. A big white's teeth are unmistakable: squat, notch-edged, triangular. The poster shark's teeth were slender, smooth-sided, slanting stilettos. Also the placement of the dentition was wrong. White shark teeth usually show only one row, especially on the upper jaw. The art work depicted double handfuls of teeth snaggling all over the upper jaw. An accurately depicted mako mouth—but it was supposed to be a great white.

Peter Benchley's book I had read at a run, skipping over the pages in between the attacks, anxious to see the shark in action, and find out who would live or die. The book, I thought, was both terrific and terrible. The first chapter contains the finest description of white shark physiognomy I've ever come across. Art out of anatomy. But when Benchley's fiction shark went into action, and the towns began to depopulate, that was pure storyteller's skill.

A great and neglected book about sharks is *Sportfishing for Sharks* by Frank Mundus. Mr. Mundus reportedly took Peter Benchley shark fishing and is, probably, the real-life model for Quint, the shark fisherman in *Jaws*.

If white sharks were really like that, all they would have to do is find any of the thousands of available beaches, and start lunching. The oceans would be red. But the real animal does not seek out man. Studies have shown sharks far prefer fish flesh to land animal meat, probably for the same reason we choose food we know over dishes we do not. When you see film of white sharks attacking the bars of an underwater photographer's cage, remember you are viewing an artificially enraged creature. Blood and animal parts (usually seal or whale) have been dumped into the water in copious quantities to attract and incite "whitey" into photogenic frenzy. Without the blood, the hoped-for villain would most likely just swim on by. How many times do sharks of any species really take advantage of the millions of opportunities they have to eat people? Well, one statistician estimates that divers have about as much chance of being shark lunch as they do of being struck by lightning three different times. Sharks do not eat very much of any kind of food. Jacques Cousteau estimates a 300-pound shark may eat as little as 150 pounds of food a year, an average of less than half a pound a day, far less than we humans consume.

Logically speaking, then, judging sharks by *Jaws* is not unlike judging brain surgery by *Frankenstein:* Both are monster movies. Logic does not, of course, make one immune to emotion. And emotionally, *Jaws* took me apart.

I read the novel twice, the first time to see what all the screaming was about, the second time to be sure I had not missed anything. It stirred my meat-eater instincts, but it also made me sick. I could never spend time with it, as I like to do with a fine book.

The movie, however, was something else again. From the moment when poor, doomed Chrissie flings off her clothes in the dark and runs for the water ("No, kid, don't do it!") I knew *I* was in trouble. On repeated viewings (the picture became my personal favorite) I could see the evidence of master moviemaking. It should have won the Academy Award for best picture. Magnificent, all the way through. Acting, editing, photography, dialogue, special effects, music—director Steven Spielberg put together a work of art that will hold up forever. All this occurred to me, later.

At the time all I could do was sink lower and lower into my seat, until from the back it must have appeared to be unoccupied. Before the show began we had talked of bringing our snorkels. If a phony part happened, we could purse lips and blow through the tube, making a nasty sound. But once the show got going, there was no more talk of snorkels. I wished I was somewhere else.

Wonder if they'd notice if I went to the bathroom and stayed for 2 hours, I thought as I closed my eyes for the forty-fifth time. I would have covered my ears, too, if I hadn't come with friends.

"Don's not taking this at all like I thought he would," said new-guy Trevisan to Dave De Nardo, but I didn't care. "Huh? What?" said Dave, rubbing the ear closest to Lindy. Kris Jensen, of the red handlebar mustache and never-failing gentle smile, said nothing. Always calm, that man. In dolphin catches, the animals would sometimes swim right up to him and surrender, giving themselves up to his careful arms. Perhaps they too could sense the inner peace he radiated. I wished I could have borrowed his calm for the movie.

Only at the last moment did I partially redeem myself, when the shark was eating the boat and I saw the air tanks bouncing around, like high-pressure bombs. "Throw the air tanks! Throw the air tanks!" I shouted to Roy Scheider on the screen. It was good advice, and he took it, and was saved.

Afterwards we wolfed down blood-colored pizza, and hoped we had not seen a major preview of our lives.

29

A Night in the Water
with a Great White Shark

Our white shark was an animal in trouble. In less than one day the female great white had half-strangled in fisherman Peter Halley's Tomales Bay nets, endured the sinking of a heavy hook through her lower jaw, been dragged behind a boat, been yanked out of the element that gave her breath and supported her ribless internal organs, suffered a hose gushing saltwater thrust down her throat, and been stuffed into a too-small holding tank on the back of a jolting, jouncing truck, which transported her to San Francisco.

At the city's renowned Steinhart Aquarium (one of the most beautiful and well-kept collections of marine life in the world), men like Dave Powell, John McCosker, and Ed Miller softly placed the comatose *chondricthyes* into the shallow saltwater of a large plastic wading pool. Their biggest tank, the "roundabout" doughnut-shaped, glass-walled exhibit was not completed yet, or they would have used that.

Aquarium volunteers began the "walking" process, wading in circles to force water through the open mouth and over the gills. And, more importantly, they worked the crescent sweeping tail back and forth, to stimulate the circulation.

The increased blood flow to the white shark's brain changed her from passive to active. Her eye moved. She snapped sidewards quickly, right and left, teeth chopping like a set of matched knives. But it was when she lunged so hard at the side of the pool that the whole thing nearly tipped over—shark, water, volunteers and all— that curator Dr. John McCosker thought about the reef aquarium tank at Marine World/Africa USA.

That night, before the telephone rang, I was as comfortable as I have ever been. Desireé Don, four years old now, stretched and yawned and leaned back against my chest, left side. My son the earthshaker, Roman Jason Patrick Reed, seventeen months old and already big enough to need all that name, shoved his nose and forehead into the right side of my thorax. On the couch on the other side of the small living room, Jeannie made soft rhythmic noises ("I'm not asleep!" she would have said if you'd waked her; "I'm just resting my eyes.") We were watching *Walt Disney Presents*, I remember.

The telephone humbly solicited attention. That insidious instrument had once been rude summoning us with a harsh, screaming RINGGGGG, but then we had found out you can *castrate* telephones. Now, with its bells clipped, or whatever the serviceman had done to emasculate it, the telephone made a barely bothersome intrusion. "Ding . . . ding?" It hesitantly said.

"I'll get it, I'll get it!" said my angel, bounding off my lap as though someone might dispute her for the privilege. It was nearly eight, and we go to bed early here: Jeannie by inclination, me because I do my writing at three in the morning, when the day's distractions are not yet demanding attention.

"Reed Residence, hello" said Desireé Don with the pride and professionalism of a four-year-old who could handle the telephone all by herself. "Yes, he is," she said, each word clear and distinct as a jewel. Speech is still a joy to her, not yet taken for granted. "It is someone from Marine World," she said, walking the phone over to me, stretching the long cord behind her like her mother does. This always makes me nervous because I feel the phone is going to yank out of the wall, so I set Roman on a soft spot and met the telephone halfway.

"What A *white* shark? As in w-h-i-t-e shark?" was practically my entire contribution to the conversation. At the word "shark" my wife sat up.

"What's this about a white shark?" she said as I severed the connection. Uh-oh.

"Oh, it's nothing, really. Just this very small—tiny! Practically a baby! Immature little (white) shark at the park, and I have to go nursemaid it for a little while."

"*How* tiny?" queried the Boss, folding her arms.

"Just 8 feet long or so, only a little taller than me and—"

"Like the one killed all those people in New Jersey."

"But that was a long time ago—1916, Matawan Creek, a freak thing. It swam up a freshwater creek, got denied its natural food, and—"

"I forbid you to go," said my wife, in the flat tones that usually announce the end of the disagreement.

"Aww, but gee, hon, Keith's in there with it already, and I'm the head diver. What's it gonna look like if I chicken out and don't show? I *have* to go." I tried to kiss her, but she yanked her cheek away. My wife is Mexican and Italian by blood and has inherited the warmer side of both those Latin natures.

"Then go, you son of a bitch! I don't care! Get the damnhell out of here!" She said, exhausting her vocabulary of undeleted expletives. I got.

The silence of the night was a surprise after the noise of Jeannie's rage, or rather, fear. The sky looked dark and starless overhead, like a black tunnel closing in, or a deadly womb, squeezing me out into death instead of life. I wished I was a kid again so I wouldn't have to go. I might get my legs bitten off tonight, I thought as the crickets started up again.

ZEE, ZEE, ZEE, the crickets sang, celebrating their territory or their love life, I don't know which. Lucky little crickets: no fisherman's coming with a jar for you. No cruel hook will penetrate your body, no flip and swish through air to flop on water, skittering, struggling till something rises from below.

What was that awful word the doctors used to describe the effects of certain shark attacks? They used it in the movie, *Jaws*. Oh, yeah: "denuded." Ghastly. When the mouth of knives closed lightly on a limb and the shark *shook* its head. Muscle, fat, ligament, and tendon severed, and the cut meat slid down, exposing bone, "denuding" it.

The miles passed too quickly under the wheels of my little car. Before I could accept it, the hour's insulating drive was over, and I pulled into the darkened parking lot. Only the guard shack was a spot of brightness in the gloom. For a moment I couldn't make myself turn the key off. My stomach felt clutched and kneaded, as if by invisible fingers.

But then I thought: If my wife's philosophy is right, and all our futures are written out for us, then what is going to happen is going to happen, and there's nothing I can do about it. And if *my* philosophy is correct, and nothing is written, but we are ourselves the writers of our lives, well then I will be pretty vigorous indeed in the defense of my own limbs. KLICKLICKLICKLICK, I put the emergency brake on, and shut off the beast of transportation.

The guard on duty was somebody new, and he scrutinized my ID card before rolling back the wheeled section of fence that is the back of Marine World. I ran. It was a time to run, for suddenly I was young and strong, and a fever for activity stirred my blood. There was nowhere else on earth I would rather have been.

Elephants rustled the straw to my left as I ran up the unpaved path, and if I had paused, I could have seen the green eyes of wolves, shining in the moonlight, on the right. But I did not pause until I reached the locker room.

I dressed in the dark. (Some electrical problem, apparently.) I could tell my wet suit without sight, by the heaviness of it. I stripped, shucked it on, got my gear, turned left at the giraffe and crossed the bridge. Even with the heavy weight belt clunking on my hipbones, my feet felt light: grabbing the ground, pulling the world beneath and behind.

o o o

A square of light broke the dark water at the bottom of the redwood steps I was crouching on. It was only the entryway to the reef tank, illuminated by floodlights set up in the hallway beyond, but that green glow was the color of hospital walls—no, *ether*, the fuzzy all-encompassing lime that is the last thing a person on the operating table sees, before consciousness cuts away.

The water was not cold. Only the faint shock of element exchange disturbed my bare arms and shoulders as I settled into the breast-deep flume between the steps and the entryway. I pressed the mouthpiece button on the regulator. RRRRRR. There was air. I ran a finger around the lip of my face mask in case some of the edging had folded under, which would mean a leak. I tugged my swim fins tighter, glad for the familiar things to do.

Anything else? Oh, yes, definitely! The shark stick. A piece of broken killer whale gate, snapped personally by Nepo, our young orca, who was getting rowdy now that he was approaching sexual maturity. Kris Jensen (the gentle diver whom dolphins gave up to) had cut up the wrecked gate, put blue bicycle handle grips on the pieces, and there we had our official shark sticks. I tucked one into my belt. Not a weapon, but something to put between me and something unfriendly.

Ducking under, I waited till the bubbles quit rising, then poked my head out into the floodlit gloom. I hesitated, in case there was traffic, but no, only pools of light and darkness and a school of motionless kelp bass. My arms pulled me out into the green dim light.

I would swim to the fiber glass reef and squat in a sheltering pocket I knew there, until I could locate the shark. My arms felt very long, like bait, and I pulled them in to me.

Something huge burst through the cloud of kelp bass. My hand yanked the shark stick out so hard my weight belt almost fell, but it was only Chopper, the loggerhead turtle, flying as if she were young again. Even her inch-thick armor is not impervious to white sharks, with their bites like the blows of axes.

I practiced pulling the shark stick as I swam, imagining how I would fight back against an all-out attack. Deflect as long as I could, but, a flat charge? Go for the gills or the eyes, I guessed; make it uncomfortable. Couldn't kill it. I had had to execute an apparently epileptic little leopard shark once, which had kept freaking and slamming into the walls and the floors and the windows, as if trying to end itself. I hit it on the head with a 12-pound weight, which would have extinguished a human but only added to the leopard shark's frenzy. I finally had to take the shark out and let the air suffocate it. I'd felt like a desperately ineffectual bully.

There! A blur in the murky distance; a slowly focusing image; a man and the great white shark. *Chondricthyes: elasmobranchii: carcharodon carcharias.* Latin words for a diver's nightmare. The man (Keith Worcester's brother, Dave, a killer-whale trainer) had very large arms and a broad sweep of back, but he did not loom over the beast he guided.

I swam prudently wide around them and came in well behind the shark. I assumed Dave had noticed my approach, but when I tapped the flesh of his shoulder, his head jerked around, and his eyes were wide.

As Dave swam away for a break, he hesitated halfway and turned and raised his thumb and circled forefinger in the "Okay?" sign. I waved him off, but I would not have objected if he had wanted to stay. It occurred to me how very little I knew about the job at hand.

"Well, shark," I thought to the wide, inverted "V" of head and back below me, "My name is Don C. Reed. I have a wife and two babies, and I will thank you to remember that."

One hand slid easily along the back to the dorsal fin. The skin in this direction felt smooth as leather, with just the faintest touch of sand. But when my other hand tried to push against the grain of the hide, forward, the skin caught and held like closely packed fishhooks. The "denticles" sharks have instead of scales look like little teeth under a microscope and are the reason sharkhide was once used to wrap the handles of swords. Even drenched in the blood of enemies, that grip wouldn't slip. When treated and labeled "shagreen," the skin made wear-forever shoes, belts, and pickpocketproof wallets. A wallet in the pants pocket couldn't be snatched because the denticles dug in: the thief would have had to steal the trousers too. For that matter, I am not entirely sure how the legitimate owner disengaged his billfold.

Beneath the hide, the muscles moved. I could feel the rhythm, swaying side to side to side, and I adjusted my body motion to it, trying to add my body's strength to hers. I wasn't there to ride, but to help push, and the exertion was like pushing a hand lawnmower uphill through tall weeds. She was magnificently streamlined, but still she weighed 350-pounds and wanted to sink. I shifted back along her till my left hand held the upright dorsal, symbol of the shark, and my right could reach the base of the crescent tail. As best I could, I massaged, worked, and stimulated the cramped muscles, trying to add to the blood flow.

She swam groggily, as though she breathed exhaust fumes from a car. Sometimes I could feel the spirit within her struggling, trying to understand the new situation. The head lifted and turned. But she wasn't really perking up, and I wondered if she was getting enough oxygen from the passage of the water through her gills.

What if I gave her a good, strong shove? I would not want a big lady like this turning around on me, like the small seven-gill shark had done when I had raised it over my head and flung it like a spear that other time: but if she could get a good rush of oxygen . . .

Kicking hard to get momentum building, I let my arms straighten out behind and *heaved* the shark forward. The hide bit into my fingers. The muscles beneath the rough hide reacted.

Like a current of electricity, life flooded into the animal. The beautifully modulated tail swept back and forth slowly, but with power and control, like an athlete's walk. Perfection of movement.

But she was headed for a window, and I didn't think deep-water sharks had much experience with glass. I hustled after-her, running up my body heat like an overstoked furnace, a racing-style crawl through the underwater.

Like a kid chasing after his Ma, I caught up. Just before her pointed nose struck the window, my straining fingers caught the backmost tip of her tail. I leaned, and the ripple of arrested movement began at the tail and shot to the head like the cracking of a whip. She stopped cold, and then shook herself all over and began again, with me tagging along behind and above, occasionally reaching down to steer her head away from a window.

It did not seem real. The broad head I touched seemed like a sandpaper-covered surfboard, or a model of a shark. I sneaked a peek around in front, to get a better look at what I swam with.

The leathery gill covers flared and contracted as the shark breathed. The jaws flexed in a tentative chewing motion. Then the eye rolled back and looked at me. I yanked back up on top, into position again. She was real, all right.

Somebody tapped my shoulder and my head whirled around so fast the column of vertebrae POPOPOPPED—oh. To have been thinking shark so hard and then have somebody touch me—whew. It was whale trainer Frank Stryzalkowski, come to take a turn.

I better go call Jeannie. She must be just out of it, poor thing, practically allergic to animals the way she is.

The telephone rang a long time. I bet she's scared to answer, thinks I'm calling from the hospital. Let's see, how had I better tell her. I know, I'll go right to the source of her worry immediately, tell her that I am—

"Hello, babe? This is your loving husband, *and I am fine.*"

"What do you mean by that? Explain yourself! Are you hurt, are you injured?"

"No, no, the only one in trouble is the shark!"

"I was going to knock you unconscious with my heavy iron skillet!" said my wife, "but I was afraid it would just dent you and you would go anyway, oh honey, I called up Stella, and

we've been praying the shark would die—I was so afraid you
would get killed while we were in an argument and not on
good terms!"

"We couldn't have that!" I said to the flood of words, and
we were both laughing and hugging as best as can be done
on the phone.

Let's see, reinforcements. Wonder how De Nardo will
react when I call him in the middle of the night for a white
shark? "Hello, Dave? We got a great white shark down
here—can you join us to take it walking?" De Nardo was
sensibly cautious—I would have understood a refusal—but,
"I'll be right over," was all the taciturn Italian said.

Should I call Lindy? She wouldn't want to miss this. But
no, better have her and Pavlos and Jensen fresh for the morning. We'll be tired then.

It was nice in the little thatched-roof hut, with the light
and warmth and quiet and the cessation of movement. So
nice sometimes to just sit still. To lean forward, elbows
propped, throat in cupped palms, and listen to the hiss of air,
in and out of the nose.

Out the window I could see the darkened canal over which
the bridge led. On the other shore a tall lamp post rose, a
weeping willow beside it. The wind was shaking the tree, and
the light on the long rippling leaves made them look wet.

Movement in the water under the bridge. Too dark to see,
but it was almost certainly an escapee harbor seal out for a
moonlight stroll. Roly-poly little guys, like spotted teddy
bears with whiskers, and flippers with claws they would
WHACK! on the water to get your attention. "You, there, boy!
Let's have some fish over here!" They would get it, too. Ever
since they had broken out of Seal Cove, we had been feeding
them in the canal. At first we had hoped to recapture them,
but the chubby, round-eyed animals were quite competent at
escape and evasion. So, since they were used to interacting
with people and their boats (the reason they are named harbor seals), we just left them there and fed them. They could
have escaped to the ocean by swimming down the canal and

crawling up and over one short beach. But they had a source of food here, and they stayed, sometimes brazenly lolling on the decks of the boats in the repair dock.

As I walked back over the bridge to get ready for my next turn, I looked down at the water and smiled: You've got us where you want us, haven't you, harbor seal.

Keith Worcester, big shouldered, reliable. Always there when you needed him. He who had been first in the water with the white shark, who had seen the stretcher open and the great white shark swim out. "At first it was like my grave opening up," he had said later, "but then I saw she was in shock and needed help, and after that we were too busy." For four hours he had worked alone, before another diver or trainer was reached.

Just now, however, he had his fingers in his mouth. "What are you doing?" I wondered aloud.

"My teef' hurt," he said.

"Your *teeth?*"

"Yeah," he said, extracting the digits and frowning. "Reverse block. When I went down, some compressed air got trapped inside a cavity, and as I came up, the trapped air expanded. Now my teeth feel like they're about to explode."

"Well, what do you think?" I said, after musing on the humor of Keith's dental problems—delicious irony: go in with the star of *Jaws*, the most feared biter in the sea, and your teeth hurt!—"Is she gonna make it?"

"If she'll quit trying to swim through the walls," he said. "I had to get out once to get an air tank, and I heard a terrific *thud*—heard it clear out of the water. Guess she charged the walls."

"How come we're calling her *her?*" I asked. "Did somebody figure out the sex?"

"Yeah. You can tell by looking underneath, in her pelvic area. Short fins. The males have longer fins, called *claspers*, by the genital slit. Apparently the male inserts one of the claspers, like a penis, into the female's cloaca . . . But then nobody has reported seeing a white shark making love, I don't think."

Hard to imagine white sharks being lovable, even to each other. Scientists do know that tiger sharks give love bites to each other, rakes with teeth that leave wounds and scars as remembrances of the affair. Rough lovers. Rowdy from the moment of birth. One species, the mako, close cousin to the great white, even begin life by eating their brothers and sisters, inside the womb. First one out of the egg sac lives.

But then compassion and tenderness probably play only a small part in the life of swimming garbage disposals, which is essentially what the white sharks are. Predators like them ensure the fitness of the sea, weeding out the sick and the stupid, the crippled and the dying. Through nature's cold efficiency, the misfits are swiftly gobbled up by a hurrying shark.

We swam into the long night, the divers and the great white shark, and only one among us was built to swim forever. Our human arms and legs quivered with fatigue, and we sprawled on the bleachers of the dolphin stadium in between our turns, with the least-wet towels we could find pulled over us. Our bodies were tired, but our minds were excited. We wanted to sleep, but we could not.

I found myself mumbling in my mouthpiece as I worked with the shark. Come on, girl. You can make it. Be the first white shark in the world to survive in an aquarium. Everybody'd come to see you, see how pretty you are. We'd feed you good, too.

I remembered a story that Jim Mullen, the head dolphin trainer, told me, about a guy who stuck his arm down a white shark's throat.

The great white had been frozen, stiff and on a shelf of a walk-in refrigerator at another park like ours. The man got to thinking: what would it be like—the muscles were ice, so the jaws couldn't spasm and close down—if he put his limb in the maw of a great white shark?

His arm slid in just fine, over the angled points and down the gullet. Fairly tight fit, but no pain.

But what the poor fellow had forgotten was that white shark teeth point inward. When the shark's chin touched the man's armpit and he felt he had experienced the full sensation, he tried to reverse course and get his arm back. *He couldn't.* The multiple daggers dug in at the top of his biceps. If he jerked, the muscles would slice open.

Now obviously a man with a shark on his arm cannot live a full and useful life. But the park was closed, and it was late. Nobody to send for a saw.

But there was a hot-water hose nearby, which was used to wash the fish guts and blood off the floor. The man hooked his heel in the coil of hose, brought the nozzle to him, and turned on the faucet with his toe. He played a stream of hot water on the cheeks of the shark, and when they relaxed he got loose.

I wished I hadn't drunk quite so much coffee. Because my system was done with the several cups, and they wanted out. To pee or not to pee, that was the question. Whether to get out, cross the bridge and wrestle-hassle-tug the wet suit up off and down—or to relax and let Mama Nature take her course.

Not quite as barbaric as it sounds. Divers' wet suits enclose a thin but circulating layer of water (the reason they are called "wet" suits, as opposed to dry suits, which are water tight), and this watery conveyor belt can carry the answer out to sea. Divers are probably the only people in the world who can wet their pants on the job and feel good about it. It warms you up when you're cold. *Thermocline:* a temperature change in surrounding water. Normally, I prefer not to thermocline in my suit. The cloth fiber on the inside retains some of the fluid, and if you don't take the suit home and wash it, you can develop itching, redness, and irritation—diaper rash. Tonight, however, I did not care. Oh sweet relief!

The trouble with doing something dangerous for a long period of time is that you begin to take it for granted. The tiredness begins invisibly to take over, sending fingers of fatigue stroking through the muscles and the mind, graying you, stealing your judgment and depth of perception. Even the width of your vision seems to narrow so that you see only what you are doing and nothing more. Anything else that happens becomes an irritation—to be ignored.

So it was when the shark stick fell from my belt, and wibble-wobbled in a spiral to the floor. I watched it fall and hit and rotate halfway under the reef, where Fred and Ethel, the reef's two morays, lived. I should go down and get it, I told myself. I'm not like some of those other guys, they don't even bother to take the shark stick along.

I congratulated myself on my carefulness and forgot about the shark stick completely. I didn't think of it again until three o'clock in the morning, when the lights went out.

One second I was shoving the shark through the center of a pool of white light; the next: blackness. Floodlights, where are the floodlights? Then I remembered the darkened shower room and the earlier electrical problems.

Of all the moments in that long night, the shark took that one to change its mood. Oh, no, I thought as I felt the different stirring in the animal I held. Don't wake up right now. Go back to sleep. Be civilized. Wait just a minute. The lights will come back on.

I heard a meshing, clicking sound. SHHCLICK. SHHCLICK. As of the closing of fitted instruments. I knew it was her teeth because I could feel the vibrations through the top of her head. Her motion accelerated. Her tail ZWOOOSHED back and forth beneath me, striking my shins like a baseball bat. I lifted my legs, and the white shark towed me. Easily, in the vastness of her strength. The pressure wash of her increased speed buffeted me.

Then, with a sudden wrench of her body that numbed my right hand, the white shark broke away. I held nothing. I fumbled at my belt where the shark stick wasn't.

I settled softly to the floor, sidled to my right where I knew the artificial reef was. So nice when I found it, touching with my bare shoulder. I squatted, relaxed, tried to think like a rock: calm thoughts, nothing thoughts, thoughts that would send out no vibrations of fear.

Denied sight, I listened harder and noticed a deeper quality in the quiet around me. Normally a faint, virtually imperceptible undercurrent of motion noise pervades the liquid atmosphere, as the fish skitter to and fro about their business. Now only stillness. The fish were doing what I was doing: holding still, making no moves to attract a nervous predator. My back liked the ridges and bumps of the fiber-glass reef. I flattened still further against it, relaxing as deeply as I could. Only my eyes moved, under the mask.

Gradually, vision returned. Details, portions of things, quick studies in outline. The variegated surface of the reef. Spines, eyes and the opercular gill covers of the kelp bass nestled symmetrically next to one another, their bodies arranged to resemble kelp leaves, among which they hide in the wild.

Then I saw her: the white shark, in moonlight. She must have turned and circled the tank and come back. Now she was a creature of the wild again. So she had lived, and so she would die, for she was heading toward the wall, at speed.

Maybe she thought she was going home, to the endless deeps where the squid and the sperm whale fight, and no human would ever be her master. Or maybe she was just shaking off the grogginess of oxygen deprivation in the only way she knew, by swimming fast. There are no walls in deep water. But whatever was in her mind, she swam forward, fast, and faster.

She struck, and the impact shook her like a bag of water. She sank, and the moonlight was her grave around her. I swam to her and raised her, and presently she began to swim again, but I think it was only the habit engrained in the giant muscles, for she did not take independent action anymore. There was perhaps some flickering consciousness left, because she would flinch when the walls drew near, but her strength was gone.

In the morning light we could see the dying shark clearly, for the first time. She was beautiful, her skin a rich brown, fading to silver, and cream-white underneath. Her eyes were not pure black but tinged with blue: the eyes Death would have if Death were a fish. Her snout was pointed like the nose of a jet, and her body structured for the torrents of pressure produced by speed. Everything about her fit together. Even the rough denticles of her hide had a special purpose, for scientists think the skin sets up special easy-flow ripples of water for the body to glide over, so the shark can swim long distances with small effort. The mouth could open to the width of the torso, with extra folds of skin at the corners of the mouth and a dislocatable jaw—even a special hinge in the top and bottom middle of the jaws—to give yet more height to the bite. She was an animal built for battle, for she would go up against the roughest, toughest animals of the sea.

I touched her eye the last time I kicked down to be with her, but there was no response. No plastic-looking nictitating membrane flicked across: nor did she flinch away. We were giving artificial resuscitation to a corpse. Divers and volunteers would continue to try, but it was over. Jensen, Pavlos, Mitchell and others would continue, as long as a twitch responded, but they were wearing themselves out over meat.

The scientists took her carcass, finally, and trucked it back to Steinhart Aquarium. There they measured (7 feet 6 inches), weighed (350 pounds) estimated age (2 years), dissected, and determined the cause of death (blood clots on the brain, occasioned by repeated chargings against the wall) and barbecued and ate her. I am told she tasted like the finest swordfish.

As for me, I put on my clothes and went home. I fell asleep at the wheel on the way and was nearly killed when my car swerved into the path of a gigantic truck. At home my sweet wife helped me undress, but then as I turned the covers down, she pressed a glass of chilled orange juice into my hand. I yelped out loud and nearly dropped it. "What's the matter, are you crazy?" she said as I danced in pain. "Take it, take the glass!" I said, and when she did, I turned my hand over.

The pads of callous on the fingertips were gone. The red, raw muscle showed plainly, and it was to be a surprise picking up anything for the next few days.

I got cocky about sharks after that. For almost a year, if I could get anybody to say, "You swam with a *white* shark? Weren't you afraid? Weren't you in terrible danger?", I would answer, "I was most afraid on the drive over. And I was in greatest danger on the road home."

30

Killer Whale Love Triangle

Kianu had been educating Nepo in the ways of killer-whale love. Night after night the older woman orca enticed the adolescent Nepo: sliding her pectoral fin like feverish fingers across the young male's flank and sides: now wheeling to glide underneath and, as if by accident, brush his genital slit with the dorsal fin on her back. Sometimes the suggestive dance would be subtle, coquettish, delicate: despite the awesome majesty of Kianu's tons, she could control the very fabric of the water between them, weaving it into her spell: her length not quite caressing his, but for the molecules of the liquid element that joined them. At other times she would take a more direct approach, and simply seize his crotch in her killer-whale teeth—and tongue the opening.

But Nepo's genitalia remained undescended. Like a bored stud in a harem, he allowed Kianu to do what she willed: occasionally rolling on his back in the moonlight to expose himself more fully to her touch, as one might enjoy a massage from a stranger. But though the lips of Kianu's vagina pulsed pink and open, engorged with the blood of most fervent desire, Nepo encouraged her not.

For there was another, younger, female killer whale. *Yaka* was her name, and she was sweet as the morning. Gentle in temperament, graceful in form, a beauty of a mere 3 tons. Her blue-sheened eyes were warm and friendly, but with the hesitant question mark of virginity. She hung off shyly at the fringes of the killer-whale pool, and Nepo watched her, even as Kianu labored to arouse him.

Nepo began to break his gates. He would lean his massive domed rostrum against the middle of the open-weave stainless-steel door and push. The inch-thick bars would bend like a cartoon rubber door. It was unnerving for a working diver to look up from the Oceana floor-scrubbing and see that gate bulging outward. Nepo would insert his "nose" (not actually a nose: dolphins have no sense of smell, and orcas are essentially big dolphins) into one of the 2-foot square openings, and either swim forward or rear up with the power of a young whale testing his strength.

Once, incredibly, he snapped one of the inch-thick stainless-steel bars—broke it with his teeth. We wonderingly removed the gate (no small chore: with Nepo's black and white bulk netted away, the divers unbolted the whale-size gate from the wall, dragged the 20-foot stainless framework across the bottom, stumbling with our flippers and our numbers and its weight: to hook it up to a chain and a crane) hoisted it out, took it to the welder, who shook his head, and rented some special equipment. Ordinary welding fire won't melt stainless steel.

When the new gate was back and in place, Nepo smacked his pectoral fins (each as long as a man's double outstretched arms) on the surface with apparent glee—and then bit and broke the weld, which is supposedly stronger than the original metal.

It got to be a game for him, I think, to break his gate by various means. He became so expert that he could break the fastening at the top of the gate, open it, and be out in the main pool of Oceana in less than ten minutes. We'd have the gate repaired, we thought, and walk by the pool to internally congratulate ourselves, and there would be "Neep," upright in the outer main tank, fairly wiggling in his glee—and the gate half off the wall. Sometimes he would content himself with merely bending the bars so that the gate could not operate: or he might rip the expandable bolts out of the concrete cinder-blocking that was the wall. Leverage, intelligence, and mountainous strength.

The only way Nepo was stopped was when welder Jeff Hall seamed stainless-steel meshing over the openwork bars. The meshing prevented the young orca from getting a grip on the bars. He could still bend them, but that was not nearly so much fun as breaking.

But both the displays of strength and Kianu's amorous ministrations were only prelude to the emotional and physical storm that was about to rage among the three killer whales.

Nepo announced his sexual coming of age in the simplest and most elemental manner. Sculling on his back in the main pool of Oceana, he wagged an enormous erection at the world. Like a pink periscope, the yard-long penis broke the water, and Nepo proudly displayed the thigh-thick phallus until it lost tumescence and collapsed sideward like an emptying bag of water, when he sucked it back inside.

Kianu was, at first, ecstatic. She knew what that thing was for! With the greatest enthusiasm she would clamber onto Nepo, submerging him with her bulk, trying to fit their bodies together like a jigsaw puzzle.

But one half of the puzzle was unwilling. For while Nepo would occasionally allow Kianu some pleasure, his love was Yaka. She was the one he would leap for, caress, and lunge his mast-sprouting groin at. She would flee coyly, submarining around the pool so that a wave would follow 10 feet behind, smacking on the stage. Nepo would give chase gladly. Yaka, like all killers, had a little black triangle on the center of her white groin-fold. Like painted pubic hair: like a target: and Nepo wanted very much to arrow that target.

But when Nepo would attempt to mount, Kianu would try to smother the younger killer whales' union by the simple expedient of leaping up and falling down on them. Four and one-half tons of impact is enough to discourage most lovers. Not Nepo, though, nor Yaka. They would just wait and try again later.

The conflict deepened. Poor Kianu! Rejected more and more by Nepo, she turned her huge head back and forth distractedly between the young male she loved and her rival. Then her gaze fixed and hardened, focusing on the slender killer form of Yaka.

There would be trouble eventually, that was certain.

31

The Shark Nobody Knows

~~~~~~

As we examined the bite the big shark had made, it occurred to me how little we actually knew about seven-gills. Fishermen knew to watch their fingers around even the smallest hooked brown shark with that characteristic broad head; swimmers crossing San Francisco Bay have reported the approach of too-inquisitive 5- to 8-foot shadows; biologists like Ed Miller of Steinhart Aquarium have made tentative beginnings of research on *Notorynchus maculatus*. But we do not even know if the sharks with no front dorsal fin give live birth or lay eggs.

"Step behind the shark—kneel behind it for a size comparison," I told Reid Dennis, a diver short in stature but muscled like a miniature Viking. He knelt behind the dead seven-gill on the asphalt and grinned for the picture.

Weeks earlier, Reid had helped Steinhart Aquarium collector Walt Schnebele, with Eric Hurst, Dave De Nardo and myself transfer thirteen seven-gills from the aquarium's truck to our reef tank. I remembered how even the smallest seven-gill had arched back, reaching its white thorn teeth for the collector's hands. The short length of shark had writhed when Walt handed it to me; it had felt like a sandpaper-covered wrestler's leg.

"Put your hand on the back where the front dorsal should be," somebody requested of our kneeling model, and the camera clicked again as Reid blinked into the sun.

I remembered how the big stretcher had looked, lowering down to Reid and me in the flume entryway to the reef. The canvas had bulged and moved, from the living weight of the enstretchered shark. "I'll pass him out the entryway," I said to Reid. "You be underwater with the shark stick in case he turns around and comes back on my legs." "Far out," said the obliging Reid and crouched down under the chest-deep water. As I opened the moving stretcher and slammed my hands down on the back and the top of the seven gill slits of the animal inside, I wondered what it would be like to have your leg torn off by a shark. Some said there was no pain, only shock; others reported excruciating agony. I did not want to find out for myself. But as I shoved the big shark out the doorway and lost him from my grip and sight—horror! Impact rocked my leg! I kicked furiously with what I hoped was not a stub of knee. Something dark rose before me, and my fist was back to punch—oh. It was Reid. Mask askew, mouthpiece out. "I jush wanted you to move back a li'l, was all," the normally crisp-dictioned diver slurred. Oops. Sorry, Reid.

"Open the mouth," somebody asked, and Reid complied, levering the end of the snout up gingerly, for a shark can always bite. Even dead, the jaws can reach and snap and sever. "Look at that!" a bystander said, not talking about the teeth, whose thorn and leaf design is unspectacular but efficient, like a power saw. "The eye!" As the jaw opened up, the white/gold/black eye disappeared. Not behind the crocodilelike nictitating membrane many sharks possess: no, the eyeball vanished inside, vanishing back into the cartilaginous skull of the dead shark so that a white, apparently empty eye socket showed. Evidently this protects the seven-gill's eyes when it bites something that fights back.

We had first noticed this peculiar property of seven-gills when Lindy and I had cleaned the windows, the day after the arrival of the seven-gills. I was safety for her, as Reid had been for me, and it was a nightmare. The reef was alive with the living shadows. There seemed more than just the thirteen thick-bodied, lazy-moving hunters. Everywhere we looked was a shark approaching—or passing by. The white, dead-looking undersides, with the inverted U-slash of mouth, with an oval of gap in the middle, like white corpse lips just beginning to part. They approached us casually, as if we did not matter. Side to side to side they slowly came, along the wall, directly at us. "They're wall-circlers," Keith pointed out later, but we did not know this then. To us they were just inexorably oncoming sharks, and I had to reach my brush to their heads and guide them around our bodies. Their eyes sucked in, disappearing as the brush bristles approached. And one, the biggest, made a sideward gesture of the jaws, like "Get that thing away from me," and veered, 6 inches over, so the implement wouldn't touch him, but still he gave us no space as he went by. His chest fin brushed my leg.

Some people think the escaping convicts from Alcatraz Island may not in fact have made it to the mainland at all: but instead had traded the hellhole existence of the old prison island for a swift execution in the water.

There was no speculation (except as to motive) about the attack on Norval Green. The Steinhart aquarist had been force-feeding a 2½-foot-long 16-pound seven-gill when the little shark broke away, whipped off, raced back, and tore into the diver's defensively upraised forearm, ripping out a chunk. It did not eat what it had taken but spat out the piece of human meat, which was later dip-netted out and, happily, surgically reattached to diver Green. A week later, the seven-gill died. Dissection revealed a broken jaw. Was that the reason for the attack?

The jaws that had taken the bite from the shark before us now were obviously in perfect working order. The limp seven-gill stretched on the asphalt was effectively eviscerated. For all intents and purposes, the guts were gone: intestines and genitals missing in a 15-inch vacancy of flesh, perhaps a quarter of the shark gone in that one horrendous bite. The half-moon of taken flesh nearly bisected the animal. And the sides of the cut were smooth, neat: as if the meat had been frozen and sawed.

I could not help noticing how the diver's flexed and folded knee would have fit easily inside the bite, with a couple inches left over on the sides.

32

The Robber Bird, the Harbor Seal, and Mother Swan

Until the robber bird came, Mother Swan had two fine, large, ungainly chicks: bundles of grayish-brown, large-boned fluff with the promise of future power showing in every awkward wingfold and joint. Like the teenage giant whose hands and feet are too big for him just now, but who will grow into them one day, the baby swans would add feather and width and muscle until they matched their mother's snow-queen majesty. Or rather, they would have.

One of the things I like best about Marine World is the casual, almost automatic way in which wandering birds are cared for. When Smelly the Peli(can) waddled in, squawking raucously, Mary Rose the bird lady was immediately hospitable with a bucket of whitebait fish, which Smelly engulfed with his hook-ended beak until the distendable neck pouch under his chin bulged fat as a shoplifter's purse. The fire-haired bird lady wasn't trying to catch or exploit the pelican: he was just hungry, and she fed him. He came and went as he pleased, demanding food as if he worked here.

When the sea gull with the 6-pack plastic wrap choking his neck showed up, at least six people made various attempts to catch the gray and white bird, to try and get that death necklace off. It was just a 6-holed, translucent petroleum-product beerholder but the gull had somehow wedged its neck through a double loop of the wrapper, and unless it came off, the bird would starve. We offered fish, small gold-and-white silver smelt, but the cautious gull would flutter on the edge of flight, and we couldn't get close enough to swoop a net over it. We left the fish, though, and as we backed away, the gull picked one up, tossed it, flipping with the expertise of long practice, so that the smooth, cool head would glide down first—it stuck. The two loops of never-degradable plastic, wedged in tight against the streamlined directional flow of the feathers, squeezed too tight. The gull could not swallow. It tried and tried, but had to keep spitting the fish out, even when we replaced it with the smallest findable whitebait, no longer than your little finger and half as thick.

Growing wary of our approaches, the gull hopped to the awning of a roofed tour boat tied up at the repair dock. We tried to follow with a long net pole, but the gull edged to the farthest point of the awning and half-raised its wings—we had to back off, or it would have flown.

But that evening, Kevin Walsh, a new seal-whale-dolphin trainer with kinky hair and mischief-loving blue eyes, settled in for a long stalk. Pole in hand, he climbed lightly into the first of the several tied-together tour boats. The big, foam-filled rubber rafts—the kind that are used to traverse the raging Colorado River—swayed gently on the canal, just a few feet from the dive locker porch where I watched. The gull on the roof of the tour boat saw Kevin's shadow through the awning.

Bird reflexes reacted. The gull fluttered, hopped, was airborne—our hearts sank as it rose, doomed to slow death by starvation; it settled, on the forwardmost edge of the last tour boat.

Kevin's eyebrows raised twice, rapidly, at his audience on the porch, as if to say, "Don't worry, I got this sucker!" Then he gave himself totally to the pursuit. Moving his weight with infinite caution, Kevin progressed slowly from boat to boat, coyly, mock disinterestedly, as cleverly as ever cat stalked bird. I sucked in a shallow breath as the trainer's feet and legs transferred over to the last boat. The sea gull raised one foot. Kevin ceased.

The gull moved back from the edge of the awning, out of the human's line of sight. Kevin waited, five minutes, hoping for the gull to hop back where he could see it. The gull hunched white wings, Feather tips tentatively tested the still air. It was going to fly.

"To your left, Kevin," said Ron Swallow, and I realized the soft-eyed vet-tech-assistant was standing beside me on the porch. "A little more," he guided, as the gull's beak swung toward us. "There." The net hunter poised; the gull flew. Kevin whipped the net backhand, up where he could not see. He'd snared one flapping wing and half a neck, and I was leaping over the railing and down to the dock, my hands up and wrapping net over, pinioning the body and head.

Seconds later, scissors snipped, and a sore-throated gull fed and flew away.

But I could do no more than stand and swear, when the skua gull swooped down. The skua, or jaeger, or robber bird, bolted down from the sky like a hawk. I had never seen one before and would not know what it was till years later when I saw one killing an infant penguin on a TV special. But there were no penguins here.

Only two baby swans, swimming in the reflection of their mother. They must have felt perfectly safe until the air hissed and the brown streak snatched the farthest chick. I could not tell whether the baby struggled in the beak or claws of the robber bird; the attack and flight took place too swiftly: one motion, no hesitation, just impact and escape and the mother swan going half-mad trying to get airborne quickly, white wings beating the water—up, but too late. The skua, which had looked like a pterodactyl when it took its prey, had become a dot in the sky. The mother swan would have had to abandon the other chick to pursue the most-likely already dead first. She flopped helplessly down, screaming.

But she could not grieve long. For in the lagoon there lived another predator, deadly as a shark to water birds. Fishermen tell of sleeping gulls knocked suddenly from the wave where they rested, a rough snout lifting them up before great teeth sheared. There was a harbor seal in the lagoon that hunted that way too. I had seen it at work.

A duck, a green-headed mallard in its prime, raced furiously down the green stretch of lagoon arm—and a shadow raced beneath. The flash of white beneath the duck's wing showed and disappeared fast as machine gun fire—PO PO PO PO PO—but fast as its takeoff speed was, the harbor seal underneath was faster, or at least as fast. The bulleting seal was playing with its dinner. Just as the duck's forward momentum lifted its breast from the water, the light gold head of the harbor seal flashed up, and the mallard disappeared.

A second's shocked silence, and the duck popped up again, dashing off in the opposite direction, with the harbor seal more clearly seen now, swimming on its back, the powerful pulls of its clawed swim-fin arms sending it along as fast as a bird through air. Just when it seemed the duck might have a chance to escape, the harbor seal reached up. The surface of the suddenly empty lagoon went slack.

When the harbor seal rose, its round eyes shining innocently with the pleasure of the kill, the feathers and blood still sticking to its muzzle, I knew I had only witnessed an act of nature. The seal had a right to a duck dinner the same as I. I put down the rock I had picked up to throw. The harbor seal fastidiously cleaned itself, combing feathers from its whiskers with its claws.

But law of nature or no, I would have interfered if I could between the seal and its next intended victim.

The mother swan sailed regally beneath the bridge where the harbor seal hung around. Her long neck was curled in that graceful arc that has inspired so many figurines. Her baby struggled along behind, trying to look dignified like Mother and not entirely succeeding. The head of the harbor seal poked up. The whiskers flexed at the corners of its face. Silent as a snake, the seal slipped under and wove its approach toward the smaller figure. I have swum underneath ducks before and knew approximately what the predator saw as he approached the two swans. The webbed feet pulling busily, vigorously, no nonsense, down to business, their motion entirely contradicting the serenity of the head and back and folded wings above. And the heavy breast of meat.

The harbor seal no doubt picked its target on the little one just before their paths collided. The neck, probably, so the seal could snatch and break and kill and run, ending the struggle quickly so it would not impede the getaway. One crunch of the needle-fanged jaws was all it would take.

But there was another neck involved here. And as the 80-pound seal made its move, Mother Swan went into action also. Her gorgeous snowy neck, looking bigger around at the base than my two hands could have enclosed, drew back like a forearm: her beak became a fist, and she *beat* that harbor seal. WHAMWHAMPECKPOW! She attacked the head and squinching eyes of the astonished would-be chick killer, and he fled for his life, with Mama Swan hot on his madly fleeing tail. If swans could talk, I bet the kid would have said, "Hit him again, Ma!"

And ever after that, if you had wanted to get a photo of the swans and the harbor seal in the same picture, you would have had to use a wide-angle lens.

33

Shark Kill

~~~~~~

The kelp bass trembled, spasming back upon itself as if, by touching filamentous tail to green-spotted head, it could rid itself of some internal agony. Cancer, probably, for the pinched-in belly almost met the backbone. The white growth would block the throat so no food could pass, and the fish would slowly starve. I had seen the throat blockages before, and they were as ugly and substantial as the calcium buildups at the base of cave stalagmites.

All I could do for the suffering bass was end it, whip a gray canvas feed bag over the fish, drag it out, and slam its head against the deck: a quick cessation of pain. And even that small mercy was an exceeding of my too-limited authority, for the park had a new policy now, regarding sick fish, and I considered it a bad one. We were supposed to leave dying fish alone, "give them every opportunity to recover," until they expired. But I had seen enough fish sink into the hopeless spiral toward death; I knew what the bending spine and palsied trembling meant.

But if I was hindered by regulation, there were those in the tank who were not. Even as I watched, a brown shadow moved in. With both confidence and caution the seven-gill shark approached. Its muscular brown body, patched with black rosette spots like leopard paw prints, wove a balanced pathway in, around, away from, and returning to the kelp bass on the floor. The spots were about the only similarity between the seven-gill and the timid little leopard sharks;

220

their safety was in nervous, jittery speed: but the seven-gill was in no hurry.

Almost as in a dance, a prearranged, mutually-agreed-on series of patterned movements, the killing proceeded. Did the kelp bass dart away when the seven-gill's figure-eight of movement crossed nearest? It did not. When the sinuous coiling brought the partners close and a dark pectoral fin almost tenderly reached out, as if to caress the scaled side, could the kelp bass run or defend itself? It could not.

Carefully, gingerly, with deliberation, the seven-gill yawned its mouth around the cancer-starved fish. I saw the white teeth, like rose thorns above, and triple rows of hook-edged leaves beneath: erect, projecting, the snout flesh seeming to pull back from them. The white thorns and leaves tapped questioningly on the back and belly of the bass: anything? But the defense mechanisms of the fish no longer operated. It did not, or could not, stiffen the sharp fin-spines on its back, to stab. Normally it could roll and poke, and the slime-covered spikes left nasty, slow-healing wounds. But now, nothing.

Delicacy stopped. With a terrific sideward shaking of its head, the seven-gill bit the kelp bass in two. Almost. For a thread of tough belly skin still connected the head and carcass the shark was swallowing to the tail that flopped back and forth almost in rhythm, as if to drumbeats.

I became aware that I was getting too hypnotized by the scene before me. A muscle tightened in the back of my neck, in the place where science fiction writers theorize a third eye might once have been. I don't know about that, but there is something especially sensitive about that area, where the spine and the great pipes of blood and the brain stem intersect. It tingled, and I spun, and the biggest shark in the tank was where he had no business being.

A broad brown head filled my field of vision. No more than 6 scant inches separated us. The mouth, which looked wide enough to take my shoulders in, had just begun to yawn. I flopped back, yanking my head away and knees up to kick, but the eye of white and gold and black had already turned away.

The shark moved on.

For now.

34

Stuck in the Mud

~~~~~~~~~~~~~~~~~~~~~~~~~~~~~~~~

The closest I have ever come to drowning was in a shallow canal I could have stood up in. A good jumper, with a run, could have cleared the distance separating the two platforms, the farther of which floated on perhaps 4 feet of water. That was the easy one.

My job was to go underneath each of the two platforms and locate and secure sixteen bolts. The bolts fastened a framework, which supported a rope ladder connecting the two platforms. The idea was for little kids to swing across from bank to bank of the narrow arm of the lagoon. Beneath them would be a plasticized canvas mat, or bag, so that if they fell, they would land on the equivalent of a water bed, in the new action-involvement Whale-of-a-Time-World playground. It was a good idea.

When I first ducked under the far, floating platform, I had the blissfully ignorant notion that the whole problem would be concluded in two hours or so. How long could it take to twist on thirty-two nuts? Of course, I didn't know exactly where the thirty-two bolts (sixteen per framework) were, they being buried in a kind of white, hard, flotation Styrofoam. But I had a heavy screwdriver and a hammer, and by running my fingers over the foam till I found a faint unevenness—and occasionally popping up to get a generalized idea of where the bolts started down from topside—I was able to chisel out and secure the first platform's bolts in a mere 4 hours.

The second platform rested on a bank of mud. I poked a length of wood doweling under the square box of wood, Styrofoam, and bolts, and the rod went in clean for 2 or 3 feet, and then I had to use force. It came out slowly, covered with bluish-black, stinking mud. Ughh. It was going to be a long afternoon. I did the first four (those I could locate easily by placing one hand on the top of the bolt and fumbling underneath for the slight bulge of the stainless shaft), nutted them, climbed out, showered, called Jeannie, and went back.

I closed my eyes as I went underneath. There was absolutely no vision under the raft anyway, and it was easier to concentrate relying on touch, rather than waste energy trying to see through mud.

A clear demarcation separated the murk from the actual mud. When I thrust my hand in, the mud was puddingy, then stiffened as I pressed further down. I had had some faint hopes of being able to kick away the muck, but no, this stuff had texture. Solidity. It clung to itself.

Experimentation taught me to press up next to the ceiling, or floor of the platform, and kick and wiggle my way backward, drilling out a tunnel with my shoulders and in-pulled head. I would wriggle awhile and fumble awhile, till I thought I had something that might possibly be a bolt. Pulling the hammer out from my belt and the screwdriver from my sleeve, I flaked away at the hard-pack foam. THUDTHUD-THUD. Short arcs of hammer motion, and not much power behind them. Difficult to get momentum in such a short swing, and also the hammer was finding my fingers as often as the butt of the screwdriver.

The mud creeping in through the mouthpiece did not taste particularly bad, but I disliked the idea of that filth invading my mouth. I tried not to think about the seals that swam down this way and the sea gulls that rested on the water. The smell made forgetting difficult, as its dank aroma labeled it precisely what it was. Liquid fertilizer. A chafe was beginning between my upper thighs, from all the accumulating hours in the wet suit, and I hated the thought of the mud working its way up the legs of my suit, all those germs coming in contact with the raw flesh.

I was not altogether happy as the day vanished into twilight, and the shadows lengthened into night. I thought about sex, and that helped for a while, but even that can only inspire a man in the mud for just so long. By ten o'clock the laughter had died out of me, when the large man in the gray business suit showed up.

I recognized him by the split between his teeth. It was the only one in the park bigger than my own.

Mike Demetrios, president of the park. Normally I would have been both slightly awed at the presence of the Big Boss and irritated at myself for feeling so. Mike was always polite, even friendly in a tentative way, but still he was the man who could fire you or give you a raise. I am an American, and a member of Earth, and I don't like to think of any man as not my equal, but still . . . I would watch what I said around The Man.

But tonight all I could think was here I was in the mud, and there he was in his suit and tie. The mud had leached my strength away, and the cold had taken my body's heat. I shook inside my wet suit, and I was not yet done.

"How are you doing?" Mike Demetrios asked. How do you think I am doing, you son of a bitch, I muttered in my mind. I'm dying down here.

"I'm fine, Mike," I said out loud.

"That water looks cold."

"It is."

"Look, I've got something in my car . . ." The president of the park turned away. Didn't even finish his sentence. Couldn't even conclude a short conversation. Nice to know how important you are to the man on top.

I pulled myself out on the dock. Walked, leaving filthy, stinking footprints all the way across the park. Picked up two more tanks of air, for the job that had to be finished tonight because Whale-of-a-Time-World opened tomorrow. I loaded the air tanks on Lindy's little wagon and dragged it back. I could not remember having ever been so tired. But I was almost done. Just two more bolts. If I was lucky, I wouldn't even need the last bottle of air. I hooked up the hose adapter to the tank, put my hookah harness on. Damn these little chest straps that always swing out of the way when you reach for them. I half-slipped, half-fell off the low platform edge and worked my way laboriously under, trying to make my shoulders dig out the first of the last two tunnel increases.

There used to be a body builder, Ellington Darden, who would take his workouts in a pit of mud. Just filled up a vat with good clean fill, soaked it with a hose till he thought it was ready, and hopped in. He'd move his arms back and forth, claimed he got a terrific workout from the mud's resistance. We all thought he was a little crazy, though he did have a great build, but I could see what he was talking about now. My elbows were tight to my sides, my hands were crossed on my chest as if waiting for someone to come with a lily, and my shoulders felt as if they had only enough strength left to tremble after struggling against the mud.

When I was a kid I used to have a nightmare about getting my head caught underwater. Same dream, over and over. I would be swimming in an underwater temple, white pillars and broken columns in clear, pale green-tinted water, and I would suddenly find my head imprisoned under a great smooth disk, like a featureless marble wheel. Probably it was only the pillow that incited the dream, but to this day I can remember the struggle to breathe, and the shaking horror when the nearness of dreamed death woke me up at last.

So I felt I had almost been in this place before, when I realized suddenly that I could not move my upper body. But, no, what am I worried about? That's been a problem all along: I can just kick free. But—nothing was happening down there, either. I could feel my feet wiggling in their swim fins, but that was the extent of it. As I tired, I had made the tunnel narrower and narrower, grudging each fragment of expended strength, and now I was wedged tight. I felt buried.

Ridiculously, I tried to sit up. Stomach muscles knotted and pulled as if they would come loose from their moorings, but of course I was not only cocooned in mud but underneath a substantial platform.

I was only a foot of mud and platform away from the air, but if I could not wriggle out, people topside would have no way of knowing I was in difficulty. And in the dark, they would not even see when the air in my tank ran out and the bubbles stopped. They might even think I had finished, and gone home, left my gear here until the morning. I tried to rock back and forth; couldn't. Make noise? Nothing they could hear. I relaxed for a moment, freed my mind, let it spin for a little, to then bear more fully on the problem. It didn't help.

Then I imagined the silt drifting silently across my still-exposed fins, sticking out in the free water. How long would it take for the sifting-down stuff to cover my feet, after my struggles had ceased completely?

No. This is ridiculous. I am not going to stay here. I do not even like it in here, I thought to myself. I am going to get out.

I pressed my right thigh and buttock against the mud wall that held me and pulled with the outside of the pressing leg. There was an increase in the sucking glue sensation of the semisolid liquid earth around me. Nothing else. But I was in no hurry. I had no other plans for this evening. I was willing to persevere.

Transferring my attentions to the other leg, I tugged with hip and thigh and side, causing a definite sludging suck against the sides of my face and mask.

What if my mask came off? To have that stuff in my eyes and nose? Didn't know if I could stand that. Might go crazy, writhe around, lose my mouthpiece, breathe mud, and my arms all pinioned. How would they dig out my body? Shovels? I imagined one of the shovel edges biting into my shoulder flesh. I tilted my head forward, what inch or two inches I could force, and fought.

The sideward-pressing edges of my thighs burned, exerting an energy I had no right to expect and didn't want. I desired only relief from pain, to not exert anymore. Was that an eighth of an inch progress I felt, an infinitesimal loosening of the grip? Yes. Truly, and I "walked" with the outsides of my thighs, a quarter-inch, an inch, until with a reluctant SLUUSHSHLUUP my body tore away, and the mud held dominion over me no more.

I broke free, into the black water of the wider section of the body-dug tunnel. I kept right on going, out and up, bursting my muddy hood and mask into the moonlight. There was Herb Reed, my semibald supervisor, tapping his foot in the moonlight. He would be there till the work was done, but he wanted to go home. So did I.

Nothing for it but to finish, to go back down now, before I could think up a few more reasons not to. I fell back on my side, that being the easiest way to get under. This time I widened the tunnel, going in at the edge of the old too-narrow one, ramming and wriggling and hating, if such a dull, energyless emotion can be given so dignified a name.

When I finished there was nothing left for a feeling of triumph or exultation or even relief. Just the job was done. That was all.

I rubbed the loosest layer of mud off underwater and then lifted my head, mask still on, and could faintly see two figures, blurred by the mud on the lens. I pushed my wet suit hood back and wiped the crud off my forehead. Then carefully pulled the mask out away from my face so the stuff wouldn't fling in my eyes—the metal clips that fasten the mask straps pinched my hair. The sudden pain on top of everything was such an unfairness I nearly sobbed, and I would have, if I had been alone.

Demetrios was talking to Herb, and Herb had a bottle in his hand. A flat bottle: wide, brown. Looked like expensive stuff, I snarled in my mind, as Herb raised the container and sipped, delicately. I must have made some small sound, because Mike turned and saw me.

"Oh," he said as Herb handed him the bottle. "This is what I wanted to get you from the car." Oh. "I don't know if you're a drinking man or not . . ."

"If I wasn't, I would start tonight," I said as I flopped on the deck. It took some effort and calculations to get to my feet. I had never realized before how many transfers of weight there can be in a simple maneuver like standing up.

Now while not "a drinking man," I am not averse to a little libation, and I brought some small experience to the task at hand. The bottle was heavy when I received it, considerably lighter when it was returned. Once I thought I saw the muscle of Mike's shoulder twitch under his coat, as if his hand had started to rise, but I certainly did not wish to scorn his gift and decided I must have been mistaken. I turned a bit and continued to swallow, and I believe I left a little slick in the corner of the container. Apricot brandy, I remember it was, and it went down like nectar.

"I don't think I could have done what you just went through," said Mike, and the words added to the glow in my belly.

Few things in life have given so much sheer satisfaction as that jolt of apricot brandy and those words. They made the long trip back to the shower room and the long, *long* shower, positively—bearable.

35

Confrontation

The skin of my exposed forehead tingled that cold New Year's Day. And the rush of my bubbles seemed an unfriendly roar in the chill green waters of the giant reef aquarium tank where the seven-gills lived. Even the air behind my mask smelled flat and dead—probably just the air compressor filters need changing, I told myself, trying to ignore the impinging evidence of all my senses on January 1, 1979.

The little leopard sharks, fifty or sixty of them, traded places nervously on the floor below me. These miniature predators were sometimes meals themselves, to the larger eaters in the tank. Several of the small, shadow-dappled sharks bore hideous red slashes, raw meat showing on their sides, where seven-gill teeth had closed but not quite caught. They did not always escape. The little fragment of leopard shark tail I had found drifting softly in a current one day told me why the leopard sharks were so alert and why their movements were such an accurate barometer of the tension in the tank.

I could see the kelp bass hiding, arranging themselves like leaves, as if there were kelp forests in the tank. Some, more adaptable than the others, crowded beneath an overhang of the reef formation, as though they were expecting rain.

Even the tough little garibaldi, California's poppy-gold state fish, seemed to be flitting ever nearer to the hole it ducked into when circumstances required.

Like a baker who can smell the bread about to burn before

230

it does, I knew there was trouble building from the moment I first set suction cup on window and began to scrub. I just couldn't believe it affected me.

The sharks and divers had been getting along so well. They evidenced little fear of us, barely bothering to alter their swimming course around us as we scrubbed the windows so that a rough-edged fin would often brush a wet-suited elbow and occasionally a human head might lift and bump into a scratchy stomach passing over. Which was terrifying the first few times it happened, but as the brown sharks with the black rosette-marks invariably flicked away immediately thereafter, we soon concluded no threat was intended.

We had in fact begun to treat the sharks with a measure of patronization, posing swimming close beside them for macho photographs and occasionally reaching out fingers to touch their smooth-rough sides. Sometimes they would make an irritated warning half-slash with their jaws, a seven-gill reminder to watch your manners, but as no one was severely chastised, we soon grew very confident, around the things with teeth that did not bite us.

So I concluded it was an accident when the first shark hit me. A sudden ram in the side of my calf knotted the muscle and woke me from my dreaming. But as I saw the neat outline of the 5-foot seven-gill race away and then turn and circle back, an ugly suspicion formed regretfully in my mind. Was this the beginning of something?

When I was a child, I saw a comic book cover depicting a shark and a fourteen-year-old boy. The kid had a work shirt on, so had clearly fallen in, and there was a dock with friends standing on it in the background. But the boy's eyes were not on them. The muscle on his neck connecting jaw to chest stood out as his head turned, and his eyes were on the brown back and dorsal fin in the water just behind him. There was no hope of immediate rescue; his only option was to fight. The comic belonged to a neighbor; I never found out what happened, and I always wondered: Did the kid have a chance?

Even when the medium-length seven-gill returned, cruising back toward me, I reasoned this could still be just an investigatory checkout. He'll smooth on by once or twice, look me over, and then go away, I told myself.

WHAMFLOPSTRUGGLE impact on both sides of my head as another shark seized and shook it while my elbow lifted and punched the shark's rough belly, but it had already let go. I jammed my back into the 4-inch recession of the window and tried to see everywhere at once.

Before me were the seven-gills. I don't know how many were involved; it seemed that everywhere I looked was something swimming: lean and sinuous and hungry. Gone was the zombielike slow-motion patrol: the sharks swam now with an alert, purposeful, prowling attitude; as different from their former endless, aimless glide as asleep is from awake.

And among them swam the biggest shark in the tank. Even in their interest the smaller sharks did not forget to make way for him. I had seen the quick sideward snaps he would take at them when the opportunity arose; but they did not bite at him.

I had a strange sensation of being spotlighted, as though the attention of the entire tank was focused on me and what was about to happen. People were looking in from the other side of the windows; most likely they would assume they were watching a regularly scheduled show. And even if they did understand, there was nothing they could do. The fish, too, seemed to be appreciating the finer points of a free entertainment, even as I had observed them, in their life-death struggles. Tomorrow they might strain nerve and sinew in the desperate attempt to kill or escape; but for now they had only to watch and enjoy and, with luck, help eat a loser.

I turned the handle of the short brush around, so I gripped the flat-backed head, and the handle protruded from my knuckles like a derisively raised middle finger. Then things began to happen, very fast.

The 5-foot shark came in at my legs, where they kicked against the wall. I bent and poked him, hard, on the top of his desk-solid head: his eye sucked back down the white tunnel into his skull as he bit at the brush. He whipped away, recircled—and then I could give him no more attention.

The biggest shark in the tank came along the line of the windows. He was 8-feet long, about as big as the species gets, and the head so wide I could see the reason why another name for seven-gill is broadhead. He could eat a fat hole in a dead whale, or anything, with a head that size. I remembered the dead seven-gill, and the size of the bite *this* shark had taken from it; nothing else in the tank could have removed so huge a gnaw. Shark, shark, shark, shark, the side-to-side weave of his advance seemed to say, and the slashing inverted U of his ugly mouth extended far down the underside of his head. I thought about the teeth that would show when that mouth opened up: like sewing machine needles, dripping down.

He veered 6 inches to go around me. Maybe he might even have changed his stupid, ratlike brain and called the whole thing off. I'll never know. I felt hunted, and I got too nervous.

I kicked him just as hard as I could. My knee lifted in the narrow space between us. My hip rotated, and my foot shot out. It would have been a great kick if it had had space to fully extend; but he was too close.

The fin tip folded as it caught the seven-gill in the side of the head. I felt the impact of my curled-back toes against the rough hide and muscle and the cartilaginous joining of the jaws. Then the teeth snapped around, and for one icy instant I thought my lower leg was gone, that the meat would be raked off or bitten through. But incredibly the jaws clopped *above* my shin as the seven-gill went crazy, exploding in a whipping frenzy of speed that defied my eyes to follow. If he'd hit the surface at that speed, the vehemence would have flung him in the air.

For a minute I thought I had killed him. The kick had been muscled by undiluted terror: could I be witnessing his death flurry?

No. The frantic motion ceased. The heavy-bodied shark

came back. No. No. I had given him, I knew, the hardest kick I could throw. All I had to offer was more of the same. If that wouldn't do the job of discouraging him, then—the gills? The eyes? I thought about the defense mechanism that protects the seven-gill's eyes, and I had the feeling of an exhausted boxer who has just flung his very best punch, and it connected, and his opponent smiles. I would keep fighting, but . . .

The gold eye of the brown shark drew nearer. The black pupil in the center of the eye may have reflected me.

And then the creature moved on. The longer upper lobe of its heterocercal tail flexed softly and diminished, as the shark resumed its rounds. Probably the incident that had bulked so large and important for me was already being forgotten by him.

I counted myself, noting delightedly—and incredulously—that I still had all my limbs. Actually, of course, the attack had ended as do the vast majority of shark aggressions, with no damage done on either side. Jacques Cousteau and his divers have swum with virtually every species of shark in Earth's ocean, and as the man I regard as a father to all divers said: "Sharks can be handled." And Ron and Valerie Taylor, perhaps the greatest shark photographers in the world (they did the real white shark footage for *Jaws*, among other films), have filmed, cageless, inside the feeding frenzy of the big oceanic blues. They had to fight—the maddened sharks were biting at anything—but they emerged unwounded. Even the kid on the comic book cover had a chance, if he'd kept his calm and remembered his work boots. Very likely he could have kicked off even a determined medium-sized shark (most sharks are around 5-feet long) until somebody on the dock thought to throw him a line.

The mood in the tank was broken. Tension fell from the water, as pollution is washed from the sky by rain. Peace returned. The seven-gills remembered their endless perimeter patrol: the little golden garibaldi reasserted itself farther from its sheltering hole in the reef: the kelp bass unstrung themselves from their imaginary kelp. Even the timorous leopard sharks settled in nervous herds upon the floor, to pump their gills and wait and watch.

But even so, I thought as I turned back to the algae on the windows, from here on in I think I will give all sharks a little bit more respect.

36

In the Feeding Frenzy
of the Moray Eels

~~~~~~~~~~~~~~~~~~~~~~~~~~~~~~~~~~~~~~

"Feed him to the (belch) morays," the purple-lipped emperor said, reaching for another grape. "No, no!" objected the proposed eel dinner, wriggling (rather feebly, I thought) in the grip of the grim-faced guards. But the ruler of ever-declining, ever-falling movie Rome waved a bejeweled hand, and the slave was tossed, to disappear screamingly under bubbles and catsup and rubber moray eels.

If it had been me, I would have asked for the execution to take place around Christmastime, when the water was cold and the eels (if they were like the ones at Marine World) would not be interested in eating. You can take a bucket of feed squid then, up on the walkway behind and above the moray eel wall tank, and throw it in, all at once or in handfuls, and all you'll get is bored. The beady, unblinking blue or yellow eyes will take no notice, even as their favorite meal lands on the sand before them. Divers would most likely have to go in and retrieve the food, lest it rot.

In summer, however, meals provoke an entirely different reaction. Then the enthusiasm is not unlike that of a shopper given ten minutes free access to the meat department.

I had been scrubbing the eel tank windows, I think, at the height of that summer when I heard a soft plopping sound, much like the *shloop* a raw egg makes when dropped onto a cold skillet. Rain? I wondered idly. Must be a summer shower because now the noise came in clumps and clusters, like—handfuls. Strange, though: the sky had been clear blue and the air hot when I went in. I had almost not worn my wet suit top.

Something white and tentacled drifted down before me, as I squatted lightly on the floor, in the middle of the eel caves. A squid. No. Nobody would be fool enough to—WHOOSH. No mistaking that. A bucketful, flung in all across the surface.

WHIP! The pale body of the octopus-cousin disappeared, replaced by a grinning eel. The heat of the summer water exploded into violence. Everywhere shadows rushed at the falling squid. There was no neutral corner for me to retreat to, for every corner was alive.

The thing to do was go home, leave the party quietly, without attracting undue attention. I pushed off the sandy floor with great control, restraining the urge to attempt flight.

A brown length arrowed for my arm. I had just time to think: It's going to bite me, when the narrow yellow-brown head lashed onto the elbow joint of my wet-suited arm. I felt the whack of impact and got busy with both hands and two swim fins, kicking and clawing. The body I scrabbled against was no longer soft, but hard in exertion like a flexing, living ax handle. Our faces were close. I saw the tiny bulblike nostrils and the black spot of gills.

But the thing on my elbow did not like wet suits, and our relationship was a brief one. It let go, ess-ing off after more cooperative food, and I broke the surface. Above me was a startled-looking man with an empty gray feed bucket. I will not tell you what I said to him. But I was just going through my list of descriptive adjectives for the second time when a tug at my heel reminded me where I was. There was a manila rope (for a ladder) hanging down into the water at the opposite end of the tank from me, but I did not bother with it.

If you go to the eel tank, even today, and look up near the

top left-hand side, you will see some holes in the fiber glass molding: ragged-edged openings that do not match the neat roundnesses of the intended eel caves. Those are my holes; I made them that afternoon, in the unscheduled feeding show. Their installation was rapid, thorough, and required no conscious effort on my part.

My skin was untouched. But there was a new flap in the rubber at my heel, and the heavy wet suit bore deep-sliced incisions at the folding of the upper arm, as if razors had slashed in. A sixteenth of an inch deeper, and the double arteries—where they pulse blue at the bottom of the bicep—would have opened.

Behind me the surface of the eel tank boiled, as forty yellow, brown, Hawaiian white, and greenish-dappled morays frenzied for the food the daydreaming feeder had dumped in.

With this background you will appreciate, I think, that I was not altogether delighted to be told that all forty of the moray eel tank occupants would have to be captured.

"They're mostly underneath the floorboards," my cheery informant said. "You'll probably need a flashlight."

37

Eels in the Dark

Under the floorboards of the eel tank was a place that morays liked and divers didn't. To us, the space between the decorative floor and the true concrete bottom was a low-roofed nightmare. I had been down there once, retrieving a workman's dropped wrench that had somehow fallen between the fiber glass and concrete walls. I knew, from that well-remembered visit, how an eel face looks when lit from beneath by a flashlight beam: like a Halloween mask you wouldn't allow your child to choose.

But what amounted to claustrophobia, snakes, and fear-of-the-dark for me was a virtual convention hall to them. Eels *like* small places. Being poor swimmers, they do not venture far from cover. They can corner unbelievably, whip-reversing in their bodies' length of space; and they can jump out with invisible speed from a coiled position. But they do not feel comfortable in open water, where any substantial shark or turtle can run them down and lunch on them. They also seem to have poor vision, so lightlessness does not affect them adversely. And they may even enjoy each other's companionship (we have no way of knowing).

Trouble was, under the floorboards the eels were not visible to the public. The artificial caves, widemouthed pipes for the eels to pull back into, were largely untenanted. Five or six of the smaller, perhaps least-statused morays kept lonely vigil in the upstairs apartments. "Not many eels in that tank," a disgruntled visitor might have thought, having no guess as to the number of *gymothorax mordax* (Latin for the majority of our eels' species: meaning "naked breast, inclined to bite") that writhed and sprawled just a few feet below the level of sight.

Management decided to remove and replace the cracked floor of the eel tank: both to bring the eels up into display, and to install a new filtration system.

The eels would have to come out. Or, when the new flooring was installed, the workers would be wading in water thick with as many morays as Ali Baba had thieves.

But, we reasoned, maybe we could catch the eels without having to go underneath with them. They were frenzying every day when their squid was dumped in (this being summer), and they all seemed willing to leave their basement socializing for food. So, we'd have a big net waiting and maybe scoop up the whole tangled, slithery, blindly biting boil?

Fat chance. Even in frenzy, the eels had more fish smarts than we gave them credit for. Five or six of the younger, smaller, more naive animals fell prey to our scheme, but the others watched and learned, and we caught no more eels by that method.

So Larry Ropa and John Pipkin turned the red handles on the water filtration pipe maze, and the water level of the tank began to lower, being sucked out into the lagoon. There was no worry about the eels being sucked out too, because that had happened once already. A moray had swum too close to the suction line, got pulled through the baffle somehow and chopped to pieces by the impeller blades of the pump. Pieces of the unfortunate were discovered all through the filter panel. After that, the eels apparently labeled the suction line a predator and stayed well away.

Too soon the sand on the fiber glass facade bottom glistened damply in the drying sun, and I could think of no further excuses to put off going underneath the floor.

My booties gritted and slipped, down the sand-and-algae covered rungs of the ladder at the corner of the moray eel tank. Down, behind the wall, beneath the floor, I clambered.

A strange, uncomfortable world awaited me. Brown twilight: the shadows seeming only deepened by the shafts of sun through the floor above. So would light on the floor of a hallway appear, if seen through the bars of a cell.

Keith Worcester bent his head beneath crisscrossed, dripping beams. A flashlight dangling from his hand penetrated yellowly into the murky water around his knees. But I could not see what interested me most.

"Keith!" I said softly, "where are the eels?" I stayed on the ladder. I am polite; I would not wish to step on any.

"They're hard to spot," he said, and I cringed at the loudness of his voice. It seemed as if we should whisper so as not to disturb them. "Got to watch where you put your feet," continued Keith. "This *light's* no good to us; just makes it harder for your eyes to adjust." He switched off the beam. I could understand the logic in what he had said, but emotionally I missed that little light, like a link to civilization.

Studying the brown water underneath the rungs until I thought I could see to the bottom, I stepped off. Wading, I slid my feet rather than picked them up, so that I would hopefully push any eels I met, rather than accidentally crimp somebody's tail.

"See? There's one."

I couldn't see it at first. But then, in the algid muck around our lower limbs, a slightly darker twist of shadow moved in our direction.

"I got a system," said Keith. "You hold the bucket." I reached for the big gray feed bucket floating beside us, but the metal handles clicked, and I jumped, and the eel switched directions, rippling, ess-ing, side to side off to our left.

But the catchpole reached out, and the noose dipped before the fleeing eel, who unaccountably swam straight into it. Keith yanked the noose tight, and the brown water foamed. "Watch yourself now!" Keith said, though why he said this I do not know. I was not bored. The writhing, whipping coil on the end of the stick had my undivided attention. I held the bucket out, arm's length away from my face. The bucket was half full of water and heavy. Suddenly it was heavier and splashing.

Keith dropped the catchpole, snatched up a dripping white towel, spread it over the gray bucket's mouth. "I had one jump out when I was bending over the bucket," the powerfully built diver said cheerfully. "Now I use the towel, and they quiet right down. Good system, huh?"

Wonderful.

"Let me do one now," I said, more to get away from the bucket than anything else. "Okay, but you've got to pull the noose supertight. You'll feel like you're hurting him, but if you don't he'll just flex right out, and we'll have to catch him again."

One hand on the pull rope that led to the noose, the other gripping at the balance of the pole, I strained to see in the semidarkness. There, the moving line. "Put the noose in front of him," said Keith. "He thinks it's a cave." I did, and the eel did, actually altering course to go inside the noose.

I yanked the rope, like socking a hook in a fish. Violent vibration, and I reared back, the eel furiously out of water.

"Watch it, Keith!" I said, and I should have listened to myself because I rushed it. As Keith extended the bucket, I let the eel on the end of the stick get too close to him. With an audible SNICK the end of the eel with the teeth passed through Keith's thumb. "Ouch," said Keith. A statement, not a shout. I pushed the stick with the squirming passenger through the towel on the bucket. Keith set the bucket down, whipped the cloth out from in between the two eels, and covered the whole thing over.

His thumb, beside and behind the nail, was split as if a sword had cleaved it. The calm fella separated the pieces of the thumb and held them upside down. "Good to let it bleed, get the infection out," he said, as the crimson digit dripped.

If only he had said something like "GODDAMYOU STU-PIDIDIOTWHYDON'TYOUWATCHWHATYOU'REDOING?!!," it would have been bearable. But that's not Keith's way.

When he returned from the nurse, his thumb all bandaged, sending out rays of guilt like a lighthouse, Keith said thoughtfully, "Now I've always got something to remember you by."

"That's what friends are for," I muttered weakly. "But I don't want you to feel bad about this." He paused. I waited.

"Because even though I will be carrying a horribly disfiguring scar for the rest of my life—at least I haven't lost the use of my hand. Unless of course gangrene sets in," he added, holding up the flashlight to the hugely padded white thumb.

"And even then I understand *amputation* is almost always effective." Keith's way is to remind me about it, for the next twenty years or so.

I went after another eel, to escape.

The rest of the catch went almost smoothly: for us. For the eels it must have been terrible, as they fought and squirmed and slashed at the thing around their middles. They must have thought they were about to be bitten in two.

The biggest eel, close to 6 feet long and thick as the top of a weight lifter's thigh, tied himself in a knot, head through the loop of his body and tail, trying to squeeze off the noose. And a good thing, too, because we had a tough time getting most of him in the bucket as it was. But strangely, once his head was in darkness, with the towel across the mouth of the bucket, even the most powerful moray shut down, like a parrot with a dishcloth over its cage.

We caught eels for hours, passing the catchpole back and forth, ducking our faces close to the water as we crawled underneath the lower crisscrossed beams. Keith kept me informed of the progress of the infection throughout what appeared now to be his entire limb, and for no particular reason, I stood at the back by the wall and shone the flashlight—up.

I sucked in breath. Nearly screamed.

A moray, dangling. Eyes and yawning open mouth, teeth like slivers of broken glass. Dried up eyes and dead. It had got pinned in somehow, between the fiber glass and concrete wall, struggling toward the water that had drained away, leaving it to suffocate: strangle: drown in the air.

We had to break the fiber glass to get it loose.

After a great deal of effort on many people's part, the last glop of liquid algae and water was vacuumed and bucketed away, and a new floor built. A beautiful floor. Lovely to look at and useful as well. White sand glowed on nylon mesh, on plastic squares and cedar framing. The water circulated cleanly through the sand and nylon mesh.

The water was turned back on, and most of the eels brought back from the bathtublike tank they had been temporarily residing in. Some few were poured into the big reef aquarium tank where they hurried into and under the hollow-walled imitation coral mountains, and a few were released in a newer exhibit, a smaller tank at the far end of the hall.

Which leaves roughly two dozen morays, all sunning themselves cooperatively in the visible half of the old eel tank?

Well . . . not exactly. Because you see we fixed the floor, but not the walls. And you remember those holes installed in the upper-left hand corner of the tank wall, installed by a certain retreating diver? The morays remembered them too.

There's always a handful of eels to be seen: yawning and puffing their black gill holes out, occasionally taking a nip at the tail of a too-presumptuous little leopard shark and occasionally meandering across their territory, for they've learned there is no danger for them there.

But the majority of the morays you still can't see. Because they're back in the walls and underneath the floorboards . . . in the moray eel convention hall.

38

Kianu Attacks

~~~~~~~~~~~~~~~~~~~~~~~~~~~~~~~~

The sheer enormous strength of killer whales makes their anger terrifying. And even when playing, their exuberance can
easily look like something more serious than normal frolick-
ing. Once, by way of irritation, fun, or strength demonstration, Nepo lifted Yaka out of the water. Chris Pavlos, trainer,
diver, and sculptor of whales, saw it happen. "Yaka was
floatin' on the surface," the curly-haired trainer said of the
young female orca, "and Nepo just dipped his snout under
her belly and heaved. All of her came out of the water except
a corner of her tail flukes." Pavlos's artist-sensitive black eyes
widened, in appreciation of that prodigious power.

The almost immeasurable might of the killer whales made
the delicacy of their love nearly unbelievable by contrast.

Once, early in the morning, even before the peacocks had
begun to call, I sneaked up behind the sloping valley of
bleachers that overlooked the killer-whale pool. Whale student David Baynes had told me that between 4:30 and 7:30
A.M. was the best time to observe the killers in independent
activity, and I had come in hopes of seeing the orcas at play.

What I saw surpassed my wildest expectations. A pano-
rama of killer-whale emotion spread before me! Hate, frustration, rejection, savage sensuality, humor, and gentle love.
On one side, blocked from the others by stainless-steel mesh
and inch-thick bars, was Kianu, raging. Again and again she
smacked her left pectoral fin hugely against the water.
HNNNnnn! HNNNnnn! she vocalized. Her vast back hunched,

more of it out of the water than usual, as if in tension she held more breath and buoyancy. She trembled along her whole arching length, and her head nodded sharply again and again, in the orca threat of violence. By both size and age she was the dominant whale, and by every indirect means at her disposal, she sought to intimidate the others. But Yaka and Nepo were of the age where romance recognizes no danger. They swam on their backs together, fluid as seals, the black-white markings on their bellies, chest, and groin like rocket ships about to take off. Yaka nuzzled nearer, rubbing the back of her head on Nepo's white acreage of chest. Yaka rolled, and the mood accelerated as she softly bit his neck. Her pink tongue extruded slightly, and she ran it down toward his genital slit. Nepo responded. A pink object burst out and upward from his groin, and Yaka—teasing woman that she was!—suddenly shoved downward, submerging Nepo's passion under tons of cold water.

She ran, and Nepo gave chase, vast shapes submarining beneath the clear dark green, and the waves of their passion inundated the stage. Nepo nibbled on the fleeing tail before him, and Yaka coquettishly smacked him in the chops, a blow that would have flattened you or me but which served only to titillate Nepo's desire. The up-and-down motions of their black-white tails were like the opening and closing of doors on a sunny day.

Nepo leaped as if to say: See how mighty I am! And, truly, he rose as a building rises, seeming in slow motion, for there was so much of him. And Yaka right behind! The two giants lifted, vertical against the sky—and when they fell back, it was in thunder, BOH-WHOOOM.

Yaka stood on her head. Nepo, his pink flagpole now to half-mast, attempted to consummate his desire, turning upside down in the water too, lunging at the moving target. The genital slit would move 6 inches to the right or 2 feet the left, and even the proudest of killers cannot make love too effectively upside down and half in the air.

Nepo pulled off, sulking. He even made a halfhearted little

CLOP! snap of his jaws at her—Yaka was instantly contrite. "Aww, c'mon, don't be mad!" I could almost hear her saying, as she reached out with her graceful tail flukes, hooked an edge around his dorsal, and pulled him back. To her. Nepo held out for at least 6 seconds. Yaka stroked her black pectoral fin languorously along his back; Nepo rolled on his side.

Their groins reached for each other and caught, connecting with obvious pleasure: drumbeats, lightning! A slow-motion no-hurry pairing of whales: pumping, thrusting, grinding in wet smoothness.

AAAAANX! AAAANX! The ugly noise of the peacock grated. Nepo's dark eye lifted and saw the sexually signaling, tail-displaying, raucous-voiced bird and a janitor named Larry Macomber, a tall man in sneakers, leaning to drag a length of fire hose into the stadium, to spray away the dust of yesterday's spectators.

The lovers disengaged, and I went away to write my notes. In a way I was glad that Larry and the peacock had disturbed the peace of the morning. Because while I could not, would not have taken my eyes away (one does not get a chance to see killer whales making love every day!), still I did feel vaguely ashamed of myself, as though I had peeped into a neighbor's bedroom window.

And behind the bars of the killer-whale gate, Kianu clomped steam-shovel jaws, in helpless rage. Kianu, who, even if she turned away from the gate, could not escape the sounds of the killer-whale lovers discovering each other. Kianu, 9,000 pounds of adult female orca, who had to endure the agony of seeing another with Nepo, whom she loved, and who had rejected her. Kianu, who now exercised in the main pool on alternate evenings from Yaka, with whom she could no longer be trusted.

Only in the shows did the trainers feel they could exert enough control to prevent Kianu from doing damage to her younger, and now victorious, rival.

And there came one day when there was no control at all.

o o o

"I could see Yaka taking her attention away from the stage," Chris Pavlos had recalled. "She drifted back a few inches from her station, and her eyes went to the gate of K.'s pen. And when the announcer got through with his spiel . . .

"LADEEEZ AND GENTLEMEN: FOR YOUR ENTERTAINMENT AND EDIFICATION, MARINE WORLD PROUDLY PRESENTS . . . THE WORLD'S LARGEST FEMALE PERFORMING KILLER WHALE—KIANU, THE MAGNIFICENT!"

The air pressure gate rrrrr'ed up. Yaka shifted uneasily. Perhaps she heard something the trainers did not.

Kianu did not even wait for the gate to fully open, but raced out the widening space on her side. Her eyes were the color of blood.

Kianu's normal entrance was designed to show her grace and majesty: a racing leap, her ink-black vastness accentuated for one beautiful instant against the painted Arctic backdrop. Then she would thunder back down in a whopping smash on her side—WHOAWHOOOOM,—and, the momentum of her first charge broken, calmly join the others at the stage. This time she neither leaped nor put on the brakes.

The water hissed as her fin tip ripped across the surface in a wide arc. Her tail flukes pumped power on both the up and the down strokes, instead of the usual rest on the up stroke, push on the down; and like a maddened submarine, 9,000 pounds of accelerating killer whale *rammed* full into Yaka's side.

Yaka could not dodge. No time. As the muscular skull rammed into her, the smaller female could only partially deflect the terrible blow, weaving like a boxer and fighting back. As the rostrum buried into Yaka's side, the smaller cetacean's jaws reached open, in agony and in antagonism. But Kianu's thumb-sized teeth were already busy, raking side to side, scoring inch-deep bloody gouges. For a terrible few seconds they fought: kicked and hit and bit, disappearing under a tangling welter of whale bodies, impact, and foam.

Yaka emerged from the foam and raced about the million-gallon arena which had suddenly become too small. As Yaka fled, a deadly bigger shadow raced behind her and tried to cut her fleeing circle short.

And Nepo, the cause of it all? At first, the young male stayed discreetly aloof, hanging by the stage, rolling an eye up at the sky as if about to comment on the weather. But, as the hunt continued into cold clarity after the blind and all-consuming rage and Kianu tired, Nepo's massive black torso with the characteristic pale "saddle" just back of the dorsal fin, began to get in the way. Unobtrusively, the black truck-door pec fins would flex at just the right moment to scoot him back, to hamper Kianu's pursuit so that she must either ram him or go around.

Kianu screamed and threatened, but she could not find it in her heart, even now, to attack the male she loved. She veered and chased around him, still determined—but again and again Nepo interposed his bulk between the two ladies who loved him. He could not (by killer-whale custom) dominate the elder female, but he could passively resist, and that is what he did, placing his too-desirable orca body repeatedly in Kianu's screaming path, interfering, slowing, damping, defusing. By the time the trainers could get nets in the water, Nepo had the situation pretty much tamed down.

But had the first explosive ram damaged Yaka internally? Granted Yaka's sides were sheathed with muscle: still, Kianu's domed rostrum had struck like a swung wrecking ball. Anxiously the trainers kept watch in the following days. Yaka moved stiffly. She had pain: It showed in her eyes and in her body's moves. But she did not pass blood; she did not stop eating. Soon her body language revealed the end of dis-comfort. She returned to her usual charming self: eager to play, delighting the people with her leaps and crashing bows.

But Kianu was infinitely more damaged. For this last at-tack had ended hopes that her increasing aggression toward Yaka could be trained down.

Kianu had to be locked away. The trainers kept trying,

hoping against reality, searching for a way to ease her pain. But I believe whales are as deep emotionally as humans; and no amount of fish or affection could make the great orca forget.

Jeff Pulaski, the young trainer who had once done a dolphin show by himself (swimming through the hoops when the animals refused to perform), tried to spend five personal minutes an hour with "K.," as the trainers called her. Wherever he was in the park, once an hour he would run to Kianu's pen and talk and do small things with her, trying to let her feel loved. Sometimes it seemed she was responding, as when she raced along the wall with Jeff running topside. In those moments, she looked happy as a young dolphin. But the largest member of the dolphin family (for that is what killer whales are, giant dolphins) could not escape her pain.

And finally, when the young trainer tried to ride her in the main pool, she threw him off and chased him out. Would she have hurt him if she had caught him? No way of knowing. Killer whales, from every scrap of research we can find, do not attack human beings in the wild. But trainers have been yanked from stages and detained underwater before being let go. Dave Worcester, husky brother to Keith the diver, still has scars on his knee from where Nepo dragged him down. Even there, of course, the whale acted with obvious restraint, for it would have been a finger-snap exertion to crunch through Dave's leg, and the orca did not. He merely held and let go, and the damage was incidental and unintended, as might happen if we cupped a butterfly inside our hands. The delicate antennae might be harmed despite our carefulness.

Denied even the solace of performance (the stimulus of their naturalistic leaps and bows and chases, buoyed by the roaring affection of the audience, which killers appear to enjoy, leaping just a little bit higher in shows than in practice), Kianu lost pleasure in life. Barely bothering to eat, she stared in leviathan loneliness at the blank walls of her pen. Sometimes when the trainers cranked her gate up, to let her have the larger volume of sea in the main pool, she would not even bother to go out. The trainers tried to stimulate her, running her through shows without an audience, just for the activity of it, but often she would not even respond to that.

I wished we would let her go. But even if I could have unlocked a door to the open ocean and set her free . . . "She would just starve," said Patrick "Bucko" Turley, his whiskered face broody and withdrawn. "She is too old and out of shape to start all over again in the sea. Muscle tone's not sufficient to chase dolphins or sea lions anymore. Only way something like that might work would be if they penned off a big empty harbor somewhere, that had seals or dolphins or a lot of fish in it, and give her just enough bucket food to keep her hungry and force her to try to relearn to hunt. And that would cost a ton of money—more money than our park could ever afford. As you know, the park has lost money (like all zoos) every year of its history so far, and one year we lost a million bucks. No way could the park afford that, to let her loose, even if she would survive, which I don't think she would."

So Kianu stared at the walls of her pen, and I feared she would go insane.

39

In Memory of Ernestine

~~~~~~~~~~~~~~~~~~~~~~~~~

Ernestine lay softly across the tops of my feet as we sat together in the night. Dark clouds, fat collections of mist, overhung the sky so that I could not see the stars. It was almost midnight. Time to do a respiration count, I thought, and reached carefully from my half-wet chair, across the beautiful dolphin with the scarred fins, nestling so quietly between my shins and the plastic liner of the portable pool.

Watch in hand, I waited for her to breathe. This was the third week she had been ill. As her kind would have done for her in the wild, we were watching her around the clock, keeping her upright in the water, lest her blowhole slip under and she drown.

PUHAAIP, she breathed, so slowly it seemed three separate operations. Puh—aaa—ip, exhale, inhale, close of the blowhole. I counted the seconds. Five, six . . . PUHAAAIP. Twelve seconds between breaths. I continued the count for three minutes. The pattern remained constant, five breaths per minute, which fact I duly recorded in the notebook on the table beside the pool: "5 resps pm." Anything else? Oh yeah. A small clump of green semiliquid matter floated beside her lower body. I scooped a sample up in a paper cup, in case the vets wanted to analyze it later. And wrote, "bowel movement, green, stool runny in texture," before dispersing the rest with a wave. There wasn't much to dissolve away.

"You better start eating, sweetheart," I said out loud, returning the notebook and watch to the table. How I hated to help force-feed her, straining her jaws apart with towels so the vet could tube-feed the white predigested fish slurry directly into her stomach. She looked so miserable when it was being done to her. She struggled, but weakly. Even the breath from her blowhole was not the clean air of a healthy dolphin but a graveyard stench. Rottenness. Decay. Death.

"But you been this sick before and come out of it, Babe," I reminded her, remembering the terrible blight of erysipelas which had made bubbles on her dorsal and flukes and when the blisters had burst they left holes. She had been almost perfect before, her delicate, multishaded gray skin so clean and fair; only one scar marked her, on her lower mandible a thin vertical line where she had tried to beat a closing gate and missed and split her chin. Now she was seam-edged where the wounds had closed; and her dorsal had a piece missing, a half-moon chunk gone, as though a shark had bitten it out.

She was still beautiful, even now, with her eyes closed and her body so strangely still. I dipped my hand in the water and stroked wetness over her, lest her warm skin dry. In the day we draped wet towels along her length past her blowhole, and there was a little homemade awning to keep her from sunburn.

"Boy, we been through some great times, haven't we, Ernestine?" I said, feeling the need to talk and not knowing what to say, as at the bedside of someone the doctor has shaken his head about. I remembered the time she'd saved me from a beating up by Lucky and the catch where she had broken my eardrum. I had never been mad at her for that; it was in a fair fight, and she had given me every warning in the dolphin vocabulary before turning loose on me.

Dolphins hear astoundingly well. I remembered once I had tried to sneak up on Ernestine in the petting pool.

It was early, and there was almost nobody else in the park. I heard the dolphins splashing from afar, and I thought: I wonder if I could surprise them. I had tennis shoes on, and you know you can walk very quietly with rubber-soled shoes.

I worked at it, setting each footstep in place with only a gradual addition of weight, never letting even the faintest vibration jar a warning to the folks in the pool. I crouched so they couldn't see me and duck-walked with legs wide so the fabric of my pants would not rustle against itself. Almost giggling at my own cleverness, I huddled at the low wall beside the pool. The dolphins stopped and listened. I neither moved nor breathed. Then about a gallon of water came over the wall to my left. Another wave splashed over to my right, and for some reason I thought about the artillery practice of lobbing a shell forward, then behind, then one right on the money—WHOOSH. A substantial portion of the pool leaped up and drenched me. Soaked to the skin, I rose and laughed and swore, and you'll never convince me those dolphins weren't laughing too.

"Hey, remember the time you got old J.B.?" John Benner, the Guamanian who loved animals so much, had been helping catch the dolphins in the lowered waters of the petting pool. And Ernestine had decided she did not wish to be caught that day, and even in the ankle-deep water where she had no maneuverability at all, she kept us hopping. One vigorous lift of her head suddenly up between my legs darn near prevented the possibility of further children for me.

J.B. was angry. This wasn't reasonable! We were not trying to hurt Ernestine, and she should know that—she had been in the park long enough to know that divers and company did not catch dolphins to be mean! "I am going to embarrass you, Ernestine!" said J.B., and he shook his big finger as he waded over toward her. I had seen J.B. embarrass Cyrus, the giant Steller's sea lion, and it was a sight to see the brown colossus cringing away from the round-faced man's finger-wagging lecture. He could never be cruel, J.B., but he felt toward "his" animals as a man should feel toward his children, and he would give Ernestine a good sound talking to.

Ernestine lifted her head and watched J.B. come. Now some scientists say dolphins can read people's emotional states by spraying them with sonar clicks, which bounce back to the dolphin and tell them of the human's hormone levels, and other emotional indicators, like X rays only with sound. I don't know if this is true or not, but Ernestine sure acted as if she knew what J.B. was up to. Her whole body posture read "mischief!" from the lift of her head to the arch of her tail, and if dolphins could wink at their pals, she would have.

She let J.B., wagging his lips and that admonishing finger, walk smack up to her, and then she kicked his feet right out from underneath him. Neat and clean and swift as you please so that J.B. sat down heavily and his mouth was an astonished O. Ernestine observed him, and her smile looked more than just muscle and bone formation. Like, "You were saying, J.B.?"

Ernestine. Sometimes when I scrubbed the grotto floor she would come and lie on the floor beside me. I would stop scrubbing, and we would do nothing together. In the classic book "Kinship with All Life," John Allen Boone movingly describes how he and the great German shepherd dog Strongheart would go together into the mountains and sit on the edge of a cliff and stare off into the blue eternity of the sky. Their thoughts soared so freely that the artificial barriers of labels disappeared from in between them, and they were no more man and dog but two lives together, experiencing the universe.

Once, through Ernestine, I experienced that "kinship with all life." I had been wire-brushing a long time and was tired. But it was healthy fatigue, the kind that makes you sleep well at night and become strong. And something more. For physical tiredness appears to increase the emotional sensitivities for a time, as if the troubles of the day become too much hassle to worry over and the mind is free to forget the past and the future and to truly listen to the present.

I heard a sweet warble, like birdsong. I didn't think I had ever heard it before or noticed it, anyway. Nothing like the normal clicks and squeaks and buzzes that go on around and on you in the dolphin tank (you can feel the spray of sonar clicks sometimes, when the dolphins emit their sprays of sound-dots, and they bounce off the back of your neck: a little like the sensation of a feather stroking your hairline, and the tweet-tweet trill was . . . pretty? Warm? Inviting?

Ernestine was before me. She arched her head and shoulders a trifle to the side. Like most species of dolphins, Ernestine as a bottle-nosed dolphin had no neck (the top two-thirds of tursiops' spines are fused), so the motion was a little stiff, but still it looked inviting, like a head-jerk "come on and play." No hint of head-nod threat.

Still I was hesitant. Lucky was still alive then, and I didn't play with Ernestine very much. The dominant dolphin had stopped me on several occasions when I had flown too long with Ernestine, hanging on to her dorsal while she raced me about the windows and the walls and the silver mirror surface—CLOP! He'd pop his jaws just once, and Ernestine would ditch me, flicking my grip away with a toss of her slender, powerful torso, and Lucky would give me The Look as his lady friend rejoined him.

So I ignored Ernestine until a thick short beak side-butted me in the elbow joint. Huh? I looked up, into the confident, large eyes of Lucky. Was I being ordered out of the tank? It didn't feel like that, but . . .

I left my brush upon the floor. Hurriedly unbuckled my belt and slid off three weights. As they clunked on the bottom, I kicked up—and flew. Some happy thought persuaded me to bring my legs together in the kick named after these great fliers of the sea, and as I aligned my arms along my side and kicked as one long unit, suddenly all four of the dolphins were beside me. Above, below, touching my arms on the right and the left. I felt the warmth of their bodies as they swam, slowly, at my pace, five lives together, Ernestine, Lucky, Spock, Arnie, and myself, four dolphin faces and a man's in the middle, kicking sedately around the tank as if we'd done it all our lives. Like notes in the same song. I had never experienced such peace and power. As if all great deeds were accomplishable: barriers existed only for the breaking or the leaping over, and love was the strongest energy of Earth. We were one blood: the dolphins, the sea, and I.

Ernestine peeled off, and I chased her, with not the slightest fear of being misunderstood, on this day. Just out of reach, she so easily glided, serenely on her back, her gray-white flukes waving bye-bye like the hand of a child in the window of a car. I pulled after her with all the swimming power of my body, hooking my hands against the blue and yanking with forearms, tricep, deltoids, latissimus, leg-roaring through the water, reaching hugely, surging—but just out of reach she so easily glided: accelerate the pace how-so-ever-much I would.

I stopped when want of breath made me stop and huffed and puffed my overheated engine: and Ernestine radiated a warm laughter that did not sting: did you really think you could swim with me?

We rejoined the watching others and soared, like happy dancers in a dream. I knew when they wanted to go up for air, and we all did, the dolphins fanning out smoothly to the side, breathing through the hole at the back of their heads without the slightest disruption of their underwater ballet.

All too soon it was over. Lucky ended it. Whipping easily in front of me, the king dolphin sank his tail down, as though he stood. He clopped his jaws, softly, just once. As though he too regretted that it must end.

I settled reluctantly back to the bottom, and my scrubbing of the floor once more. . . .

But if I had to choose one dolphin memory to warm me as I grow old, it would be the day I took my daughter in, to swim with Ernestine.

Desireé Don, then two and a half, wore a red and yellow Hawaiian-print swimsuit, with little ruffles on the seat. Her mother wore a look of fixed anxiety—her baby going in with all those *animals*! Despite the fact that Roman had hugely taken up residence in her tummy, Jeannie waddled swiftly around the pool's perimeter. "Watch out!" she called, "Be careful! Ooo, oo!" and other advices.

As I slipped into the water, shielding my baby with elbows and forearms and hunched shoulders, I realized I was being stupid to take a chance with her. I did so want her to know dolphins, but—Arnie was in the pool.

Arnie. The dolphin we called the hit man, or assassin, because he was the only dolphin I have ever known who would deliberately set up a diver for an attack. Other dolphins inflicted violence on us, but after warning; they would increase speed, nod, snap their jaws, but Arnie could fake me out. He would deliberately trick me, falsifying his body language so I could not "read" him, even playing with me for several minutes until my defenses lowered—and then WHAM! He would charge, ramming with his rock-hard rostrum, raking with his eighty-eight white teeth. Once he cracked several of my ribs for me so that I walked like a complaining Quasimodo for a week or ten days: and another time he gave me a bite-scar on my left hand to match the one I got from Chopper. But even after I had learned he was capable of such deception, still he worked the same maneuver on me on several occasions because I just couldn't accept that a dolphin would do that! I would keep one hand on the wall, and everything was fine. I must have been mistaken that other time, I'd think. Arnie would slide along beside me, his muscles all relaxed, perhaps even presenting his smooth stomach to be rubbed. But as soon as I released my grip on the escape route and committed myself irrevocably to the water—he would beat me up again.

But I figured if worst came to worst and Arnie attacked— and I did not think he would because dolphins are above all else curious about new things—I could shield Desireé with my body and just absorb whatever damage I had to until I could lift her out.

Ernestine came rushing over. Just for a second I thought fear, but no, her attitude was that of any matronly hostess, bending over a baby carriage. Her gray snout edged inquisitively close—but not too close, as though she sensed I was a little nervous. She seemed to understand the situation perfectly. This was my little one, the young of my species, and no threat whatsoever was presented or called for. Introductions were in order, and as I said, "Hello, sweetheart," and reached out a tentative hand to stroke her (while my gaze remained fixed on Arnie, cruising in the background) Desireé said "Hello, sweetheart" and reached out her tiny, soft-boned hand.

I heard my wife suck in breath from the side of the pool. But Ernestine could not have been more courteous and considerate. She allowed the touch of the two-and-a-half-year-old's fingers, only squinching her eye shut when a wandering digit digressed too close. For a moment or two, perhaps longer, they enjoyed each other's company.

Arnie rammed me in the right buttock: there where the muscle cups and the hip socket operates. Bone met bone, and it wasn't a comic kick in the pants. But I couldn't swear or say *ouch*, or Jeannie would think I had lost control. "Things might get rough here, we better get out," I believe I said, and Desireé screamed and started struggling because she did not want to get out.

I kicked for the wall, covering my daughter, thinking about my spine exposed to Arnie's ram. But Ernestine was there. As she had done once before, against Lucky, she stood between me and a bull dolphin's wrath. She shot beneath the surface and said or did something to Arnie, because I saw the arc of his charge veer off, and he surfaced on the far side of the tank from us, and *now* that dolphin did not trouble to hide his emotions! He snapped his jaws and nodded his head and made slashing noisy motions with his teeth and in general acted very frustrated indeed.

And to this day my daughter remembers the kindness and courtesy of the dolphin lady.

Memory faded. I remembered where I was, several years later, and in a shallow portable tank with Ernestine, who now kicked softly against my legs.

"Do you want to go swimming?" I asked, straightening carefully so as neither to put pressure on Ernestine's sides nor to push the chair legs into the plastic liner. Ernestine's swimming motions were strange: weak, but determined, and with a peculiar rhythm I did not remember ever having seen before. I leaned and helped her out into the deeper center of the pool.

But when I let my hands off the sick bottle-nose, and she had to open her eyes to navigate, she looked around her, and stopped. Her brown eyes closed again. She rolled over on her side and would have sunk, but I was with her before her blowhole could slip under.

I raised her awkwardly because we were in 6 feet of water, and I had not put my fins on. I did not understand why she had seemed to want to swim, but then declined when given the opportunity. Did she want the motion but not the exertion? That would be fine, "just let me get my fins on, okay?" and I lugged her over to the chair and held her with one arm while I finned up.

The black clouds above us opened. We swam (or rather I did, with Ernestine neither helping nor resisting) for an hour in the rain. It was not easy paddling in the middle, so I took my fins off after a while and walked around near the edges where I could get footing, gripping with my toes on the ridged folds of the liner. It made no difference to Ernestine, so far as I could tell.

I stopped, finally, and took a respiration count and let my own harsh breathing slow. I had turned the notebook over when the rain started and the fake wood clipboard had shielded the paper, but the drops fell as I wrote, and the words were blurred as though by tears. I turned the notebook back over and set it down.

Hemmed gently between my legs and the liner, Ernestine began again that strange, peculiar-rhythm'ed kick. Long strokes, slow swells, rising and subsiding . . . I thought: what if she thinks she is free?

She did look like she was dreaming. The tail strokes rose and fell, rose and fell, without haste: pushing on the down stroke, resting on the up-glide: the kind of swimming a dolphin might do, if she was with her herd again, and with a great distance to cover, in the deep sea. Her eyes stayed closed: there was no tension in her: no sideward struggles to break loose: only the long but slowing waves of the flukes' movement, weakening, as though the tide was going out. A pause lengthened at the top of the up-stroke glide, before the exertion of the push-stroke down. I kicked away the chair so I could hold Ernestine better.

In a little while she convulsed and vomited. I struggled to keep her from striking anything in the blindness of her final frenzy. But there was no need. She was past being hurt. She shuddered and grew still. And sighed. With a long hiss, like the slow collapse of a blacksmith's bellows, the air emptied out of her lungs. There was no answering inhalation. Just that too-long hiss of expiring air, and silence.

She had gone where Lucky had gone before.

40

Good-bye, Big Woman

~~~~~~

Kianu weighed 9,000 pounds: as much as an Asian bull elephant or forty-five large men. The female orca's 4½ tons
floated quite nicely in the sea; but on land, denied the supportive qualities of her normal liquid environment, the
whale's own bulk would soon kill her.

The vets estimated Kianu could live 24 hours out of water;
the flight to Japan, if everything went as scheduled, should
take 18. There must be no slip-ups: no delays, no unnecessary stress. Whales have died on moves before.

Larry Bosdeck, electrician, checked the condition of all the
floodlights and wrapped the connections of each extension
cord, against the forecast rain. Filtration men adjusted
valves, seeking that magic water level, neither so high the
animal could swim nor so low she stranded and we could not
work the stretcher under. The crane operator was already
present, and a big flatbed truck, on the back of which waited
a white, iron-frameworked cradle. Into this cradle Kianu in
her stretcher would be set, and old Mack would drive the
truck to the airport, where a 747 would fly the killer whale
to Osaka, Japan.

Dr. Martin Dennis described Kianu's destination, Kai
Ybarra's World Safari Wildlife Park, as "the finest marine
mammal facility in the world." I had never seen it. I hoped
the people there would be nice to her. There had never been
a killer whale in an oceanarium in Japan before. I was glad
some of our folks would be making the trip with her and

staying a couple of months until she got settled. There would be other whales there (though not orcas), and the tanks were supposed to be gigantic. Her holding pen alone was reportedly as large as our main pool at Oceana. And there was even talk about getting her a companion.

A second chance at happiness. To be taken out of the endless frustration-rage-jealousy trap she was in, having to watch Nepo love her younger rival Yaka—aahh! Even now the killer-whale lovers lay motionless together, length by quiet length, outside the watertight door sealing Kianu's draining pen. Without them, the orca we had named "Big Woman"—Kianu—could begin afresh.

But there was no way she could understand that she was going to what would most likely be a better place for her. If I was a giant alien, captured from a water planet and brought to Earth, my problems would have been the same as hers. What would I have thought, as the water which supported me disappeared, and the little two-leg creatures—my captors—edged closer?

WHOMP! WHOMP! Kianu crashed her flukes on the surface of the lowering water, and her eyes were red as she glared at the men on the wall. And Kianu screamed, SQUEEOWEEK! SQUEEOWEEK! as the stretcher lowered down from the night.

It was time. One-thirty A.M., and drizzling strings of mist connected the black sky with the ring of people hesitating on the edges of the lowered pool. For a moment the only sound was the buzzing crackle of the floodlight's power and the whistle of small wind that whipped about us, chilling our bare shoulders. Lying on her side, Kianu looked like a black and white moving van. I felt proud to be allowed to try to help her. I did not feel afraid, except for her. If she hurt us, I was sure, it would be by accident.

Jay Sweeney, great whale and dolphin vet, climbed down the wall via a fishnet which had been lowered over for that purpose. Lightly, unostentatiously, the slender but taut-muscled veterinarian moved. I have always loved to watch Sweeney work, taking blood from the tail of a struggling dolphin which I would be trying to hold still. His face, like a gentle hawk's, would be intense but thoughtful while his thick thumbs (all vets I've known have heavy, workers' hands) rooted firmly around on the tail flukes or pec fin until he found just the right slipperiness of flesh. That flexibility of skin indicating a vein, Sweeney would insert the needle— TSSSIP!—and an answering rush of released blood would almost invariably push the plunger of the syringe right out on the first attempt, although many experienced doctors might need fifteen or twenty "hits," poking the needle in again and again, trying to find that exteriorly invisible vein.

Behind Jay Sweeney climbed down Dr. Marty Dennis, as always looking on the verge of rage, his wiry hair being that particular shade of rust-red and his freckles so thick, his nose so fiercely hooked, and his eyes so glacially blue. On appearance alone you would never guess Marty is as nice a vet as ever risked himself standing behind a zebra, a freckled arm thrust to the shoulder inside that evil-tempered animal's vagina while she tapped the heavy hoof that could kill or cripple the man who was trying to find out why the zebra's baby was having trouble being born.

As those designated followed down the net, making no splashes and talking low or not at all as they entered the crotch-deep water, a short, muscular figure in a wet suit bounced (that's the only way to describe John Racanelli's energy-filled walk) on the wall above. He wanted to get involved in the action, and he couldn't. Not yet.

Kianu stirred uneasily as Jay Sweeney approached.

Rain started. It rained the night Ernestine died I remembered. Then I shook off the chill false premonition—a coincidence only—as I waded through the crotch-deep water. It was warm, despite the rain, and I was glad I did not have my jacket on. I loosened my arms and shoulders, shaking the stiffness out as though before a fight.

Kianu pivoted on her side, "walking" around the tank in giant's movements, and we followed, pulling ourselves through the water with our hands, our feet light and almost purchaseless on the slippery bottom.

She stopped, having made three-quarters of a revolution around the circle of her pen. Her tail trembled, lifting up in a tentative gesture—but her 20-foot, 6-inch length remained stationary—"that's her security position," said Pat Bucko Turley, his mustachioed face calm and humorous as always. "She likes to face toward the gate. This is where she will most likely stay."

"SQUEEUHWEEK!" Kianu vocalized.

"I know, sweetheart, it's rough," said Jay Sweeney and rubbed a wet hand soothingly along the mass of back before him. Steam rose from the hot black hide. Kianu's eye, beneath its jellylike extrusion of clear, tough, protective mucous, was virulently red.

"SQUEEOHWEEK!" said Kianu. "I hear you, sweetheart," said Jay very softly and then, "Coo-oo-ee. Coo-oo-ee," a little snatch of imitated whale song (coo-oo-ee, the notes the same pattern each time, middle-down-up). The large red eye faded pink, then white, around the bluish-brown ball with flecks of gold as the blood vessels slowly unengorged.

Presently the vet made a circling motion with his index finger, and Mike Demetrios at the wall top signaled to the man who ran the crane. The stretcher, which had been lowered into Kianu's pen in gradual stages to accustom the whale to its presence, eased down. Kianu's big eye followed it. She might appreciate Jay's soothing remonstrances, but she was not missing a thing.

The stretcher was impressive. The white poles looked bigger than you could put your two hands around, and the great hanging wad of nylon, canvas, and army blanket was approximately the size of a captured manta ray, but still the whole thing put together did not seem large enough for what it had to do. Only the ropes inspired total confidence, being nylon and very thick, as if you could lift a battleship with them. Or a whale.

The nylon rope ends were lashed, secured against unraveling (John Racanelli's work). I glanced briefly at the young diver, crouching on the wall, miserable in his enforced passivity. He was supposedly only here to tie the knots securing crane to stretcher around whale: that being the only way I could get him involved at all. The number of people actually laying hands on the whale had been deliberately kept small, which I could understand. But still, there he was in a wet suit, and I knew that sooner or later there would come a confused moment during which I would get him into the water. Until then—well, if there was ever a model needed for a statue of impatient youth, John Racanelli was it.

Quiet Ron Swallow and fish curator Eric Hurst unhooked the stretcher and dragged it through the rain-dimpling water, toward the whale. Kianu lifted her head to see better. As her head sank back down so that one eye was underwater, her tail began to twitch, nervously, as a man might drum his fingers on a desk. She was not being aggressive, just expressing dissatisfaction, but still those flukes were wide. WHOOM, WHOOM, WHOOM, WHOOM: the tail levered back and forth, creating foam. As I took an edge of the canvas and worked it underneath the struggling whale, I kept a wary eye on the black fluke-top and plotted my escape route, just in case. I would have time to dodge, I thought, but I would find out later, I was mistaken.

Our gripping fingertips tugged the canvas, nylon, and army-blanket mat beneath Kianu, who allowed it. The only hang-up occurred when the forward edge of the advancing mat caught between the floor and Kianu's 166½-inch chest. I knew exactly how big her torso was because I'd helped to wrap a tape around it, in the first of the two rehearsals we had made for this move. The first had taken only 45 minutes to wrap her in the canvas. The second, an hour and a quarter. If she would just hold her patience this one more time and not fight us, we could get her to her new quarters, and she might never have to endure being moved again.

Kianu flinched, and the reaction helped us. The leading edge of the composite mat slipped beneath her semisupported bulk. I stood at the back of a killer whale's head.

PTOOOHUP! She breathed, a quick hook of sound and air-flow, not the slowly slowly out, slowly slowly in of her normal respiratory pattern, but quick, as if there was no time. The C-shaped blowhole opened, the muscular plug of flesh pulling back, and I had one quick but clear look down the divided white hallway to the animal's lungs, and then the stopper popped back, the breath done. Handy arrangement, this breathing through the back of the "neck." If she had to inhale through her mouth, she'd have to lift her head out of water for each breath, like a skin diver with no snorkel tube. Instead she need only brush the surface, arching, gracefully breathing in a coordinated continuity of movement, while her head and eyes could remain under, looking.

Carefully, we began to raise the side pole and canvas around the side-lying orca. Hey, if she kept helping, or rather not hindering, like this, we—SHURROOM, she rolled, and the effect was not unlike mechanics working on a 4½-ton truck which came alive. She buried the stretcher in a white boil of foam and then returned to her original position.

Fumbling underwater, we located the poles and lifted the stretcher side again, but more slowly, giving her more time to accept the rough touch of canvas along her stomach and chest and pectoral fins. She let us, though her pectoral fin trembled and her tail worked back and forth—incredibly the pec popped through the hole in the canvas, just as it was supposed to do. Now for the touch one, the pec that's underwater. Our fingers wrestle with the heavy canvas under her, groping hurriedly for the woven pec-holes, and the search is made tense by the knowledge that if she rolls, we'll lose our progress and have to start over, and the longer this takes, the harder it will get. If she becomes too stressed, if the tension in her mounts too high . . .

"Don, would you trade places with me?" Drat. It was Ron Swallow, Marty Dennis's vet tech assistant, and he wanted, understandably enough, to work with his boss. The soft-voiced man had been doing the harder work of holding a stretcher pole over the top of the tail of the whale.

Oh good, I thought as I waded back, at least it was

De Nardo on the other pole. The heavy-shouldered, taciturn
Italian raised dark eyebrows in greeting, and I said something
about this being the action end. The tail we were supposed
to contain swooshed back and forth, apparently unmindful of
our presence. Water flung in whole chunks. Whoo! A
scooped tailful dumped cold down the neck of my open-
topped wet suit, all the way down, as if my sweat-warm front
was suddenly naked in the water. I felt vulnerable as I
stretched above the hurled foam and the wide, side-swinging
tail.

"Sure could use a mask," I heard somebody mutter at the
front of the whale, 20 feet away. Aha, John's chance! "I got
a mask topside," I mentioned casually, and then broke pro-
tocol. We had been instructed beforehand not to call topside
for any reason, but—"Racanelli! *Bring* my mask down here,
would you? It's by the floodlight." There was a small stiff
silence, and I waited for someone to say, "Just throw it
down," because John was technically a standby and not supposed to get in the water until . . .

But Racanelli, John, is not one to need his opportunities
underlined. As the words left my mouth, he was snatching
up my mask and hurtling down the rope ladder like a me-
dium-height Tarzan. And, being John Racanelli, he did not
merely deliver the mask, but put it on and ducked under the
shallow dark water. He immediately bobbed up, too buoyant
with half a wet suit but no weight belt.

"Sonny, put your foot on my back and hold me down,
would you?" he asked, and the marine mammal director
obliged. The young diver disappeared under the water. Under the whale.

The great tail towered to one side of our held-together
poles. The white underside of her flukes and belly lifted—
quivered, held high—I could see the 4-foot slash of her genital slit with the two dimples at the sides where nipples could
protrude to nurse young—I was 10 feet from the poles,
blinking, with no recollection of how I got from there, to
here. As if I had been in a movie and some of the frames of

film had been snipped out. No memory of the tail flashing down, nor of the impact, just there I was, staring at the whale and hearing Dave De Nardo yell, "Watch out, Don!" Which was thoughtful, though a little late. But then he most likely couldn't see me through the foam and, besides, he was a little busy himself.

I rushed back in around the tail and yelled to David, and this time we rewrapped the poles around the still struggling whale from the inside of the flukes, and it was so nice to lean panting against the warm moving side of the whale in the rain . . . John! Where was Racanelli?

A dripping head emerged from the darkness at the front end of Kianu. "Everything's fine underneath," he said calmly, completely oblivious to the small terror his absence had just occasioned.

Jay Sweeney raised his hand again, and the long arm of the crane extended over, dangling a heavy ball and hook and swaying nylon ropes beneath it. Now was John's official moment, to rig the ropes to support Kianu. John knew knots, having done some rigging when he was a fisher of king crab in Alaska. But never had a life hinged on his knots before. If Kianu fell from height, she would surely die.

The young diver's fingers moved swiftly, and all our eyes followed the tugs and jerks and ties. He paused and checked his work, as we all did, to the limit of our knowledge of ropes and hooks and eye loops. John spread his arms out like an umpire. "Done!" he said.

"Take her up a little, straighten her," said Jay. The crane groaned and creaked. The poles sagged, and the outline of the whale with her pecs out showed as the crane lifted and righted her. Nine thousand six hundred pounds (counting the stretcher) rose slowly. My eyes tried to grip the knots. Let it be okay . . .

"Bring her back down," ordered Jay Sweeney. "Her pecs aren't right." The canvas around the pec holes was an inch too far forward, cramping the joint of pectoral fin and smooth white chest.

"Unloose her," said the vet in charge, and John untied his knots, as the whale balanced on her brisket: tail up, pecs out.

"Stretcher's got to come forward," I heard Jay say, and then Marty Dennis said, "Donald, I need your weight down here." The red-haired vet grinned like a freckled leprechaun, and I was very happy to oblige. Vet-tech Ron and I traded places once more. At the front we all gripped the stretcher edge with our finger and thumb tips and pulled, hard. The whale moved, almost entirely supported by the water.

Only problem was, the stretcher moved too. We tried repeatedly, but all we accomplished was to move the whole situation a couple feet closer to the watertight door. And time, Kianu's enemy, sneaked by. Every minute that passed made Kianu that much more stressed, that much less likely to live through the move. There would be no gross, easily seen warning signals if her mortality limits were reached: killer whales show almost no symptoms of disorder, even when they are just about to die. They go off their feed—that's about all. Something to do with not wanting to appear helpless before the other predators of the sea. If Kianu got on that plane too tired and uncomfortable and down from the struggle to catch her, she might not be able to raise the will to keep lifting her dinosaur-sized chest and back, all those long 18 hours in flight. Somewhere over the Pacific, she might simply cease to breathe.

This vast life, this personality, this almost-friend could be extinguished by the detail of not being put in the stretcher right.

I heard myself saying, "Hey, guys, can I pull back on her while you pull forward on the stretcher?" "Well . . . okay," said Jay, and I wondered if he thought I was playing some foolish macho game because obviously this was a 9,000-pound whale, and nobody was going to budge her by himself. But he couldn't see any harm, so he didn't say no. And I knew what I was doing! As a former competitive weight lifter, I had a good feel for mass and leverages, and if we could just all pull together . . .

I rushed to the upright dorsal fin, hooked my elbow high around, and locked my fingers. When Jay's almost whispering voice said *one*, I added a bellowed "TWO, THREE!" loud as my son's outdoor voice, which be can be like a bull in a cave. The shout and our will united us: we were a people together; and there is no stronger force than that, on all the earth.

I leaned with my back and legs, and Kianu moved. "All right!" somebody yelled and slapped me on the shoulder, as though I had done it, and I was trying to explain that the smallest person there could have done what I did, which was just to provide some countervailing balance to their force on the stretcher, and she was 99 percent resting on the water anyway.

Kianu made a joke out of my great idea by calmly rolling onto her side. Oh! But I was not going to be cheated now! "John, Dave!" Three divers strained against her in-the-water dorsal, straining gut-wrenchingly so that John's arms and shoulders rounded like rock and Dave's bull neck seemed about to separate into individual fibers, though his face, even in the midst of total exertion, remained imperturbable, as though he really had another appointment and was late. Kianu, thus encouraged, rolled upright in the wide-open stretcher—and continued on over to her other side. All of us, whale and people, began again.

Two hours blinked by before the stretcher and the whale and Jay Sweeney agreed, and we banged our shins against the wall clambering up the net ladder, as Kianu rose. She looked graceful as a bird, with her pectoral fins spread out like wings and her tail and huge head high.

As the crane lifted her out of the circle of light, into the night sky, a rope fell from the back of the stretcher. For a horrible instant I thought the stretcher had come apart, but no, that was just the guide rope, and as it brushed across the partition at the back of "K." 's pen, I saw it tighten as somebody grabbed on.

I hurried around the divider, and there was Mack, pushing sixty years old but with a turn of that rope around his waist and backing up guiding the whale in the stretcher toward the white framework cradle on the back of the open bed truck. I added my weight to his, and we leaned into the long slow settling of the stretcher down.

Then something small and wonderful happened. As the stretcher came down and the truck springs groaned and sagged under the more than 4½ tons, somebody yelled, "There's too much weight on the back end!" The cradle did stick out a bit off the bed—nothing serious, but . . . There was an old sawhorse, standing as if forgotten, by the side of the road.

Someone snatched up the simple carpenter's device, just two upside-down V's of wood supporting a two-by-four, and thrust it hurriedly under the whale cradle. The sawhorse was clearly past its prime. Rusted nails barely held together the lengths of warped and weathered pine, and dribbles of multiple unmatched colors of paint hinted at how many times it had been used.

When its portion of the whale's weight came down it, the sawhorse's wood legs widened, and I guess the nails tore loose internally. But it held together, supporting what it could, until the truck moved off, to go to the airport. Only then, with the final torsion and release, did the old sawhorse break and fall softly to the ground.

Could a person ask much more than that: to wear out in honest work, and break at last in the successful completion of a great endeavor? I would like to live my life with that much usefulness, and die with that much honor.

I did not learn the fate of Kianu for several weeks. I had heard of course that she did not die on the plane trip; but the larger question of her well-being went unanswered, at least for me. I did not know and was hesitant to make inquiries for fear of what I might find out. Then one day I could no longer avoid it.

I had just finished scrubbing the main bottom at Oceana and was wearily lugging my hose through the back when a shy-faced man looked up from the outdoor sink where he had been pilling fish, popping blue vitamin tablets into mackerel for Yaka and Nepo, our two remaining orcas.

His hair was copper colored and curly, and his face bright pink. Probably sunburn, but it looked the color of embarrassment. That plus the broad shoulders packing his shirt, and the awkward way he bobbed his head saying hello, made me think of a backwoodsman, more used to the society of the wild than any two-legged company. His name was Dan Cartwright.

So many people come and go at Marine World. I couldn't remember what it was he had done when he'd been here before, so I asked him what he was doing now, expecting him to say college or something.

"I just got back from Japan," he said.

"Japan? Did you go to see Kianu?" Suddenly my breath came different, and the weight of the coiled hose on my shoulder was forgotten.

"Oh, yeah, I see her every day. I'm one of her trainers," said Dan Cartwright.

I almost didn't ask the next question. "How . . . is she? Is she happy? What is she doing?"

"Real good."

"What do you mean? How do you know?" The words gushed out, and I immediately wished I could recall them. Why had I pushed it? Should have let it alone because I was sure he was going to say, well, actually she's miserable.

"You know how an *un*happy whale is? Sit in the water, stare at the walls, eyes get red? Head nods, jaw snaps?"

"Yeah, uh-huh."

"Kianu's *nothing* like that," said Dan, and suddenly the day brightened, and he didn't look the least bit shy.

"A *happy* whale does a lot of . . . unnecessary behaviors. Swimming fast for no reason. Tail-walking without being asked. Leaping just for the crash it makes. Investigating her environment and the people who come near. Curiosity, and enjoying the trainer's company, even sticking up her stomach to be rubbed. Vocalizing. Talking up a storm. Playing."

"That's what *Kianu* does now?" I had to ask again, almost unable to fit that image with the memory of the sad and angry whale she had become here at the last.

"That's what she does now. A lot," said Dan Cartwright. "Hey, and the people really dig her! They come and see her by the millions. They're doing a documentary on her: she's a celebrity, if that means anything to a whale." He grinned, then turned serious. "She's doing good." he said.

Dan understood, I think, why I shook his hand so hard and so many times.

41

Afterword

~~~~~~~~~~~~~~~~~~~~~~~~~~~~~~~~~~~~~

In the past ten years, I have spent approximately 9,000 hours underwater, possibly more than any other person in the world. And in all that time of feeding fish and scrubbing floors, one thought has become increasingly urgent in my mind.

I think that we as a world should look to the sea.

I wish that every person on Earth were a diver, because then we would look at the ocean with the same eyes, and we would cherish, nurture, and tend that blue eighty percent of our planet's surface, and she would repay our care with the most incredibly bountiful harvests imaginable.

We can farm the ocean's shallows, and mine her deeps, carefully: and produce enough wealth to tackle the giant problems that confront us now—problems like hunger, homelessness, joblessness, war—we can defeat them, and make them only memories.

If we are wise and brave (and we are humanity, we can do anything), we have it in our power to break the chains of need that bind us; we can replace shortages with plenty. We can usher in a new age: an age of exploration, discovery, adventure; of enormous challenge, and greater reward. We can build security, comfort, and beauty for all people. We can live the beginning of Earth's golden age—

The age of the ocean.